Her Daughter
The Engineer

The life of
Elsie Gregory MacGill

NRC RESEARCH PRESS BIOGRAPHY SERIES NO. 3

Her Daughter
The Engineer

The life of
Elsie Gregory MacGill

Richard I. Bourgeois-Doyle
National Research Council of Canada
Ottawa, Ontario

NRC Research Press
Ottawa 2008

ISBN 978-0-660-19813-2
ISSN 1701-1833
NRC No. 49722

Library and Archives Canada Cataloguing in Publication

Bourgeois-Doyle, Richard I.
Her Daughter the Engineer: The Life of Elsie Gregory MacGill / Dick Bourgeois-Doyle.

(NRC Press Biography Series, 1701-1833; No. 3)
Issued by National Research Council Canada.
ISBN 978-0-660-19813-2

1. MacGill, Elsie Gregory, 1905–1980.
2. Women aeronautical engineers – Canada – Biography.
3. Aeronautical engineers – Canada – Biography.
4. Women – Canada – Biography.
I. National Research Council Canada.
II. Title.
III. Series.

TL540.M32B68 2008 629.130092 C2008-980177-6

NRC Monograph Publishing Program

Inquiries: Monograph Publishing Program, NRC Research Press, National Research Council of Canada, Ottawa, Ontario K1A 0R6, Canada.
Web site: http://pubs.nrc-cnrc.gc.ca

Front cover: Elsie MacGill upon graduation from King George Secondary School in Vancouver (1921). (Courtesy of Elizabeth Schneewind.)

Back cover: The shadow of Elsie MacGill leaning on her cane to take a photo of her Maple Leaf Trainer II (1939). (Courtesy of Mr. Ian Leslie Canada Aviation Museum Library.)

Correct citation for this publication: Bourgeois-Doyle, R.I. 2008. Her Daughter the Engineer: The Life of Elsie Gregory MacGill. NRC Research Press, Ottawa, Ontario, Canada, 332 pp .

To my dear Mrs. B-D

Contents

Prologue

At 24, she was bright, pretty, popular — and even a little famous. She was, after all, the first woman in her country to graduate from university in electrical engineering. Now, she was thought to be the only woman in the world completing an advanced degree in aeronautics, and she was preparing for marriage. Her future burned bright.

Then a slight tinge of tenderness, barely noticeable, floated across her lower back. It was an odd feeling, different, but not initially disturbing because she had been fighting a flu-like cold for days and sitting long hours at the desk studying. Unconcerned, Elsie MacGill pushed aside the discomforts to join other University of Michigan students celebrating the end of the school year with a night out across the border in Windsor.[1] It was May 1929.[2]

That evening, her dress seemed to chafe her skin, and at times she was numb and stiff.[3] But once back in her room in Ann Arbor, Elsie went to bed as usual without telling anyone. The next morning something was clearly wrong. When she awoke and touched her back and legs with the tips of her fingers, she felt nothing. Within a single night, Elsie had become completely paralyzed from the waist down. The diagnosis, acute infectious myelitis,[4] suggested an inflammation of the spinal cord, likely related to the mundane virus that had caused her cold. But there was talk of "poliomyelitis",[5] and the University Hospital staff pronounced her likely to "not walk again".[6] She was far from her childhood home, her closest friends, and family.

Over the next few years, Elsie would spend most of her time confined to home, sometimes in pain and often engulfed by the dismal prognosis of a life in bed or, at best, in a wheelchair. In fact, the damage that befell her body that spring never fully left it, and eventually would lead indirectly to her death. Yet, 50 years later, those who knew Elsie best would say that the enduring disability engendered by this day was "the least important thing about her".[7] Such was the life of Elizabeth Muriel Gregory MacGill that a dramatic, lingering event — devastating for some, defining for many — proved ultimately to be a mere sidebar to a greater story, a story that changed the history of Canada, established illustrious milestones in the United States, and touched lives beyond. This book strives to tell her story.

"Daughter of the late Helen Gregory MacGill ...", Elsie's Professional Engineer's Curriculum Vitae 1971. (*Courtesy of Ann Soulsby.*)

Chapter I

The Golden Thread

"passionate, yet objective"[8]

The golden thread is not hard to find. It shimmers, standing out from the surrounding hues and tints. It is stronger than the other strands. It neither tarnishes nor corrodes with time.

Elsie Gregory MacGill maintained that a life is best described and understood by grabbing onto this "golden thread",[9] the package of beliefs and values that motivates and binds diverse, seemingly random actions, events, decisions, and achievements. Elsie suggested that "loyalty" was the golden thread in the lives of some of her ancestors and that "a faith in the rule of law" defined the lives of others. In this way, she would explain the various stands taken, successes, and setbacks in her family history.

Her Mother's Daughter

In her mother, Judge Helen Gregory MacGill, Elsie recognized "a passionate, yet *objective* sympathy for the hurt, the helpless, the exploited"[10] as the consistent and constructive force that harnessed and mustered her mother's full, multidimensional life.

Although Elsie was the product of many influences, the most consistent, the golden thread of her own life was clearly built around her admiration of her mother and what she regarded as her mother's honourable passion. Yet Elsie's life was more complex. The shimmering thread of confidence and passion, spun during childhood, was made useful by the knowledge and technical skills she developed on her own in later life. The emphasis on the qualifier — *"objective"* — hints at those other, later-life influences that helped define the person Elsie eventually became. A proud, firmly entrenched scientist and engineer by the time she penned the words describing her mother, Elsie would have had found it difficult to omit the notion of objectivity when describing anyone she considered worthy of admiration and emulation.

Passionate, yet objective. This was her golden thread.

Although Elsie's life was undoubtedly bolstered by many positive experiences and uplifting forces, she was structured and made effective by an objectivity, thoughtfulness, and pragmatism born of reflection, hard work, and her experience of challenging times. This is why she often told her friends that she accepted life's rewards and reversals with equal gratitude.

The application of her objective engineer's mind to a methodical analysis of her own experiences and her mother's passions also led Elsie to develop a distinct perspective on life. Life's purpose and the process of giving something back, she said, were not to be found in uncertain goals or ephemeral career accomplishments. Far better, she said, to celebrate the simple adventure of life, the impacts that flow from each individual's struggle to function and do their best whatever the circumstance.[11] This approach served her well in both good times and bad, and she seldom lost sight of life's joys or flinched in her quest to do and make things better.

More than a quarter century after her death and a hundred years after her birth, it is easy to admire Elizabeth Muriel Gregory MacGill, the woman known mostly as Elsie MacGill, as someone whose story can still inspire and instruct those who might seek to do something exceptional in the face of intimidating obstacles.

The Engineer

Elsie was the first female aeronautical engineer and professional aircraft designer in the United States, Canada, and likely the world. She was both highly educated for her time and smart in a practical way. A confident bulldog of a personality, Elsie was just the kind of person North American industry needed as it geared up for the demands of World War II. Her engineering skills produced innovative designs and earned her senior positions in the production and development of famous aircraft. Later on, she filled the roles of wife, mother to two stepchildren, businesswoman, community leader, and author, and towards the end of her life became a social activist who was said to be "one of the most important individual women"[12] of her time, a woman who "entirely change[d] the nature of [a] country, legally, economically, and certainly in terms of the quality of life".[13]

While Elsie was dismissive of her own accomplishments, others were impressed, particularly when they learned that the powerhouse behind these achievements was a small woman who had spent part of her life in a wheelchair and then succeeded in a male-dominated trade, often struggling to walk with canes. For many, disability and discrimination would be sound reasons to shrink away from the challenges of a dynamic career and rich personal life. Elsie, however, rejected that path. Studying her story is largely the process of asking why she made the choices she did and what one can learn from them.

Elsie hinted at the answers to such questions and exposed some of her feelings in the early 1950s by writing *My Mother the Judge*, a hagiographical but heart-felt biography of her mother, who had died in 1947. There is no doubt that Helen Emma Gregory MacGill, an adventuresome, daring, and formidable suffragette, journalist, and judge, set a standard that motivated and directed Elsie throughout much of her own life. Helen provided inspiration to her youngest child in many ways: by confronting serious injury and disease, by bouncing back from career setbacks, by breaking down barriers, and by advancing social reform. Given that well into her eighth decade of life and 30 years after her mother's death, Elsie would still begin her professional curriculum vitae with the credential of "daughter of the late Helen Gregory MacGill, Judge of the Juvenile Court of Vancouver", it is clear that a biography of Elsie would be pierced with a gaping hole if it downplayed her mother's influences, including some that may have been less than constructive.

Yet Elsie was much more than her mother's daughter. Her life could even be described as the fluctuating tension between her mother's influence and the pull of Elsie's own identity as a scientist and engineer. When these two forces resolved into one in Elsie's later life, they produced a climactic and powerful effect that would help define her life, her country, and her enduring contribution to our world.

Elsie's life was bound by other fibers as well — her writing, her playful sense of humour, her pride, her stubbornness, her loving husband, her especially close relationship with her sister, and other passions — and

Vancouver's West End
and the wilderness of the
North Shore around the
time of Elsie MacGill's
birth in 1905. (*Vancouver
Public Archives LGN 697;
photo by Norman Caple.*)

these add colour and texture to Elsie's own story and truly help to explain it. For no matter how instructive it is to identify the "golden thread", it is only a small part of the rich tapestry of ideas, circumstances, and events that fill out and strengthen a life.

Vancouver 1905

Elsie's life and 1905 birth thus owed a debt to several streams. One of those significant, early, and enduring other influences was the city of Elsie's childhood, Vancouver, British Columbia (B.C.).

Even today, a century later, standing in downtown Vancouver in the shade of towering concrete and steel and in the midst of the tightly-packed homes of millions of people, it is still easy to accept Elsie's favourite observation — *"in Vancouver every street ends in a view... the flowers bloom from early February into December... you won't want to leave"*[14] — as an appropriate description of a city likened to the mythical Lotus Land of dreamy contentment. For the great part of Elsie's youth and throughout difficult times, this city was a touchstone, refuge, and uplifting place to call home.

At the dawn of the 20th century, Vancouver radiated the charm of a small town even though it was firmly established as a community of about 30 000 people.[15] It was anchored by a solid commercial infra-structure, a vibrant year-round port, and a railroad linked to the industry of eastern Canada. Nevertheless, it had a simple quality to its daily life. There were stately homes of stone and cedar, but even these affluent residences featured stables and a barn to accommodate the most popular means of transportation. Gunfire aimed at wild animals was still a com-mon sound in the residential areas of town. Vancouver was very much a last frontier.[16]

Although it had been inhabited since the last ice age by increasingly artistic, cultured, and inventive Aboriginal people, British Columbia was largely undeveloped in modern terms until mere decades before Elsie's birth. The region was among the last parts of the Americas to be explored, claimed, and cultivated by Europeans. It sat at the end of a long ocean journey around the tip of South America, and the towering mountains of the interior created a formidable barrier to those who dared to travel overland.

In three hundred years after Columbus first visited the New World, only the omnipresent James Cook, especially adventurous seaborne traders, the curious Juan Pérez Hernandez, and a handful of California-based explorers ventured north to check out the Pacific Coast extremities of the Americas. Only in the last decade of the 18th century did fur, fish, and minerals prompt the British to assert themselves by sending cartographer George Vancouver to the B.C. coast. This voyage, combined with England's successful standoff against the Spanish over access to Vancouver Island's Nootka Sound, served to plant the first Union Jacks in the region and to lay the foundations of the very British society that would envelop Elsie MacGill's childhood.

The area around today's City of Vancouver did not, however, take hold as a settlement until the late 1850s, when the search for timber was coupled with the boom of the Fraser and Cariboo gold rushes. British Columbia began its sustained growth with the arrival of the cross-Canada railroad in 1885, built by the new Dominion of Canada in order to bring the colony into the federation. The city's role as an important crossroads did not really become established until the launch of steamship traffic across the Pacific and the horde of gold seekers heading toward the Klondike arrived in Vancouver just as the 19th century ended. These city-shaping events followed the incorporation and naming of the City of Vancouver by a little over a decade and preceded baby Elsie MacGill's birth by just a few years.

The impact of these activities meant that shops and roads, factories and multistorey buildings, doctors and barbers were all present in British Columbia's largest town by the year of Elsie's arrival. Indeed, it was a city of substance and organization, with a wonderful park, mountains, green landscape, and, everywhere, the sea. Although it remained very British,[17] Chinese, Japanese, and other Asian immigrants who had worked on the railroads and in the mines were residing in Vancouver by this time and beginning their unique struggle for a place in the city. The Aboriginal people of the region had already been segregated and pushed to the side, but remained a modifying backdrop to life in Vancouver.

The Vancouver of 1905, echoes of which still resound through the city's streets today, was not yet held in the clench of modern pressure. This would change dramatically over the next decade as the outside world entered a new era of technological development. In the United States, the

Wright brothers were building on their breakthroughs in flight; in Switzerland, a government patent examiner was completing a series of papers that would contort human thought forever; and around the world, ominous economic and military alliances were being forged.

Elsie MacGill's life would be shaped by all these developments and more, yet Vancouver would retain a special place in her heart as a reminder of simpler times and the largely stable, supportive environment that welcomed her into the world.

Her parents had already fallen in love with the city by the time Elsie was born even though they had strong ties to eastern Canada. For different reasons, they were comfortable with life in a town just emerging from its pioneer days.

Helen, her Mother

Certainly, the city had much in common, both in size and trajectory of development, with 19th-century Hamilton, Ontario, the town that Elsie's mother, Helen Gregory MacGill, considered her childhood home. Helen was at ease in such places and may have sensed a happy and complementary symmetry between the unexploited potential she felt inside herself and that of her Vancouver surroundings.

Helen's many passionate interests and projects put demands on her time over the years. But in 1905, she was at a stage of life that arguably positioned her, more than at any other time, to be an attentive and involved parent. Just over a decade later, Helen would plunge into the consuming, multipronged function of groundbreaking juvenile-court judge, role model, and champion of social and legal reform. Before Elsie's arrival, Helen had been fully absorbed by the drama of her travels, her personal tragedies, and her quest for a career.

Tragedy had taken the form of the heart-rending death, just a few years earlier, of her first husband. Lee Flesher, a physician working in Minnesota at the time, was a strong, energetic man until cut by a "crazed",[18] knife-wielding patient. Blood infection ensued, and though this incident was not the direct cause of his death, it was the beginning of a trend toward weakness. In 1901, other afflictions induced Lee's body to hemorrhage, lapse into coma, and expire. Helen was left to support her two young boys and her mother.[19]

Fortunately, she had the skills and means to deal with the situation, having had more education and life experience than many of her contemporaries. Born in 1864, Helen had been raised in the upper strata of 19th-century Ontario society. Her family's relative affluence and prestige in Hamilton had many roots, but its most important source was the career and life of Helen's maternal grandfather, Elsie's great-grandfather, the Upper Canada barrister and judge Miles O'Reilly. O'Reilly was a combination of distinguished establishment man of the courts and daring reformer whose early career was highlighted by his successful defense of a group accused of participation in the ill-fated 1837 Upper Canada rebellion. His blended example provided both inspiration and structure for his extended family and the generations who followed.

In this and many other ways Helen led a privileged life, and some family members would later suggest she was actually quite spoiled.[20] Yet her early life was also spent under the shadow of the prejudice and high barriers to practical education and professional careers confronting 19th-century Canadian women. Her route out of the confines of these attitudes came in part from the example of defiance and involvement set by her mother, Elsie's maternal grandmother Emma, and in part through the influence of her father Silas Gregory, Emma's second husband, whose failures in business and weaker qualities were offset to some extent by his talent for and interest in music. With her father's support and access to a piano and lessons, Helen developed a musical skill that in the 1880s helped her to breach the doors of Toronto's Trinity College, eventually graduating as the first woman in the British Empire to receive a degree in music.[21] She built upon this achievement with a B.A. and eventually an M.A. from Trinity in 1889.[22]

These accomplishments drew the attention of the editor of the U.S. magazine *Cosmopolitan* and an invitation to write as a journalist with a unique perspective. She developed an adequate ability in the trade and a reputation that resulted in 1890 in an assignment to cross the continent and the Pacific Ocean to cover the opening of the Diet, the first Parliament of the enigmatic and mysterious Japan.[23]

At a personal meeting in Ottawa with Prime Minister Sir John A. Macdonald, a family friend, Helen was armed with letters of introduction for her trip and a formal mandate to report on life in western Canada and, Sir John A. hoped, to celebrate the development of the Canadian

Excerpt from a hand-drawn
MacGill-Gregory Family
Tree prepared by Elsie and
her sister Helen. (*Photo by
M. Bourgeois-Doyle; cour-
tesy of Elizabeth Schnee-
wind.*)

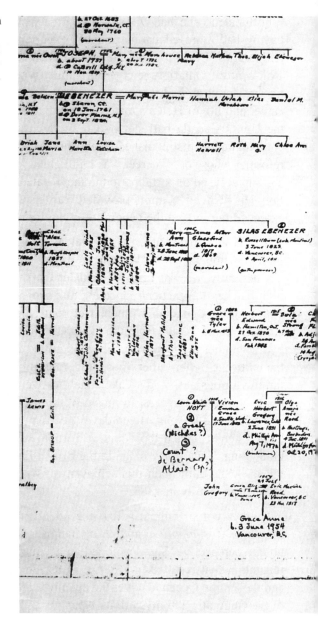

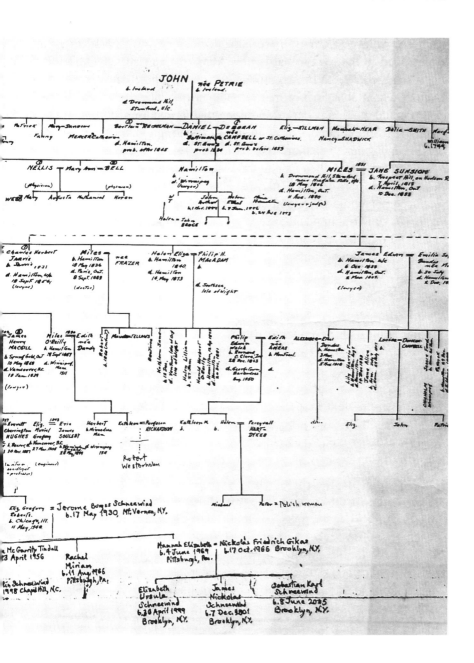

prairies. While performing these duties on her way westward to Japan, she stopped in the region that is now Manitoba to visit her half-brother and was introduced to his neighbour: the rancher, poet, and charmer Lee Flesher, whom she quickly married after a romance measured in days. Helen could not consider abandoning the prime ministerial-endorsed assignment and continued her journey to Japan, pregnant. The trip took her through Vancouver more than a decade before it would become her home and at a time when its cultural charms were decidedly limited. The steamship ride across the Pacific was also not without incident; the heavy seas accompanying a typhoon tossed her around and gave her a broken leg. Now both hobbling and expecting, she completed her working tour of Japan and returned to North America equipped with a modest knowledge of the Orient that was to feed much of her money-earning writings in the years ahead and would later help colour Elsie's perception of her mother as an audacious and unusual woman.

Meanwhile, her new husband Lee had rented out his Canadian lands to allow him to lease property in Lawrence, California, where he hoped to grow fruit in a more inviting economic and physical climate. Back in Ontario, her parents, Emma and Silas, were arguing over Helen's impulsive marriage, and when Helen fainted while visiting them, Emma used the event as a pretext to spend time away from her husband Silas, leaving with Helen to settle in California. Emma's commitment to her daughter's family was magnified when Helen brushed death with the difficult, painful birth in California of her first son, Elsie's future half-brother Eric, on June 2nd, 1891.[24]

Failure in the fruit-growing enterprise, and perhaps the trauma of Eric's birth, prompted Lee to embark on a medical degree in San Francisco. The second boy, Elsie's other half-brother Freddy, arrived more easily in May 1894. As the family prospered over the next few years, Helen and her mother Emma worked together with considerable impact in U.S. women's organizations to advance social reforms in the region. The family eventually moved to Minnesota where Lee had relocated to work with the already-famous Mayo brothers. There Lee had his run-in with the patient, fell ill and, in 1901, died.

Helen mourned deeply, but with her mother Emma's support, the urgent need to care for her young boys, and a modest life-insurance payment, she moved on, picking up work once again as a journalist. Sometime in the year after she was widowed, she began corresponding with a friend from her college days in Toronto, the awkward but admirable Jim MacGill. This soon led to her second marriage and the immediate move to Vancouver in 1902. A year later her third child, a girl destined to be Elsie's older sister, was born. This second "Helen", fully Helen Elizabeth Gregory MacGill, was soon dubbed "Young Helen", a nickname that would endure as a means, in conversation and in letters, of distinguishing her from her mother and the other Helens in the extended family.

In just over a year, the MacGills established roots as deep as most of their fellow citizens in the infant city of Vancouver, and they shared a steadfast intent to stay forever. Helen's second marriage had thus been solidified with a baby girl, a home, and a sense of comfortable love.

Helen's two boys from her previous marriage, now on the threshold of their teen years, were entering a stage in life where they were old enough and independent enough to allow their mother to dote on her new daughter. She certainly had more time for the baby, Young Helen, than might have been the case had her children been bunched together at intervals of two years, as was common at the time. The arrival of her children had been delayed by her longer than usual education and had later been interrupted by widowhood. The space between her first and second families had given her at least a fragment of time for reflection and perhaps to hone the independent thought that underpinned her approach to life.

Nevertheless, the daily concerns of the MacGill household were to limit Helen's outside interests and the full exercise of her talents. At least for a while.

Although Helen was approaching her fortieth birthday, she was healthy and exuded the appearance and energy of a much younger woman. Given an affluent family history, a lawyer husband, and the support of house-keepers, Helen did not have to carry the physical burdens of a pioneer. Yet the still-rustic, frontier quality of B.C. life nevertheless presented her with many opportunities for outdoor exertion and work, for the family kept a cottage up the coast at Buccaneer Bay, a location that to some seemed isolated and remote. There, throughout the summers and almost always without Jim, whose work kept him in the city, Helen and her septuagenarian mother Emma would monitor the activities of the children as well as a mix of wild and domestic animals. The steamship carrying people to the bay would have had to be met by a rowboat, a dangerous and difficult operation in rough-weather conditions.

At the cottage, Helen and Emma, on their own, had to learn new skills, including how to swim, and the two women worked together to fish, gather firewood, and prepare food for the new baby girl and her male siblings. Even when the group was staying at the family's large home in Vancouver, Helen's daily life had a rural quality, with chickens and a cow in the backyard, an orchard, and large gardens, and horse barns scattered throughout the neighbourhood.

Jim, her Father

A child's life is influenced by people they might not want to emulate as well as those they do, and in some ways, Elsie's father fell into the former category. Although others felt that Elsie was not as generous as she could have been in her accounts of her father, it is true that he appeared at times to be uncomfortable, mean, aggressive, hypersensitive,[25] and, to his younger daughter, a pale, dour contrast to Helen's sense of adventure. Still, James Henry "Jim" MacGill was a handsome, well-built, multidimensional character with a modicum of wit and enough perception and charm to appreciate and engage others outside the family environment.

He also knew what he liked and wanted. While at Trinity, one of Helen's chauvinistic professors, resentful of the presence of a female student, forced her to sit alone, like a dunce, segregated from the rest of the otherwise all-male moral philosophy class. Jim, a fellow student in the class, was impressed by the stoic dignity of the pretty young woman put on display solely because of her gender, and he sought to make her his friend.

By 1904, the man who would be Elsie's father was a clearly committed lawyer operating at the heart of the legal dynamism of the Vancouver business community. Yet he had arrived in this position only via a circuitous route that began with his graduation from Trinity. Helen had been what Elsie later termed his "beloved companion" during those college years, but after graduation the two parted ways. Whether this constituted a heart-wrenching breakup for Jim or not, he soon determined to leave his Ontario home and head to the far-flung West Coast, citing health problems as the reason.

The MacGill side of the Family — (standing) Elsie's father James Henry (Jim) MacGill, her mother Helen Emma Gregory MacGill, Jim's brother-in-law Dr. Jesse Williams, Jim's sister Jennie Williams, his mother, (seated) Grandma Elizabeth MacGill and Elsie's sister Helen and Elsie. (*Courtesy of Elizabeth Schneewind.*)

This brought him to the unfolding opportunity of Vancouver around 1890, just a few years after its incorporation. Before settling into the legal profession, however, he survived financially by teaching school on Vancouver Island, working as a land surveyor in the Fraser Valley, and later earning intermittent pay as a reporter for several West Coast newspapers. Throughout his experimentation with career options, he continued to study for pleasure, reading history and thinking about a return to school nearer his family in the east. Thus, by the time he was 24 years old, he had secured a position with prestigious Vancouver barristers and been called to the bar. Yet barely two years after achieving his B.C. credentials as a lawyer, he quit this job, jumped on a train, and returned to his alma mater Trinity in Toronto in order to pursue another degree, this time in the School of Divinity.

Elsie's future father studied hard and was ordained as a deacon in the Church of England after graduation in 1897. But shortly after completing divinity school, a seemingly eccentric urge sent him back to British Columbia and work in his former pattern as a lawyer and part-time journalist. Finally, by the time he resolved to propose to his newly widowed university friend, the former Helen Gregory, he had determined to make Vancouver his home for good. When they married in 1902, he decided that the best area of the city for the young couple, a couple with an entourage including a mother-in-law and his bride's sons from a previous marriage, would be Vancouver's new residential district, the bush of the West End. Sitting on a strip of land sandwiched between great slices of salt water, the neighborhood's homes were within modest walking distance from the attractions of the business district and the solace of the great green space of Stanley Park. Schools, playgrounds, churches, stores, and baby-birthing hospitals sprouted between the buildings. This combination of the rugged rural and the practical urban seemed to nicely balance Jim's biases from a prolonged bachelorhood with the needs of his instant family.

After briefly boarding in cramped space in a house on Hornby Street, Jim moved the family into a two-storey house complete with water, electricity, modern appliances — and land for the chickens — on Comox near bustling Burrard Street.

Around this time, Jim began volunteer work at St. Paul's, the church that gave him spiritual strength, later baptized Elsie, and provided him with fruitful business connections. Jim's networks also flowed from his involvement in grassroots B.C. politics. His many associations allowed him to prosper for years.

For Jim, however, life at the MacGill home was not always as rewarding as were his outside interests. He had great difficulty in the role of stepfather. He found Helen's young boys, his stepsons, to be distant, unruly, and aloof, leading him to feel isolated and lonely, as separate from the tightly bound group of Helen, her mother, and the boys.[26] He tried to be affectionate and had some success when out duck hunting and boating with his stepsons. But even these opportunities were limited since the boys, their mother, and grandmother spent much of their summers up the coast at the Buccaneer Bay cottage while Jim stayed in town with his home, his work, and his church.

A new door on a sense of family opened when the new baby, a physical entity who shared Jim and Helen equally, arrived in 1903. Jim sensed an opportunity for redemption as a father in the birth of "Young Helen", their child and the girl who would soon be Elsie's older sister.

Helen understood Jim's feelings. But unlike him, her sometimes draining experience as a parent was by then reaching into its second decade, so that when the new baby, the younger Helen, suffered with a severe case of whooping cough in her first months of life, Helen felt she had all she could handle. She thus balked when Jim raised the prospect of another baby and would have welcomed a break instead. But her new spouse pushed the idea in a persistent way, seemingly fuelled by love and joking that his wife's protests were just the product of a rebellious woman.

The conception and approaching March 1905 birth of a second Vancouver baby were thus worth celebrating. He resolved that were it to be another girl, the baby would bear the first name of his own mother, Elizabeth MacGill.

Eric and Freddy, Her Brothers

The news that another baby was on the way, adding a second bright, exuberant little sibling who shared both their parents' genes, could have presented daunting competition for two boys, sons of another man, entering the age of trouble and testing. Jim's difficulty with his stepsons was real and a source of tension in the home. But Eric and Freddy had their own anchors and attachments and places of comfort within the Gregory-MacGill household. Eric had a strong bond with his grandmother Emma, and Freddy was known to be Helen's pet, a function of their early life experiences in California.

Eric, the older son and the one whose 1891 birth had been so violent, had come into the world with such trauma that the event had threatened his mother's life. A long period of recuperation had ensued during which Helen was considered at risk of becoming a permanent invalid. But, with dry weather and his struggles with the family's farm, her husband Lee already had his hands full. Further, the baby's left eye was damaged at birth, and initially it was feared that he would be blind. While Eric did retain his sight, he would suffer recurrent eye problems all his life and have to wear glasses, a visible reminder of his rough start and an enduring prod to maternal anxiety. Fortunately, Helen's mother Emma had stepped into the gap. She was still searching for a reason to stay with her daughter in California and found it in caring for the boy, who despite his bumpy arrival showed "a lighthearted and affectionate" disposition and touched a soft spot in his grandmother's heart. She idolized him, and he responded with a cheeriness and warmth[27] that still coloured her interactions with the now-troublesome teenager in Vancouver.

By the time Frederick Phillip, the second boy, arrived in May 1894, Helen had returned to a healthy state and was again active. In comparison to her first, this birth was easy, even light, even though the baby was a round little person doomed to be nicknamed "fat boy". She rebounded from the birth quickly and not only maintained her work and outside interests, but also attached more fully to Freddy, this younger son, whom she supported wholeheartedly, calling him her "lamb".[28] It was a bond still evident during those early years in Vancouver and eventually grew so tight that it may have, 50 years later, constrained the length of her life.

When the boys' father died in 1901, it had, of course, been a shock for everyone. Eric was 10, Freddy only seven. They were old enough to have known their father well and retain both memories and the skills like horseback riding he had taught them. Eric, the eldest, was aware of and touched by the trauma around Lee's Minnesota death to the extent that, for a while, he feared growing up "because you get sick when you do".

A few years later, as they began life in a new country, the boys would present a complex package, with much in common and bonds that ran deep. They were at times tough, daring, and at ease with their rough surroundings, which ranged from swamps, wild animals, and a jungle of fallen logs, to city streets, school, and the people on the Kitsilano Reserve. They were also, at times, lonely, dependent, awkward, and even, some say, mean-spirited. They added a Huckleberry Finn dimension to the family who welcomed Elsie into the world in 1905.

Grandma Emma, Gong, and the Others

Parents and siblings were not the only significant human fixtures as the home prepared for a second Vancouver-born MacGill baby.

Included were also a string of people who worked in the house as cooks and servants.[29] Elsie would come to think of one, a young man named Gong, as almost a member of the family. He was friendly, genuine, and concerned, but also focused on daily chores, and his interactions were limited by language and the monetary nature of the relationship. Gong, like his successors, would leave at the end of the day to return home into the mysteries of Chinatown. Wages for house staff were often minimal, even in the better-off homes, although Gong received what was deemed by the MacGills to be an "ample $15 a month". The presence of paid staff of any kind in the household was a reminder of the MacGill family's relative status, sense of position, and means.

It was also a reminder of the flavour and history of their community, which was prospering as a function of the labour of those Chinese rail workers who were now settling in the Lower Mainland and thus ensuring an enduring Asian influence on the character of Vancouver. Elsie would feel this influence in her home and recognize it as an integral feature of Vancouver despite what her sister would label as their decidedly "Wasp"[30] upbringing in the starchy British layer of local society. More immediately, Gong and his abilities around the house made the prospect of a fourth child a more comfortable idea for Helen.

The other significant, supportive presence in the house in 1905 was, naturally, Grandma Emma. Although not destined for a firm place in Elsie's memories, Emma was a force behind the pervasive personality that was Elsie's mother. Helen and Emma were now even closer than ever. Together, they embodied the spirit of two generations of the women's movement involved in the fight for general suffrage in Canada and the United States. At this point, however, they mainly saw themselves as a team that cared for the children and oversaw family life.

While Elsie's grandmother Emma never completely broke free of a world that regarded quality careers and higher education as male pursuits, she did poke holes in those notions and challenge the related social institutions. She could understand her daughter's perspective on home and family in this context. Mother of a relatively small flock of three, Emma, like Helen, had also experienced a gap between babies that allowed her to pause and contemplate her situation. She was granted this unexpected and uninvited opportunity because in 1857 her first husband died of a gunshot wound on the very day her first child was born. A young widow with a newborn surrounded by rumours of the death as a suicide, by feelings of confusion and uncertainty, Emma had no choice but to stop and reflect on her life. Yet she also used this period to look beyond her own circumstance, to consider injustice in general, and to advocate for change beyond what was common for young women in the polite society of mid-

19th-century Upper Canada. Emma was, in her own way, a trailblazer and liberated like her daughter.

Elsie's Grandma Emma had never considered herself a favourite in the family of Judge Miles O'Reilly. Still, she had a front-row seat from which to watch the special attention lavished on her brothers, and even listened in on their lessons despite being warned against absorbing an uncomely level of knowledge.[31] She persisted in learning on her own and in following current events, eventually becoming a staunch abolitionist, a point of view she found was shared by Silas Gregory, the older man who was to become her second husband. Silas, who had come to Hamilton for business, had an interest in languages and the arts that Emma also found appealing.

Silas and Helen had two children together, Herbert and Helen, both of whom left home at an early age for education and travel. Emma might have seen this as an opportunity to settle into a comfortable pattern for the latter part of her life, but, as shown when concern over her daughter's health provided a pretext, she was ready to grab any opportunity to spend extended periods away from Silas, an attitude that led her into those unique experiences she shared with Helen in California, Minnesota, and finally British Columbia. These experiences, which included campaigns for social reform, helped to forge the strong bond between the two women.

Emma did not come to California totally unequipped for social justice work. Earlier in Canada, she had joined women's organizations with a political bent if not an active suffragette agenda. She had acted for a while as treasurer of the Dominion Women's Association, advocated for the rights of convicts, and cultivated her talent as a public speaker. In California, with her daughter Helen at her side, she became known as a highly effective orator, writer, and organizer for reform. A combination of what Elsie later described as "fierce sympathy for the weak and oppressed" and distain for self-pity and slough, Emma was well placed to support her daughter with an image of purpose and strength. Helen needed Emma's support — as a suddenly widowed, 37-year-old woman with two boys in Minnesota, and then again when she contemplated motherhood once more in Vancouver.

When, little more than a year after Lee's death, the two women moved to Vancouver with the boys and with Helen's new husband, Jim MacGill, they were a pair who had built a unique relationship through a string of shared challenges and conquests. From the difficult childbirth and widowhood to learning the formula for turning social concerns into action, the two were a strong team. Although Grandma Emma's presence in the Vancouver home was to be limited in time, it was important, for it too made the advent of Helen's final pregnancy easier to accept.

Baby Elsie

The baby, another girl, was born healthy, and her March 27, 1905, delivery at the Burrard Sanitarium on Georgia Street was unremarkable.[32]

A debate over which grandmother's name the girl would carry was the only event of the day that lingered as a family memory. Unlike the eye problems afflicting the newborn Eric, or infant Freddy's chubbiness, there was nothing to suggest anything other than a relatively healthy life for this, the MacGill's second child. She was physically sound in appearance and movement, and there were thus no particular concerns when she later encountered the routine childhood illnesses, took part in vigorous activities, or jostled for a place in a home with older boys and rowdy friends in the bush-filled neighborhood.

Jim won the naming debate, and the baby was christened Elizabeth Muriel Gregory MacGill for his own mother, as he had intended. As the youngest and smallest object of affection, the baby soon heard her name massaged into something smaller and more tender: "Elsie".

Her Sister and HelNelsie

Even though her mother Helen naturally dominated her early life, Elsie soon came to see her sister Young Helen as the shining star of her existence, a star that over time would glow with a brighter and brighter light.

The episode of whooping cough, prior to Elsie's birth, may have been the only time her sister Helen occupied the entire attention of the family. Not that Elsie hogged the spotlight, although the youngest child often has that capacity; it was more that Elsie presented a need to share attention and experience. Almost from the day Elsie was born, she and her sister were viewed as a special, near-inseparable pair identified with the new

Buccaneer Bay Cottage in August 1906, (standing) MacGill family cook Gong, Elsie's brother Eric Flesher, Elsie's sister Helen, (sitting on the ground) Elsie's brother Freddy Flesher, one-year-old Baby Elsie is sitting on her maternal Grandmother Emma Gregory's lap. (*Courtesy of Elizabeth Schneewind.*)

home in Vancouver. Describing her childhood later in life, Elsie would most often cite this connection with her sister, comparing the two of them to a "team of horses" or a "vaudeville pair", almost as if the two girls had morphed into a single being.[33]

Indeed, the duo of "Helen and Elsie" soon became cited as the slurred "HelNelsie", a pairing that was to be the most enduring relationship of Elsie's life, stretching as it did from her birth in Vancouver to her Toronto memorial service 75 years later. Young Helen would be there at all the major junctures of her sister's life, a source of support and strength nurtured in those first years in West End Vancouver, a place that Elsie's sister would equally see as home and the base for her own growth and personal development.

Their close association included sharing germs and times in sick beds. As Elsie later recalled, they "took croup, chicken pox, measles" together and later "suffered chronic bronchitis" in tandem, always at the same time and with the same intensity. Through such shared experience, their childhood wove ties perhaps only fully recognized years later; at the time it seemed natural to bundle HelNelsie for every occasion and event.

Elsie was the precious little one, but Young Helen could also sparkle along with her little sister. Later, she would hold her own in the areas of education and social work so important to older members of the family. With little or no differentiation between Young Helen and Elsie in terms of the benefits of family life, material or spiritual, there were none of the jealousies that can taint even the most mature sibling relationships. The two little girls thus had the ingredients and special opportunity to build the close and loving relationship that would buttress the rest of their lives.

From their earliest years together, Elsie and her sister played and learned in the warm light of their mother and grandmother's love in a place of privilege as daughters of a prospering, connected lawyer. They had ready playmates in each other, laughter, and opportunity, both social and educational, in a city on the edge of a golden era of cultural development, urbanization, and economic growth. It was in many ways an ideal launching pad for a life that would be propelled forward by a positive outlook and unhindered aspirations.

Chapter II

My Mother the Suffragette

"From plague, pestilence and famine, from battle, murder, sudden death and all forms of cowlike contentment, Good Lord deliver us".[34]

Soon after the MacGill's new baby Elsie opened her eyes and took her first breaths, her life was affected by an army of men with picks and shovels at a place thousands of kilometres away. The hole they were digging would grow into a deep, wide pit some 80 km (50 miles) long, a hole that would boost Vancouver's economic growth and draw international attention to the skills and daring of the professional engineer.

The dream of a navigable canal across the Isthmus of Panama had been a topic of conversation for hundreds of years. Even the first Spanish explorers, in the 16th century, could see the potential for a short cut between oceans at this site. But the scale of the project had intimidated everyone until the mid-1800s, when the Americans built a railway along the route and when realization of the Napoleonic-era dream, the Suez Canal, proved that such mega-engineering feats were not only possible, but politically popular.

Work on the Panama Canal began formally in the summer of 1904 and was completed a decade later. A renowned project championed by U.S. president Teddy Roosevelt, construction of the canal held the drama of a daunting challenge, capturing the imagination of the ambitious and technically skilled around the world. It also pointed to a promising future for the year-round port of Vancouver.[35]

New investment was attracted to the city as it prepared to break free of dependency on the rail line to the east. The fledgling mining and forest industries saw the potential of new markets, and moneyed visionaries in Britain and other countries shared the optimism. Banking, insurance, and branch-office businesses planted themselves in Vancouver, bringing new traffic to Jim MacGill's law office. The population of the province more than doubled to almost 400 000 in those first ten years of the 20th century, and Vancouver became the anchor city of the province, with well over 100 000 people by the time Elsie MacGill entered public school.

Against this backdrop of industrial and urban growth, the MacGill family lived with some affluence in a softer, more thoughtful milieu. For Elsie, the city's growth and development were manifested in a secure home, a comfortable childhood, and a parade of interesting people. This parade would shape her early life and eventually lead her away from Vancouver.

The Classroom in the Mustard-Coloured House

By 1908, growth in the Vancouver economy made it possible for the MacGill family to afford a new house in Vancouver's West End, not far from the rented homes they had occupied before but much roomier and more comfortable. This house, more than any other, would be remembered by Elsie as home. A big, wood-frame building surrounded by a high fence and clad in cedar shingles, it had three levels, a little land, and lots of room for children, their friends, the adults, their guests, a series of pets, and some farm animals.

The specific house number was 1492, purportedly picked by Jim because the historic number was easy to remember. Its exterior was a yellowish golden colour, and it irritated Elsie that the neighbourhood children called it the "mustard-coloured house".[36] But the name stuck and that is how she would always refer to it.

With several university degrees between them, Elsie's parents were unquestionably inclined toward education in all its forms, including pre-school tutoring and private lessons, which they arranged for Elsie and her sister as soon as they emerged from infancy. The third floor of the mustard-coloured house was converted into a classroom, and the little girls were joined by a few friends to be taught academic subjects such as French and artistic pursuits such as painting in water colours, and to enjoy other organized play. It was a formal setting that required them to dress up for class and adhere to a schedule echoing that imposed on their older brothers, who were in public school at the time. The high-quality preschool and association with her older sister gave Elsie an educational leg-up and began a process that would eventually see her entering university almost two years earlier than the norm.

The mustard-coloured house in Vancouver. Elsie's beloved childhood home. And the Lord Roberts School — still standing today. (*Photos by M. Bourgeois-Doyle.*)

When Elsie was old enough to begin formal schooling, she was thus very well prepared. Happily, the West End was well equipped to educate its youngest residents. In particular, the Vancouver high school had a range of programs and a special credibility because of its affiliation with

McGill University as a sort of higher-education outpost of the venerable eastern institution.[37] Lord Roberts, an elementary school on Bidwell Street down near English Bay, had been in operation since the spring of 1901, when a large red wooden structure was erected to house eight classes and a few hundred students. Elsie's brother Freddy had gone to the wooden schoolhouse, but by the time his sisters arrived, it had been replaced by an impressive brick building that still stands today. Lord Roberts — or "Bobs", as the students dubbed it — was a lively place, growing every year, and would reach an enrolment of as many as a thousand students over the next decade.[38] As the West End was a place of relative affluence, students, like Elsie, at Lord Roberts were supported, stimulated, and advantaged.[39]

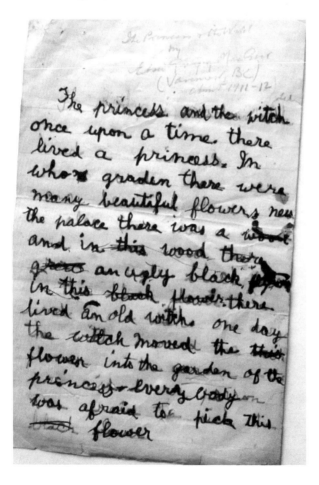

Elsie's handwritten story "The Princess and the Witch", marked 1911–1912. (*Library and Archives Canada.*)

Emily and Old Joe

Elsie seemed to enjoy learning to read and write and at the age of seven impressed herself and her family by scribbling an original piece of fiction, a saga of few pages entitled "The Princess and the Witch".[40] She and her sister Young Helen were also fortunate enough to have outside instruction in sports and arts. Their private lessons even included drawing lessons with the future Canadian luminary Emily Carr in her studio across False Creek in the area known as the Fairview Slopes.[41]

Carr, who would later be acclaimed as a painter and a unique expression of the Canadian character, was still struggling for acceptance in the art world and for a livelihood when little Elsie crossed her path. In the years after her 1912 return to British Columbia from study in Europe, Emily Carr raised animals, sold produce, and made pottery as well as taught to make ends meet. Elsie later described the time of her classes with Emily as likely the most challenging of the artist's life. This was a significant observation; Carr, whose innovative work was not always well received by critics, had confronted "ridicule" and "even hostility" before this time.[42]

British Columbians made for stimulating and inspiring teachers. Carr, for example, had stories of her life-defining sojourns to West Coast native villages and other parts of the world, but had also tasted the bitter side of life, burdened by male-defined convention and attitude. Elsie's mother Helen, who had broken out of the rigid prescriptions of Upper Canada through her interest in music, could empathize with Emily's rigid upbringing in Victoria, B.C., her orphaned circumstance, and her sometimes lonely pursuit of art because of her own escape from a stiff British upbringing. In addition, both women had lived in San Francisco in the 1890s and knew the vitality of the women's movement in that part of the United States.[43]

Elsie's exposure to people like Emily Carr was, therefore, a typical feature of life during this dynamic period of B.C. history and the resulting variety of personalities, often strong and committed, whom the MacGill family encountered. The parade through Elsie's early years also included the memorable and doting Joe Fortes, the self-appointed lifeguard who encouraged her and many other Vancouver children to "kick 'oo feetz"[44] as they learned to swim under his eye in the waters of English Bay.

Old Joe Fortes

A hero to many and one of the few notable blacks in the city at the time, Joe Fortes was a unique personality. He had come to Vancouver from the Caribbean, likely Trinidad, via England three decades earlier on a ship said to have run aground off the coast and then been towed into the harbour. Joe fell in love with the West End, especially the English Bay area, and lived there for the rest of his life, supporting himself with odd jobs but always seeing himself as the protector of the beach and the people, like the MacGill family, who shared his enjoyment.

Eventually, the City of Vancouver put him on its payroll as a lifeguard and special constable, and he was well honoured during his life and after. Known as "Old Joe"[45] by the children who loved him, he was a symbol of the comfort and security surrounding Elsie as she was growing up. She and other children were given great freedom to explore along the water precisely because Joe was there and trusted utterly by Helen, Jim, and the other parents.

The MacGill children's experience of British Columbia was not restricted to the urban Lower Mainland. When Elsie and her sister contracted a persistent case of bronchitis blamed on the dampness of coastal Vancouver, Helen took the girls into the high country for a summer to dry out their lungs on a ranch overlooking Okanagan Lake. The spectacular view of rolling hills and big water was permanently implanted in Elsie's mind, as was the sight of her mother riding horses and working around the ranch.

In part because of the girls' preschool and extra-curricular experiences, Jim and Helen felt confident enough to take their daughters out of class for a six-month family trip across Canada and on to Europe. Jim, whose connections with the Liberal Party in Ottawa were bringing him more and more government business, had legal work in England involving the Privy Council. At six years of age, Elsie was too young to absorb the full benefits of the trip, but knew that her mother was happy to have the family together.

Her family, the West End of Vancouver, the Roberts School, Old Joe Fortes, Emily Carr, riding in the Okanagan, travel… It was a rich and pleasant childhood.

The Beach of Vancouver's English Bay near Elsie MacGill's childhood home (circa 1905), and her swimming teacher and friend Old Joe Fortes. (*Vancouver Public Archives: Be P5.1 and CVA 677-440; photos by Stuart Thompson.*)

Comings and Goings

Yet the MacGill family's circumstances did not stand still. For Helen, change began in 1907, a year before the move to the mustard-coloured house, with one of life's hard but predictable blows. Her mother Emma, while still in her early seventies, died of cancer almost immediately after diagnosis and a hasty, vain operation. The death terminated what Elsie would later recognize as "the longest and most harmonious association"[46] of her mother's life. Helen, Elsie said, grieved "in every way that a woman can". Emma had been Helen's best friend, business partner, caregiver, confidante, colleague, and role model. Together, in both Canada and the

United States, they had written and published newspapers, crusaded, and learned the trade of social change. In Vancouver, they had shared child rearing and learned, as mature women, to manage in new settings. Walking away from her mother's grave in Mountain View Cemetery, Elsie's mother Helen MacGill felt alone and distressed.

For Elsie, however, Emma's death would have its greatest direct impact through those who came into the MacGill home to fill the vacuum. One was Elsie's maternal grandfather, Emma's husband Silas Ebenezer Gregory, a vivid, albeit aging figure who would become a firm image in Elsie's childhood memories.

Elsie's Grandpa Silas had spent much of his married life separated from his younger wife. Although he joined her and his daughter for extended visits in California, he may have felt misplaced around the tight clutch of Emma, Helen, and the two boys. Back in Quebec, on the other hand, he had siblings, French Canadian roots, and recollections of younger days filled with promise and fun. Elsie's Grandpa Silas loved the violin and associated it with his youth, when he was deemed to be the top amateur in a province that fervently celebrated fiddlers. He set his passion aside to pursue a business career, which had led him to Hamilton, Ontario, and his marriage to Emma.

Silas was living again in Quebec when, in 1907, his wife, his luck, and his strength all came to the end of the road. Then 84 years old, he welcomed the invitation to come to Vancouver and live with Helen and her band. A genial man with a big white mustache and long wavy hair, Silas tried to remain active and social, ultimately leaving another soft, smiling mark on Elsie's childhood home even though his time with them was limited to less than five years of steady decline, aches, pains, blindness, and eventually terminal illness.

Many others — friends, the occasional visiting relative, and strangers in need — passed through the MacGill home during the years when Elsie and her sister were growing up. But if the pair "HelNelsie" was ever to be stretched into a triumvirate, the leading candidate would have been their grandmother's cousin Sarah Ann Kerby, whom they called "Cousie". A substantive and formidable woman, Cousie was a product of the poorer side of the family, one who maintained her lack of wealth by devoting much of her life to working for the church and for the people of the Six Nations Reserve near Brantford, Ontario. Later in life, she earned her

Elsie, a teenager, with her cat at her
West End home, and a few years earlier
on a trip to the horse country of British
Columbia's Okanagan Valley (near
Penticton 1915). (*Courtesy of Elizabeth
Schneewind.*)

keep through housework with family in eastern Canada and then finally
with Elsie's family in Vancouver. She came to the MacGill's shortly after
Emma's death. Cousie was 60 and would live out the last three decades
of her life with the family.

The months passed, and with the influx of new faces, the stimulus of the new house, and Vancouver's dynamism, Helen started to emerge from her sorrow over the loss of Emma. She spoke to Elsie, Young Helen, and others more and more comfortably and positively about her late mother and specifically about her work in social movements and women's groups.

As she renewed her interests in social reform and activism, Helen's home life was also changing. Elsie and Young Helen were busy in school, and the boys took major steps toward adulthood. In 1909, when Elsie was barely four years old, her older brother Eric went away to university, to study arts at Trinity College in Toronto, as did his parents. Going east was the only viable option for higher education at the time, but it had the added advantage of avoiding the increasingly tense relationship between Eric and his stepfather. The next year, at only 16, his younger brother Freddy also travelled east, to attend Highfield, a private school in Hamilton.

Helen would miss them deeply, and although Elsie was still very young, she was aware of her brothers' absence, for they had provided her home with a male-driven, rough and tumble environment. The boys seemed to rule the Buccaneer Bay cottage of "old clothes and canvas cots… rowboats, rafts, tents, swimming, fishing, and campfires". The property was sold just before Freddy moved east, and while the MacGill women would later dominate another cottage, Elsie's early and enduring associations and memories of her brothers were intertwined with those happy, effortless times in a rustic, physical setting, in a cottage often in need of repair.

Mother and Suffragette

The mustard-coloured house was certainly quieter. With the passing of Emma and Silas, her children far away or occupied in school, and with the support of Cousie and Gong at home, Elsie's mother was increasingly free to pursue her social concerns. Although Helen had involved herself in a few charitable organizations and the women's auxiliary of the church,[47] she did not initially see the same opportunities for activist involvement as she witnessed in California and Minnesota. Then music, the skill and talent that had lifted her out of the mundane and nudged the course of her life over 20 years earlier, provided her with a vehicle to pursue her interests anew.

The Vancouver Musical Society, a club conceived while she was pregnant with Elsie, would soon grow to engage hundreds of educated and motivated Vancouver women like Helen. It was to have an influence on education and society beyond its stated goals of music, refinement, and provision of a place for like-minded women to gather and talk. For Helen, who still practiced the piano at night after the children were put to bed, music education now meant the opportunity to break out of a home-based social mould and participate more fully in the world. The Musical Society was more than a mere cultural nicety.

With this foundation, Helen regained her professional footing and refreshed her skills as a journalist by contributing to magazines and daily newspapers and by assuming influential roles within the Vancouver Women's Press Club and the city's fledgling University Women's Club. She became a proud "joiner" of women's organizations,[48] and soon these associations led her into friendships with iconoclastic Canadian feminists.

Helen's Friend Nellie

Among the new friends and visitors who dropped by the MacGill home, Nellie Letitia McClung was, in many ways, the best example of an embodiment of the times. Nellie surely was the human epitome of the early struggle over women's rights. She stood out, a special power flowing from her easy wit, her intellect, and her unique gifts as an orator and writer. Nellie McClung became the person who most "personified Canadian feminism"[49] during the period and who fostered the atmosphere of confrontational debate and passion that Elsie MacGill would associate with this feature of her early experience. "Never retract, never explain, never apologize — get the thing done and let them howl"[50] was Nellie's renowned slogan. With a prayer asking the "Good Lord" to "deliver us" "from plague, pestilence and famine, from battle, murder, sudden death", and, perhaps most of all, "from all forms of cowlike contentment",[51] she urged other women to avoid comfort and complacency lest their souls "atrophy".

Elsie's mother was cut from the same cloth as the celebrated suffragette Nellie McClung, and the two women enjoyed "a warm and merry friendship"[52] as sister journalists and members of women's professional organizations. In 1914 and 1915, when McClung was engaged in the landmark campaign for women's suffrage in Manitoba, Helen Gregory MacGill was busy as a leader of delegations petitioning the B.C. provincial government for "the vote". With her daughters acting as parliamentary pages, Helen even helped stage a mock parliament in Vancouver to ridicule the male-only institutions denying women the vote,[53] a stunt that later inspired Nellie McClung and her colleagues to do the same with a more celebrated version on the prairies.

Later, in the 1920s, when Helen started breaking new ground in the B.C. legal system, her friend Nellie was helping to make laws as a member of the Alberta Legislative Assembly. Towards the end of the decade, as one of the Famous Five, Nellie would join other women to build on the earlier gains in suffrage through the renowned "Persons Case" — their successful fight to overturn a Supreme Court of Canada decision and to confirm that women were legally defined "persons" who could therefore hold public office as Canadian senators.[54]

Association with such motivated feminists led Helen MacGill to investigate the laws affecting women and children in her own province. When she first dug into the subject, she was stunned to learn that British Columbia's family laws were among the most archaic and out of date in the modern world. Many provisions originated with the imperial proc-lamation of 1858, which applied early-19th-century English law to the mainland of British Columbia. As much of the authority in this area fell under provincial jurisdiction, the laws remained unchanged through Brit-ish Columbia's entry into the Canadian confederation and beyond while the rest of North America and jurisdictions abroad progressed to recog-nize increasingly the rights of women and children.

This situation added a unique legal edge and B.C. dimension to the local version of the fight for women's rights and suffrage aflame across Canada and the United States at the time. Educated, erudite and engaged, Helen turned her writing skills to the task of documenting the relevant laws in a booklet that became popular, serving not only to support those who needed such legal tools, but also to highlight areas of weakness. Her self-published "laws handbook"[55] magnified her profile as a suffragette and her appeal as someone who could help out. Strangers approached her after meetings, on the street, and eventually at the MacGill home. Elsie came to accept it as the norm when someone seeking legal advice, cash for groceries, personal support, and even medical attention knocked on the door of their house in the evenings.

The classic image of big hats and banners, politics and petitions, and placards and parades conveys only part of the story and of the ultimate success of the early 20th century suffragette movement. The campaign to secure equal voting rights for women had many sides and was fought on many fronts, in many ways, and by many personalities. Through her mother, Elsie came to see that the work for reform brought together different ideas and different people.

The feisty and witty Nellie McClung may have personified Canadian feminism in most minds, but her cause — "the Cause" — also attracted women with very different skills, attitudes, and motivations. Canadian suffragettes counted upper-class snobs and vocal racists within their ranks as well as struggling defenders of human rights,[56] while their male allies included many political opportunists and hypocrites as well as the enlightened and bold. The movement also drew in elements of all major political parties in Canada.

The heterogeneous nature of the early Canadian suffragette movement is illustrated by people like Helena Gutteridge, another of Helen MacGill's associates but also a socialist and labour activist destined to be the first woman on Vancouver City Council. Gutteridge, like others, was committed to securing the vote for women, but as just one element of her broader interest in social reform. Born to a working-class family in England, she brought a cockney accent and blue-collar mindset to Vancouver in 1911. She had worked alongside the Pankhursts and other militant suffragettes, who tutored her in the organizational tactics of the British class struggle.[57]

Unlike Gutteridge, Elsie MacGill's mother often acted more as a member of the elite and a legal scholar than a fighter. She was passionate and involved, but less radical and more inclined to practical approaches and to influencing the system from within. The same practical inclinations prompted Helen MacGill, a life-long supporter of the Conservative Party and product of the affluent, upper-class east, to support the Liberals in British Columbia when that party seemed the one most likely to introduce the vote for women.[58] Helena Gutteridge and her colleagues, however, were suspicious of the Liberal leader when his commitment to the vote changed into a simple pledge to respect the results of a referendum on the issue.

A few years later, Helen MacGill found herself once again at odds with women like Gutteridge when she started to work for the British Columbia Minimum Wage Board. Helen was made a member of the Board and, as periodic chair of its meetings, was responsible for refereeing very public and heated negotiations over sector-based minimum wages. While sympathetic to the needs of the workers and the circumstances of women in particular, Helen did not have the freedom to indulge in a whole-hearted position on any side of the issue. She sought instead to be impartial, to seek what was possible. Helena Gutteridge, predictably on the side of the workers, felt that the snobbish "Helen MacGill had been party to… betrayal"[59] and was merely seeking favour with the employers and the provincial government. Elsie, a young teenager, knew only that her mother faced challenges, had lively debates around social reform, and did not flinch in facing them.

The Suffragette Becomes Judge MacGill

In any case, Helen and her political stands were well known to the provincial Liberals. She was widely respected and an evident, even obvious choice, when in 1917, British Columbia was induced, in the wake of women's suffrage, to follow the Alberta example and appoint its first woman jurist, technically the first in Canada with the title "judge".[60]

She was 53 years old. Her youngest daughter was 12.

Her appointment as Judge of the Juvenile Court of Vancouver flowed from the persistent nation-wide campaign to advance the interests of women and children with a focus around the right to vote. While the women of Quebec had to wait another 20 years and federal enfranchisement was extended in a fragmentary, hiccupping way, western Canada moved quickly. In January of 1916, through that crusade led by suffragettes like Nellie McClung, the women of Manitoba were the first to breach the wall, to formally gain not only the right to vote, but also to hold provincial office. Saskatchewan and Alberta followed suit later in the year, and British Columbia in 1917. It was in this atmosphere of imitation and pressure that governments sought to engage women in the courts and other venues.

The next decades would be enriching and gratifying in many unforeseen ways for Judge Helen MacGill. Her life would assume a new vibrancy, dignity, and worth. Her daughters, HelNelsie, were aware of her stature and works, and became increasingly proud. But they would see less and less of her around the house.

In fact, in that first year, the most visible and notable personal impact of Helen's appointment to the bench for Elsie was new clothing. Helen used her first $50 monthly pay cheque to buy herself a black dress for court and new clothes for the two girls. Elsie and her sister, who were then facing the complicated social interactions of the teenage years, were said to be clearly in need of new outfits.

The worn-out clothes and the evident need for Helen's modest income were signs of other changes in the MacGill family's circumstances, changes that had been building for a number of years.

Jim's legal work continued to be the main source of support for the family, and they remained affluent in a relative sense, but Jim struggled. He suffered from poor investment decisions and from a change of government in Ottawa. A staunch supporter of the Laurier Liberals, even when his wife was a committed Conservative, his tight connections had included the senior official and future prime minister, William Lyon Mackenzie King. Jim, therefore, saw his politically based fortunes evaporate with the 1911 election, which replaced the Laurier government with the Borden Conservatives. Jim's legal income and investments would suffer further when Vancouver started to feel the ripples from an international economic recession in 1913. World War I would make the situation worse. Although armed conflict can stimulate heavy industry, the outbreak of the Great War in 1914 cut off markets and induced new demands on Vancouver business, causing the city's economic fortunes to decline.

Meanwhile, a nastier side of B.C. society started to rise. The main benefit of Jim's association with the governing Liberals had come in the form of immigration-related legal work, largely directed to him as the authorized government immigration agent for the Port of Vancouver. Immigration issues had, for many years, been a lively and stimulating source of discussion at the MacGill home. Now, as Elsie and her sister were becoming aware, immigration, the law, and the Port of Vancouver were discussed in the atmosphere of lost income and the tense and sometimes sad mix infusing local newspapers and permeating city life.[61]

Not only was the city home to eastern Europeans and thousands of Chinese and Japanese struggling to find ways to make a living, it was also the first Canadian city to see the arrival of numerous South Asian migrants, largely Sikh men who during the first years of the 20th century left families and farming in the Punjab in search of better circumstances in Canada. Those who hoped better circumstances included equality and basic rights would be disappointed.

The pressures created by the new and increasing flow of immigrants to the city were blamed in early years on the federal government and its agents, like Jim MacGill. Instead, the province acted first, passing laws to deny newcomers the right to vote, to hold office, and to work in the professions, the public service, and even as labourers on some projects. Within a few years, the federal government joined in the discrimination with regulatory requirements that effectively stopped further immigration from India and permanently separated those already in Canada from their families. These legislative assaults were coupled by periodic riots, street fights, and violence directed at Asian citizens both new and old. While the privileged in Elsie's West End neighbourhood were spared direct exposure to the conflicts, there was no avoiding talk of it, particularly in the connected and concerned MacGill home.

Komagata Maru

It is powerful testimony both to the natural appeal of British Columbia and to hardships in the Punjab that those who came stayed despite discrimination, and more wanted to join their ranks. Conditions reached a loud, vehement pitch in May 1914 when the freighter *Komagata Maru* arrived from Hong Kong with close to 400 prospective South Asian immigrants on board. A standoff of two months, during which the sweltering shipload sat in Vancouver Harbour, ended in ostensible victory for Canadian regulations, the ship returning home with its full human cargo.[62] These events marked a turning point in Vancouver's reputation, and even young children, like Elsie and her sister, would know about them and be touched in a permanent way.

Jim MacGill's politically based security had long dissipated, therefore, by the time trade and business activity were disrupted by the demands and pressures of the Great War. Although Helen had inherited money from her mother's line and seen insurance paid out with the deaths of her first husband and her father, those funds were gone. The family, which once had property and investments valued in six figures, lurched in and out of debt during World War I. Jim's legal practice waned along with his personality.

The war, the economic downturn, and the racist reactions combined to suck the joy from many souls, and Jim MacGill's personal, financial, and professional struggles pressed even harder on his ability to laugh and enjoy himself at home. He maintained a capacity to support Helen in his own way, to nurture their partnership, and to provide, and for the most part, Jim MacGill remained a solid structure in Elsie's young life. Yet Elsie later recalled her father as becoming more and more defined during these years by his more unpleasant qualities —overly sensitive, strict, domineering, anxious, and uncomfortable.

But even a different attitude on Jim's part could not have fully shielded his family from their changed financial circumstances. In 1915, when Elsie was just 10, Jim sold the beloved mustard-coloured house and moved the family to a rented place on Haro Street. Still in the West End and closer to Stanley Park, the new house had nice features, but not the pleasantness and open joy the family associated with the mustard-coloured house. Elsie saw great pain in her father, whom she later described as "tragically" hurt by the financial pressures and the need to move. She did not, however, recognize any contribution her mother might have made to those feelings of hurt.

Elsie and her sister were forming a very clear and positive image of their mother that did not allow for the notion that she might have been "a rather difficult woman to be married to", who "was used to money", and who may have done "less to assuage [Jim's financial] humiliation, than a more sensitive woman would have done".[63]

Although aware to some degree to these changes affecting their parents, the HelNelsie duo was generally blind to anything negative around their home and focused on concerns that were less political and financial and more social in the girls-and-boys, clothes-and-school, friends-and-fun sense manifested in some manner in the minds of teenagers of every generation and every social context.

For the girls, the loss of the mustard-coloured house would also be mitigated in part when the family acquired a new cottage at a spot known

Elsie upon graduation from King George Secondary School in Vancouver. (*Courtesy of Elizabeth Schneewind.*)

as Greyrocks, off Burrard Inlet. Helen bought this cabin in her own name with her judge's salary in 1920, when the girls were moving into their late teens. Initially purchased as a place for Elsie's sister to recuperate from appendicitis and the lingering illness that ensued, the cottage was embraced by her mother as a symbol of the personal security afforded by land ownership and as a sanctuary from the myriad pressures and tensions of town — and of her marriage.

In recalling her Greyrocks cottage experiences years later, Elsie said that her father came up to the cottage "only occasionally" as "he no longer cared to rough it, and adolescent commotion wearied him".[64] In fact, Jim went with Helen on a preliminary tour of the property and never returned. It was a place for Helen and her children, and the girls adored their times there. Yet "no one succeeded in making Jim feel it could be a family place where he too would be welcome", and some family members wondered later "whether they tried very hard".[65] Jim's unease with Helen's family circle even in Vancouver was such that, on at least one occasion, he disappeared for days.

Like Elsie, Young Helen also played down or avoided discussion of their father's absences from vacations at Greyrocks and the Vancouver home, possibly sharing Elsie's discomfort over it and certainly not desiring any stain on the family reputation that Helen worked so tirelessly to preserve.

For whatever reason, reminiscent of the earlier cottage on Buccaneer Bay, for many years this was a place clearly reserved for women — Helen, Cousie, the girls, and their friends — to relax on weekends, holidays, and summers. Surrounded by tall trees, rippling salt water, and rocky cliffs, it was a strenuous place demanding the skills of the "woodsman", "handyman", and "fisherman", and Elsie absorbed it all with relish. A visit there meant climbing up rocky slopes, dragging the canoe, cleaning fish, cutting firewood, wearing old clothes, and assembling mechanical devices. Elsie and her sister enjoyed the place as a diversion and refuge and were formed by their experiences there throughout their teenage years and beyond.

University Begins

In 1921, the flow of change in the MacGill family home took another turn when Elsie, who had just turned 16, and 18-year-old Young Helen began classes together at the still-new and forming University of British Columbia (UBC).

The MacGill girls had shared childhood experiences, education, and relationships that Elsie would later cite as the most dramatic and noteworthy of those years. Even into their teen years at King George High School in a building that Elsie always called "the Old Dawson School" for its previous occupant, the two continued to move as a near-inseparable pair, learning and growing in tandem as a mildly comical team. They discussed, assessed, and shared almost everything: parties, formal and informal; picnics on the beaches of Vancouver's Spanish Banks; rustic, active weekends "climbing Grouse Mountain and Hollyburn Ridge".[66] They shared friends, parents, brothers, and extended family. Now, although still living at home, Young Helen was finding new friends, new ideas, and new notions about her home and future at the university. She liked the challenge, the atmosphere, and the new circle, and, perhaps, felt a little less coupled to her younger sister.

Elsie's grandparents had been gone for many years, her brothers had moved away a decade earlier, the mustard-coloured house had been sold, her parents were absorbed fully in their professions and financial pressures, and now her sister was growing up. Elsie MacGill was in many ways alone more than she had ever been. Yet she would soon discover someone new — herself, with her own distinct personality and her own separate identity. Within two years, this confidence and self-awareness would take her far away from the family home, UBC, and Vancouver.

Chapter III

Toronto and Ann Arbor

"It never occurred to me I couldn't be an engineer" [67]

As the steam train jerked away from the station on a late summer day in 1923, 18-year-old Elsie MacGill looked out the window, knowing she was heading off for an adventure and into the unknown. She was leaving behind, in a way forever, a comfortable, happy life. She loved the sea and sky of Vancouver, her parents, and their cosy West End homes. But growing up, she had also developed a deep attraction to the unorthodox and exciting. She sensed that she was destined to do something different with her life.

This youngest of Helen MacGill's children had been a solid, industrious student throughout her teens and many options beckoned when she finished high school. She could easily have succeeded as a teacher, a nurse, or in any of the other professions considered appropriate for women at the time. But Elsie did not feel constrained by what was considered the norm. She even felt obliged to ignore the conventional. Because her mother had been an active, even prominent suffragette and had been celebrated at home and beyond for breaking through barriers as a judge, Elsie was aware that, thanks to the years of struggle, women in the 1920s were entering professions once restricted to men. As a young girl, Elsie had been conscripted by her mother into protest events to promote women's suffrage, had helped prepare meals for needy mothers, and had worked for women's charities.

As a student in high school, Elsie thought about what it would be like to continue the work in the political and legal arena where her mother and her friends had fought with enthusiasm and commitment. She also wondered about the personal rewards of a scholarly life because she had

The Greyrocks cabin where Elsie spent her weekends and summers.
(*Library and Archives Canada PA-203361.*)

come in contact with a number of people with that bent at Vancouver's growing new university.

But as she toiled at her studies, helped her mother in community work, and did her chores around home, she was developing a special identity of her own and recognition, within the family at least, as a "Miss Fix-it",[68] a small, delicate girl who enjoyed repairing broken mechanical devices, who excelled in assembling new equipment, and who did some of the heavier work around the house. Elsie's talents were, of course, particularly valuable at that remote, austere family cottage at Greyrocks, Helen's rough-hewn hut on a rugged lump of land at the junction of Burrard Inlet and its north arm.[69]

The boat ride from Vancouver to the Greyrocks cabin, which could take the best part of a day, now became a nearly weekly routine for Elsie. The cabin sat amidst trees and was a stiff climb up from the water's edge, making it a secluded and peaceful site for roughing it. As a university student, Elsie still loved the cabin, and it was her favourite weekend haunt, sometimes shared with a cluster of young friends and her siblings, sometimes alone with her mother — but still never with her city-bound lawyer father. Like her mother, she had no choice but to gain a degree of mechanical and physical independence if she was to enjoy this special place as often as she wanted.

As Elsie's reputation for fixing things merged with talk of a career, her circle of influence pulled in a boyfriend who had access to a ham radio set and a window on the magic of the emerging electrical world. This mix of social life and science seemed to crystallize her ambitions; she decided to become an electrical engineer. More precisely, she "started... planning to be a radio engineer".[70] Elsie knew that engineering was the profession for people who could fix things and use their minds, and she now saw electricity as something more than just power generation, as the force behind increasingly important household appliances, industrial equipment, and exciting new communication tools. Elsie knew it would require an advanced knowledge of math and other sciences — a challenge, since she had not taken such classes at King George Secondary School. Still, something in the challenge appealed to her, and the thought of a career in engineering took hold.

Decades later, she would quip that even though relationships with her Vancouver boyfriends, including the one that evolved into an engagement to be married, did not last, her teenage fascination with engineering and technology stuck with her forever.

The Christmas Graduate

Like other universities in western Canada in the early 1920s, the University of British Columbia (UBC) was still in its infancy. Spurred into action by "the Great Trek", an impressive student protest march in 1922, the provincial government eventually announced plans to build permanent facilities and launch expanded programs.[71] But when Elsie was accepted into applied science studies, UBC classrooms were still housed in temporary buildings, known as "the Shacks", that were becoming increasingly crowded.

Whether crowding and limited resources affected his thinking or not, the Dean of Applied Sciences soon determined that the engineering program could do with one less student. Elsie was asked to leave after only one term, and while the man would live to be embarrassed and to openly regret the decision, he was firm at the time. The reason for his ruling, he told Elsie, was that he simply did not want women in engineering studies at UBC. Although women were not explicitly banned from engineering, Elsie may have been allowed to enroll simply because, as was still the case at some institutions for many decades after, "the idea of women in engineering had seemed so preposterous that no one ever bothered to exclude them officially".[72] Elsie was shaken, but continued on at UBC in general studies. Her sister tried to soften the blow by euphemistically calling Elsie a "Christmas graduate" in engineering.[73] Elsie's parents tried to console her as well, supporting Elsie in her decision to stay at UBC for a while, but they had another suggestion.

They had been told that the best route to a Canadian education in electrical engineering was at the University of Toronto (U. of T.). Elsie knew the risks. She would be a continent away from her parents and friends and likely once again the lone female in the class. Worse, her career opportunities on graduation might take her even further away from Vancouver. Nonetheless, she applied to the U. of T. and was accepted.

The notion of an 18-year-old girl leaving home to live thousands of miles away can be unsettling for parents even today. In 1923, it was dramatic and unusual. But Elsie's parents were comforted by a few facts. They were both from eastern Canada, had fond recollections of Ontario, and had graduated from Trinity College, one of the many institutions that by 1923 had joined into the University of Toronto. Helen and Jim MacGill often recalled their many warm memories of university life, including their first meeting, praising a Toronto education and the greater availability of opportunities for higher learning in the east.[74]

Elsie was well aware of her mother's adventures as a young woman, of her travels alone across the untamed west and by steamship to Japan. Members of the MacGill family had also taken many train trips back east over the years. As a young child, the family had visited their relatives in Toronto and travelled to Europe by boat. So Elsie had experienced a little of the romance of travel and, after all, her father's sister and other relatives were still back east.

But her siblings were most responsible for erasing the stress of leaving Vancouver. Her much older brothers, Freddy and Eric, had left for school in Ontario a decade earlier. Although it was hard at the time, the boys seemed to have survived the experience quite well, making friends and later finding careers. While they would not be in Toronto waiting to greet

Elsie, the fact that they had earlier charted a trail to the east made it seem only natural for Elsie to follow in their footsteps. Both the California-born Freddy (who had joined the U.S. military at the tail end of World War I) and Eric (who stayed longer in school) would use their eastern education as stepping stones and would marry, eventually returning to the West Coast to build their lives in farming and business, respectively.

Still, the summer 1923 train ride across Canada could have been lonely and anxious if it were not for the person sitting beside Elsie: her older sister Helen. Like Elsie, Young Helen had already been a university student for two years, studying languages and economics at that scramble of buildings labelled the University of British Columbia. She was doing well, but knew her parents had always wanted their daughters to study in Toronto. Young Helen investigated the regulations and arranged for a full transfer to Toronto to finish off a degree there and, more importantly, to accompany Elsie on her quest to pursue engineering. The two sisters were excited.

For someone contemplating a career in the field, the train trip east across Canada from Vancouver presented a spectacular pageant of engineering marvels. Down deep river canyons, over snowy peaks, and through the long spiral tunnels of the Rocky Mountains, the trip showcased brilliant, obvious testaments to the skill of Canadian engineers, builders, and surveyors. The forests, the lake-filled scenery, and the excitement of the voyage made it easy to forget the tragedy and sacrifice entailed in the track's construction. The towering mountains, fields of wheat, the winding miles of forests and rock even now inspire awe and feelings of wonder in sophisticated 21st century travellers. When Elsie and her sister rolled into Toronto's old rail station, they were filled with an appreciation for the expanse and the engineering challenges of their country. And on leaving the train, they immediately sensed the difference between their countrified home in Vancouver and life in a big eastern city.

Toronto

By 1923, Toronto's rapidly growing population numbered in the hundreds of thousands. It was still in the shadow of Montréal, the country's top business centre, but an increasing number of industries and institutions were making Toronto their headquarters. The Royal Ontario Museum was over a decade old, and the previous year the Toronto Symphony had been established.[75] Toronto felt like a place destined to be one of the world's great cities, and its university fitted the mould.

The University of Toronto was well established and also much larger than UBC. Its history stretched back almost a century to the creation of its primary predecessor, King's College, as an institution under the control of the Church of England. The university's development was hesitant and complex. Over the years, several forms of affiliations and associations with other religious and non-denominational colleges were tried out before the fully amalgamated institution of today became reality. Nevertheless, progress was steady and all the major disciplines had been brought into the fold by the time Elsie was filling out her entrance forms and figuring out her class schedule.

Engineering at the university was in some respects well defined, in others still finding its way. For example, it was just starting to stake out ground in engineering research, building on work begun during World War I. Although the engineering faculty was gaining a degree of recognition as a source of answers to industrial problems, it had only begun to sense its future as a research leader following the 1917 creation of the School of Engineering Research (SER).

Its programs of instruction, on the other hand, had been developed and refined for almost 50 years. Even though Elsie's part of the university, the Faculty of Applied Sciences and Engineering (FASE), was barely two decades old, the university's experience in the field dated back to the early 1870s, when the Ontario Government established the School of Practical Science (SPS) at a location physically close to the core of the campus, yet retained administrative and financial control through the provincial Department of Education. This separate status was, in part, a product of differing views on what was needed. One political element envisioned the school as something more akin to a technical skills and trades training program for workers as opposed to an academic concern. Consistent with the former view and its name, the School of Practical Science developed with a clear no-nonsense, hands-on bent under the leadership of its founding principal, the industrially trained "man of sound ability" John Galbraith.[76]

At first, even during the years when the university supplied some of the teaching staff, the SPS was not recognized as a university organ. As a consequence, the students were initially required to study for only three years, receiving diplomas instead of engineering degrees during the school's first decades. The diploma was later subsumed within a four-year Bachelor of Applied Sciences (B.A.Sc.) program that became the mainstay of the transformed SPS when it evolved into a U. of T. faculty just after the turn of the century. This is the very practical and technical program to which Elsie applied and gained admission two decades later.

The much admired Galbraith continued with the FASE as dean, and his bachelor's program maintained its strong technical, hands-on core. A little over a decade before Elsie's arrival at the U. of T., the customary means of acquiring the engineering-related B.A.Sc. degree was still to complete the three-year diploma, work, and then return for a graduate year, only *then* focusing on a specialty such as civil engineering.

In the early years, mechanical and electrical engineering were considered the same field for the purposes of the B.A.Sc. at Toronto. But long before Elsie decided to pursue a career in electrical engineering, the U. of T. recognized the field as a distinct area of study worthy of attention in the four-year degree program. There were other places to study engineering at the time, but for Elsie and many other Canadians, Toronto was the best venue by far, largely because of the dedication and vision of Galbraith and his colleagues.

Nevertheless, engineering at the U. of T. was still viewed as an infant in the early 1920s by some in the senior disciplines of physics, chemistry, and biology. Some in other fields regarded it as a form of industrial arts and properly the work of mechanics. The evidence they used to support this view included that lack of substantive engineering research programs at the university. This was about to change.

At the time of Elsie's arrival, the engineering dean was a former brigadier general named Mitchell, an 1892 graduate of the SPS who had absorbed all of the industrial prejudices of his predecessors through his training and later his own consulting work. A decorated soldier, Mitchell had taken his technical knowledge to the battlefield and understood the consequences of engineering and technology in this venue. In fact, as early as 1895 Mitchell had shown an interest in mechanics as they apply to aeronautical research, and he brought such interests to his new position at the U. of T.

Therefore, although Canada and the world were at peace and money was not particularly abundant when Elsie joined the U. of T. in 1923, the wartime appreciation for scientific and technical research lingered, and universities and governments across Canada were making new investments in facilities. Aeronautics was among the novel fields attracting talent and funds to the university although still as a sideline to mechanical engineering programs. In 1917, a young lecturer named John Hamilton Parkin built a small wind tunnel for wartime aeronautics studies. Six years later he secured funding from the federal government to construct a much larger facility and expand his research program.[77]

When Elsie MacGill walked onto the campus in 1923, she was ready to break down barriers as a young woman enrolled in electrical engineering. Yet her experience would be easier than the one her mother and her mother's female contemporaries encountered in fields like medicine in the 1880s. The women of her mother's generation routinely had to battle ferociously for admittance to college, were ridiculed by classmates, and suffered blatant hostility at the hands of their own professors. Elsie, on the other hand, was entering a university fully accustomed to women students. Although still relatively few in numbers in many disciplines, women were a visible, enthusiastic, and often exuberant presence at Canadian universities.

While most, like Elsie's older sister, filled classrooms in the arts and social science faculties, some women could be found in the science labs and a few had even earned advanced degrees and professional positions in fields like geology, long considered exclusively male domains. In 1918, almost a decade before Elsie was to graduate as Canada's first woman electrical engineer, Grace Anna Stewart became the country's first woman geology graduate after studying at the relatively new University of Alberta.[78] At least one female geologist, Llewellyn May Jones at King's College in Halifax, had even earned a degree through a science and engineering program.[79]

Elsie's future title of first woman graduate in electrical engineering, however, did not mean should would be the first woman engineer in Canada. A number of female analytical and applied chemistry graduates had gone on to professional careers effectively and sometimes officially as chemical engineers in the years before Elsie's entry to university. One early graduate in the field, Hildegarde "Emma" Scott, had even earned a

B.A.Sc. at the U. of T. in 1912.[80] In short, Elsie was exemplary, but not completely alone.

Elsie was not even the sole female in the Faculty of Applied Sciences and Engineering when classes started that September. Her 191 classmates included one other female student: Miss E.M. "Betty" Lalor, who had registered as a student in architecture, a discipline by then said to be "accustomed to the presence of ladies"[81] in the university's studios and lecture halls. In addition, many classes in the first year of engineering studies were generalized and often shared with students from other sub-disciplines. Elsie was again not always the lone female.

But there was one first-year classroom where Elsie's presence was felt and where she was clearly establishing a precedent. The male engineering students considered the drafting room a crude, rough "sanctum", and many were said to have been "astonished" when what they perceived as a "tender and unspoiled creature" appeared in their midst. Despite the initial shock of her appearance in class, Elsie managed to fit in, and her male classmates recalled her holding her own, being accepted "as one of the boys" in 2T7, Toronto's Class of '27 engineers.[82]

One reason that drafting class might have been considered a particularly male arena at the time was its relatively casual atmosphere, like a shop where as much hands-on work took place as formal lecturing and note taking, a place where students would joke and swear casually and where male professors were comfortable telling their "stories". Drafting class was also very much part of the initiation into the profession of engineering. Also known as engineering drawing, drafting was more than a technical skill and trade. It was part of the engineer's language.

Students in a 1923 drafting class learned to use tools, a steady hand — and imagination. But, more importantly, Elsie and her classmates absorbed the standards established by the engineering profession to communicate information and ideas effectively. Before the introduction and development of elegant, computer-aided design technologies in the last part of the 20th century, a "draftsman" would record the details of machinery, structures, and their components in specific ways, using specific profiles, perspectives, and scales. Their drawings allowed craftsmen and machinists to turn dreams and designs into reality, and they made it possible for engineers to share new ideas and build on old ones.

Whether early engineering students anticipated a career in a drafting room or not, they were taught from the beginning the need to know both the process and language to even exist in their chosen profession. Because this was also fundamental to trades and technical work in that era, many of Elsie's classmates arrived at university with some technical-school training and drafting experience. Consequently, students who were technically inclined and male would have had a real advantage.

However, success in the drafting room, like many other classes, is dependent as much on what you do there as on what you bring, and Elsie's inherent discipline and intelligence served her well. She was also on level ground when it came to other elements of the trade of drafting, such as geometric art. Her art lessons with Emily Carr may not have been the same as technical school drawing, but they were part of the helpful, stimulating package of formal and informal education that characterized her Vancouver childhood and prepared her for new experiences.

She may, in fact, have been more comfortable in the engineering classroom than outside. On the whole, the engineering students at the U. of T. were a rowdy bunch. While many of their pranks and extracurricular activities were harmless and even edifying, it is also true that they routinely drank, partied, and talked of women in unflattering terms. Celebrations around the image of a naked Lady Godiva and the "demolish forty beers" chorus of their anthem were expressions of an international, male-defined esprit de corps and a widely accepted understanding of what it meant to be an engineer, a profession with its roots in the military and manual trades.

These traditions, still haunting a more politically correct era, were manifest in 1923.

The atmosphere might well have been intimidating and even frightening for a young woman, but Elsie hid any concerns well. Indeed, historians of the faculty have uncovered no clear evidence of "unwelcoming professors or a threatening student culture" during this period, and conclude that Elsie and her few female colleagues "seem to have found their experience in the faculty quite acceptable".[83]

In Elsie's case, there may also have been the buffer of support and fortification from several would-be suitors; many of her male classmates were said to have become "quite stooped"[84] from carrying her books to class.

At least one of them carried things further to kiss his new classmate on occasion, naturally in private.

Her first uneasy steps at the University of Toronto were also taken knowing that her older sister, her best friend, was close by and would be there at the woman's residence of St. Hilda's College at the end of each day. Within weeks, this all changed. Helen was having her own problems. Arrangements for the orderly transfer of credit for her two years of prior study at UBC had fallen through and the university bureaucratic entanglements threatened Young Helen's chances of keeping on track with her studies. She was extremely apprehensive and stressed, especially by the prospect of embarrassment at being perceived as anything other than a top student.

Anxiety about reputation was part of Young Helen's character and would later play a part in her professional life. Although outwardly accomplished and confident, inwardly she was an anxious person, "a nail-biter even as a very mature adult"[85] and prone to digestive trouble "of a nervous origin". She had a sense, cultivated by her mother the judge, that it was unthinkable to expose one's human frailties. The judge had, perhaps purposely, fostered "the family feeling that they were 'better than most people' and could rather expect to be at the top". Unwilling to admit to poor eyesight, Young Helen "worked hard at school so as to rank top" of her classes in order to "be allowed a seat in the front row, the only place she could see from".[86] Now, at the U. of T., Young Helen's status as a top student was threatened by mid-program transfers and change.

Elsie, who had completed similar university courses in Vancouver, was harbouring the same ingrained concern about family appearances. But since engineering was an entirely new program, she did not face the same bureaucratic challenges as her sister.

By the end of their first month in Toronto, it was clear that her sister's problems could not be resolved. Young Helen was compelled to cut her losses and head back to Vancouver to salvage her pride and academic year at UBC. To what extent, if any, homesickness played a part in the decision, Young Helen never acknowledged. She made her decision apparently assured that Elsie was on solid, safe ground and "gleefully"[87] pursuing her engineering courses and life in Toronto. Their mother, however, was disappointed that things had not worked out and was now very concerned about Elsie, all alone in Toronto with a heavy course load. The

Elsie at the University of Toronto 1927 — Canada's first woman graduate in electrical engineering. (*Courtesy of Ann Soulsby.*)

judge also felt that Elsie was not receiving the respect and treatment she deserved as an "industrious" student who had more university experience than most of her classmates and was, in the judge's view, more mature than the other students in the women's residence.[88]

Although she may secretly have felt lonely and somewhat isolated, Elsie stuck it out on her own and, unlike many male students, survived the first year of classes with relative academic ease.

An Introduction to Aeronautics

In her second year at the University of Toronto, Elsie's courses moved from the technical and practical of the drafting room and the shops to the theory and higher-level knowledge that distinguishes a professional engineer's education from that of a technical tradesperson. Her 1924 courses included Elementary Machine Design and Theory of Mechanism. The latter covered topics ranging from fundamental aspects of machine construction to the properties defining the motion of the parts of a machine, meaning that students like Elsie had to comprehend the mathematical methods for determining velocities, both linear and angular, and the physics of the forces underpinning the relative efficiency of machines as well as the various applications of toothed gearing systems, flywheels, and other important components. Yet although the courses were increasingly theoretical, they retained the workshop atmosphere of the faculty's forerunner, the School of Practical Science. Whenever possible, Elsie and the other students visited shops and factories to gain a better understanding of the perspective of machinists and other tradespeople responsible for taking engineering ideas and making them real.

The second-year lectures were designed with the specific intent of addressing any lack of practical experience in the trades, which earlier generations of B.A.Sc. graduates would have gained through first-hand processes. Elsie, who worked during her summer breaks at a machine shop repairing electric motors,[89] also sought every opportunity for practical experience outside the classroom.

The aim of blending flexible, omnipotent theory with the in-your-face practicality of the machinist was to prepare students for the later years of their degree program and to help them reach a stage where they could together pull the fibres of their program into an understanding of whole systems and, perhaps, lay the groundwork for future work designing entire machines themselves. Elsie's professors, the dedicated ones, liked to give their lectures life with modern examples, including some from the nascent field of aeronautical engineering.

For the first time in her life, Elsie heard someone talking about aeronautics as a separate discipline, one that drew upon a wide range of engineering knowledge. It was amazing to think the forces, mechanisms, and physics of an airplane could be so complex and deep that they could consume the entire career of a university research professor. Yet despite the popularity of these informal discussions and the U. of T.'s early research in aeronautical engineering, the faculty would not inaugurate formal courses in the field until years after Elsie had left Toronto.

"Unfortunately, there is no course in Aeronautical Engineering nor any instruction in aeronautical subjects given here", Elsie's Machine Design and Mechanics professor would say with frustration. "The work at Toronto is confined entirely to research or experimental studies of aircraft or aircraft components [and] there is [still] no place in Canada where such instruction can be given".[90]

Elsie had her hands full with the existing courses. She was a bright, enthusiastic woman with the right combination of traits to benefit from the U. of T. engineering program and the drive to fill in the gaps in her earlier education. Nevertheless, as the course in machine design and mechanics proved, there were hurdles to overcome and some awkwardness to endure from her special status as the lone female engineering undergraduate. Her fellow students, man-sized boys in many cases, would titter and giggle in class whenever a professor was obliged to use terminology with sexual innuendo: male fittings, bastard file, female threading, and so on. It was uncomfortable. Yet however self-conscious Elsie might have felt, she could have taken comfort in realizing that she was not alone. Her professor, a man normally stern and confident, had the charm to blush in the circumstances and ultimately edited his lectures to save "Miss MacGill" and himself from embarrassment.[91]

While such stories seem quaint and misguided today, they hint that the atmosphere in the engineering classes was more inclined towards the gentle, light-hearted, and accommodating for the lone woman, than the hostile and resentful alternative. They are also a reminder that much of the opposition to female entry into Canadian universities a half century earlier was not based upon an assumption of inferiority in women, but rather angst over the potential impact of coeducation on the male students and consequently on campus life.[92]

In fact, the admission of women to some universities was resolved not by a decision based upon equity, but rather the availability of resources needed to properly segregate the two sexes in residences and in certain classes. The behaviour of some male engineering students might give validity to those concerns, and remained a clumsy burden for the women students to bear.

Elsie and the other female students were known as "co-eds" since their presence meant that an institution had become "co-educational". "There are more co-eds on campus this year", "The co-eds live in that building", and "There is a co-ed in our class" were common elements of conversation.

Elsie may have wondered why the boys were not called "co-eds", since there are two sides to coeducation. Still, she and other women wore the label with pride as the vanguard of something new and exciting in the decade after women's suffrage took hold in Canada. They wore knee-length skirts, loose clothes, bobbed hair, small hats, and smiles. It was the "flapper" era of the roaring twenties, and some people linked the masculine look to the newfound feeling of emancipation. Elsie sought to fit in, adopted the styles, and later remembered feeling superior as a result.

Generally speaking, it was a great time to be a student at the University of Toronto. Everyone at the university — students, faculty, and administrators — knew that they were part of an institution on the rise. A year before Elsie's arrival, the first successful treatments of insulin were administered in Toronto following its discovery by Frederick Banting and Charles Best and its effective development by a highly respected team led by J.J. Macleod at the U. of T. The discovery would bring the university a Nobel Prize and instant international recognition. At the same time, graduate programs, research, and other advanced studies were being introduced in an obvious drive to transform Toronto into the country's leading university in direct competition with the revered McGill in Montréal.[93] Feelings of pride and optimism flowed into the latter half of Elsie's time in Toronto, and later official historians would authoritatively brand this period as "the Good Years".[94]

Elsie was like many university students today. Anxious at times, over-confident at others, always blending the books with what it meant to be young. She was, for the most part, a proud and confident reflection of her surroundings. In her final years at Toronto, Elsie increasingly thought about building on the knowledge gained through her university studies with her own original ideas, and was one of several fourth-year B.A.Sc. students who embarked on research, carrying out original experiments worthy of a graduate thesis. Again she confronted the challenge successfully.

In the spring of 1927, as her last semester was coming to an end, Elsie was celebrated by her classmates and professors as the first woman in Canada to graduate with a degree in her field: "Canada's first woman electrical engineer"[95]. In pursuing her degree in the decade after the widespread acceptance of women's suffrage, she never considered the notion that she should avoid a career in engineering because of her sex. But some engineering schools still refused admission to women, and women in Canada were, astoundingly, still engaged in the battle launched by her mother's friends for legal recognition as "persons".[96]

Michigan

Elsie, however, had her own framework and was already pondering new frontiers and challenges and, once again, moves that others would see as unorthodox and unusual.

In 1927, the U.S. automobile industry was expanding dramatically and had become one of the most powerful magnets for young, technically trained people. The Detroit area and specifically Pontiac, Michigan, was a site of future growth and a hotbed of well-paying jobs and opportunity. Elsie now accepted one of these jobs and moved to Pontiac, leaving Canada for what would be years.

Looking at the heavy, clunky, grinding vehicles of the 1920s, young engineering graduates like Elsie might well have thought that the automotive industry could benefit most from the skills of a mechanical or design engineer. In fact, however, all the major car-makers were aware of the importance of electrical engineering to their industry.

Electricity was more than a luxury or add-on to the basic machine to power the headlights and make instrumentation easier to read. It had been integral to all successful motor vehicles since 1911, when the American genius, industrialist, and electrical engineer Charles F. Kettering invented and developed the electric starter motor. Although efforts to market electric automobiles fizzled, Kettering's electrical innovation made motor cars significantly more acceptable to consumers, facilitated their marketing, and generated the pressures leading to Henry Ford's use of mass production techniques. Mass production and a blending of electricity, motors, and men — such was the technological atmosphere that characterized the booming industry 22-year-old Elsie MacGill entered in the summer of 1927.

Today the United States lures many highly trained Canadians to its industry. But despite the unique opportunities and pull, many of Elsie's fellow graduates in 1927 would not have considered leaving their country for the United States as an option, no matter what the career implications. Canada was not merely home; it was a nation still defined by ties to Britain and Europe, and students with wanderlust often looked across the Atlantic instead.

To the extent that Elsie may have fussed about the merits of crossing the border for a career opportunity, her concerns would have been mitigated by her family history. Her mother had, of course, spent many years in California and Minnesota as a fully committed resident of the United States, working as a journalist, businesswoman, and active suffragette. This work and commitment to life in the States even endured through a difficult period on her own as a widow responsible for two young boys, Elsie's brothers, both of whom were born in the United States and identified themselves as American at times with Freddy going so far as to join the U.S. Army. When Elsie's mother Helen joined the suffragette cause in Vancouver, it was considered a very "American thing" for her to do because women had much earlier successfully agitated for the vote in several U.S. states. Notwithstanding the British flavour of Vancouver, in the MacGill house it was a far from negative thing to resemble an American. Elsie, for her part, considered Americans to be "wonderfully friendly, wonderfully open-handed" people and throughout her life would celebrate her family's past, present, and projected American ties.

Moreover, Elsie's beloved sister Helen had moved to Chicago two years earlier, would marry an American, and was pursuing graduate studies at the University of Chicago with every intention of making her career there. Indeed, Young Helen would eventually take out American citizenship and live out the bulk of her adult life on U.S. soil.

Elsie's new home in Michigan would be close enough to Chicago for visits, and her sister's example and personal successes in the United States may also have had at least a slight influence on her decision to move to Michigan. However, the main reason Elsie MacGill chose to move to the United States, aside from professional opportunity, is probably the same one that characterized most of her major decisions in life. She did not recognize the same boundaries as other people, men or women, and made her decisions despite factors that others might consider as not being proper, normal, or safe.

In any case, in 1927 the energized U.S. auto industry clearly offered a promising future for young engineers, and Elsie was seduced by the opportunity in Michigan. She would soon regret the decision, and for much of her life, she spoke little of the disappointing experience other than to acknowledge it indirectly as a transition phase in her life.

Although Elsie rarely, if ever, cited this work experience in her own writings and accounts of her career, several secondary sources identify her employer in Pontiac as a manufacturing plant owned by "the Austin Motor

Elsie's sister Helen's wedding in August 1927 at the Vancouver family home. Elsie on the right, her sister-in-law and friend Rosel on left with young cousins.
(*Courtesy of Elizabeth Schneewind.*)

Company",[97] which would have made it part of the British firm founded by Sir Herbert Austin in 1905, a sometimes prestigious element of British auto-industry history. But the suggestion that Elsie worked in such a plant is certainly incorrect. Even though it was harbouring ambitions for operations in the United States at the time, the Austin Motor Company did not have a plant or even an office in Pontiac.[98]

It is more likely that Elsie was hired by the Austin Company, a U.S. engineering firm still vibrant in the 21st century and in Pontiac in 1927 just launching a megaproject that demanded the recruitment of engineering talent from across North America: a contract to build a plant for the Oakland Motor Car Company, a firm that would later become the Pontiac division of General Motors. The Austin-built, 35-acre auto plant was "the largest man-made physical structure in the world"[99] at the time of its completion, and its construction was a complex undertaking promising exciting career opportunities for engineers and would-be engineers alike.

This "Austin" company was already a respected multinational with aeronautical engineering facilities and operations across the United States and in Canada, making its recruitment of Canadian graduates from varied fields a natural practice. It is "highly possible",[100] company historians say, that Elsie was employed briefly by this particular Austin Company in its 1927 Pontiac auto plant project — but with one important qualifier. If she did work there, she was not recognized in the records as one of the company engineers. The firm did not have an acknowledged female engineer on its payroll until 1969, and this at its office in Chicago.

Perhaps frustrated within an "Austin" company that did not recognize her professional status and disappointed with the tasks assigned her, Elsie began, within months of arriving in Michigan, to reconsider her plans. The aviation industry beckoned. Unlike the unskilled production line of the auto manufacturer, airplane design and construction was still, in the 1920s, an activity characterized by the work of individual craftsmen, artisans, and visionaries. The appeal of aeronautics grew every day. When in May 1927, around the time of Elsie's move to Michigan, Charles Lindbergh's sleek, shiny *Spirit of St. Louis* carried its pilot from New York to Paris on the first solo flight across the Atlantic, the whole world was caught up in the excitement and romance of aviation. No city felt the magic with more intensity than Lindbergh's 1902 birthplace, Detroit. That summer newspapers and radio broadcasts overflowed with the celebration of a native son and the future of aviation, and the ambitious young workers in Pontiac must surely have been affected.

These events and forces rekindled Elsie's memories of classroom discussions in Toronto about aeronautical engineering research, and revived her interest in pursuing studies at the master's or doctoral level, as her sister was doing. Canada was still not an option for such studies in aeronautical engineering in 1927 or even, formally, for a degree at the undergraduate level. Foreign institutions with active programs included the

Imperial College of Science and Technology in England and a few U.S. universities, the latter having been spurred by an infusion of funding from the mining millions of the Guggenheim family and via other industrially driven sponsorship. The American institutions touched by such support for aeronautics in the 1920s were the Massachusetts Institute of Technology, the University of Washington, New York University, and one not far from Elsie's Austin workplace, the University of Michigan.[101] Elsie's U. of T. professor with the aeronautical bent knew them all and would rate them for his interested students.

The University of Michigan, just down the road from Pontiac in the town of Ann Arbor, was well known to the auto industry as a critical source of engineering talent. To those with an interest, it was firmly recognized among the leading institutions in the United States and thus all of North America for aeronautics education. Elsie collaborated with the staff at the university and studied part-time, evidently while still with Austin, and this led to her to enroll as a graduate student in November 1927.[102] Offered a fellowship in the Master of Science of Engineering (M.S.E.) program, she joined the class scheduled to graduate in 1929.

The story of how the University of Michigan came to pioneer aeronautics education is, in part, a function of the open-mindedness instilled by the early presidents and professors who established novel programs in fields ranging from history to medicine in the 19th century. They made sure that Michigan was among the very first U.S. colleges and universities to admit African Americans, doing so years before the Civil War.[103] In 1870, the same thinking led the University of Michigan to become the first large post-secondary institution in the United States to admit women even though the University's Board of Regents feared the move as a very "Dangerous Experiment".[104] Twenty-five years later, Marian Sarah Parker became the first woman to graduate from the University of Michigan in engineering. A civil engineer, Parker brought an artistic sense to her career and applied it to work that would play a role in the design of iconic American buildings such as New York's Waldorf Astoria Hotel.[105]

The University of Michigan can rightfully be proud of its record of encouraging diversity, which it celebrates today by noting that as early as 1841, just a few years after its first post-secondary courses began in Ann Arbor, it was even prepared to open its doors to a student "from Canada!"[106]

Elsie's aeronautical engineering mentor, University of Michigan Professor Felix Pawlowski. (*University of Michigan Archives.*)

Professor Pawlowski's Pride

If he had known this history of open-mindedness and novelty, the young Polish immigrant and Elsie's future mentor Felix Wladyslaw Pawlowski might not have been surprised when the University of Michigan responded positively to his unsolicited 1912 letter proposing that the university establish courses in aeronautical engineering with him in charge.[107] An engineer who had built his own plane, taken aeronautical engineering courses in Paris before coming to America, and was to play a key role in Elsie MacGill's advanced education, Felix Pawlowski had sent similar letters to universities all across the United States in a desperate attempt to find work in his favoured field. Aside from the University of Michigan, only the Massachusetts Institute of Technology (MIT) replied with anything other than outright rejection. The innovative MIT, which would in fact muster the resources to launch its own program within a few years, said, essentially, "nice idea, maybe later" in its response to Pawlowski's letter. Several other universities sent replies indicating that they took the Polish immigrant's proposition and letters to be a joke. Flying was still a novelty with little perceived practical application, and aeronautics was not the stuff of serious science in many minds.

Pawlowski, like many immigrants of the era, had arrived in the New World looking for the professional equivalent of streets paved with gold and rivers flowing with milk and honey. His reality, while less traumatic than his early life (which had included seeing his father exiled to Siberia and being jailed himself at the hands of Russian secret police), was disappointing. With his fortieth birthday approaching, and having failed to find permanent work in anything related to his expertise let alone his specific passion of aeronautics, he was anxious.

Pawlowski had been enthralled with aeronautical studies since witnessing Wilbur Wright's flying machine in action during a 1908 visit to France. The year after, he enrolled in classes at the University of Paris, which was offering the first courses in the world under a professor holding a chair specifically in the field of aeronautical engineering. Pawlowski graduated in 1910, worked on his own businesses for a couple of years, and then made the move the United States.

As a consequence of his bold enquiries, Pawlowski was hired by the University of Michigan to work in the mechanical engineering department where in 1914 he began "lecturing on aeronautical subjects". Yet, even at the generally receptive University of Michigan, his classes were initially slipped into the curriculum "hid[den] in the Department of Marine Engineering and Naval Architecture".[108] Despite his difficulty with English, he was keen to teach and immediately began to promote more specialized courses.[109] At first, his aeronautics classes were given as part-time, non-credit courses for flying enthusiasts. Soon, however, the popularity of the subject became clear, and a formal program leading to a full bachelor's degree in aeronautical engineering was established, with the first class due to graduate in 1917. The pioneering nature of the program is illustrated by the fact that the early students trained on equipment made by the Wright Brothers.

Thus, when Elsie MacGill decided to enroll at the U. of M. in 1927, she entered a university that was counting its aeronautics grads in the many dozens, and had been offering graduate programs in aeronautics for close to a decade, with the capacity to bestow an M.S.E. in aeronautical engineering.[110] This being unique in a North American context, Elsie, as the program's lone and first female student, was yet again on a path towards unique status.

Ann Arbor was different from Toronto. Labelled for the love of a woman, some say two women, named Ann and for its arbor-like envelope of greenery, the town was rural, picturesque, and just far enough away from Detroit to push thoughts of the big city beyond the horizon. Yet the University of Michigan was Toronto's match in many ways, just as diverse, and it was large. The growing auto industry had been pouring tax money into the coffers of the State of Michigan, and some of it had found its way into new buildings and facilities that would benefit Elsie MacGill while at the Ann Arbor campus of the state's great university.

The combination of small town and large university augmented by other, albeit smaller educational institutions made Ann Arbor a place dominated by students, a community that catered to the interests of young people and marked student events to a greater degree than did the big cities. It was lively both academically and socially in the late 1920s. Because of the university, Ann Arbor also enjoyed many big-city amenities, including an excellent hospital with health services linked to the university's long-established medical school and research community. Reasonable rail access gave students easy means to go home or away on vacation, and students with cars could drive to Detroit and Windsor regularly. Despite prohibition-era restrictions and curfews, the late 1920s was a great time for many of Ann Arbor's temporary residents. Elsie made several good friends and was pleased to encounter other Canadians, even a couple of British Columbians, among the grad students.

Women accounted for more than a quarter of graduates from the university in the 1920s, and they even represented the majority in disciplines such as literature.[111] Elsie's campus was firmly "co-ed" amidst the "Jazz Age", a time when dances were held every night at local restaurants and coffee shops, and periodically at high schools and the university. Motion pictures were shown to enormous crowds, and before Elsie finished her days in Ann Arbor, the town would host its first showing of a talking picture. The lively young people who came from across the United States and abroad had plenty to do.

It was also an especially exciting and challenging time for students in the aeronautics department, which was just starting to show hints of future greatness. In the years since, the University of Michigan's Department of Aerospace Engineering has produced a string of accomplished graduates. Mementos of the university, including the seal of the department, can be found on the surface of the moon, having been left behind in tribute by some of the many NASA astronauts who received their initial training at the U. of M. Famous pilots and business leaders also count themselves among its proud alumni. They include some of the world's top aeronautical engineers.

A legendary example from the students in the department during Elsie MacGill's time is Clarence "Kelly" Johnson. Listed among the greatest aircraft designers of all time, Johnson joined Lockheed after graduation in the 1930s to form and lead the company's celebrated "Skunk Works" design team, which would generate many of the firm's greatest aircraft successes. While the university and its aeronautical engineering programs would suffer and slow down in the decade ahead under the strains of the Great Depression, they were still riding high in 1928 and 1929, and freshmen like Johnson and M.S.E students like Elsie were benefiting from an exciting atmosphere energized by the introduction of new research equipment, notably a novel wind tunnel built under Pawlowski's direction in the new East Engineering Building on the eve of Elsie's arrival.[112] The wind tunnel, one of many aeronautics projects across North American then being financed by the increasingly robust and activist Guggenheim Fund, was a first-class research facility that inspired new studies particularly those aligned with aircraft design.

A few years earlier, the professor had visited facilities in Europe in preparation for construction of his wind tunnel. During the tour, he renewed his contacts and learned firsthand about the latest research being conducted in the major centres abroad. Consequently, when aeronautical engineering research took hold at the University of Michigan, Elsie was exposed through Pawlowski to the latest ideas and opportunities.

Although Pawlowski, with his well-trimmed goatee, distinguished appearance, and confident air was, as department head, the most influential and commanding figure in the overall aeronautics program during Elsie's time at the University of Michigan, he was not the only instructor Elsie would cite as important to her personally. She also worked closely with a brilliant and ambitious young professor named Edward Archibald Stalker.

Stalker had been hired as an instructor in the aeronautics department in 1921, ostensibly to relieve some of Pawlowski's increasingly heavy teaching load. But it may also have been an acknowledgement of Pawlowski's limitations as an instructor; his heavy accent proved daunting for students for much of his career. In one exemplary account, he is said to have once asked his grad student Elsie to fetch some "kitchen soap"; she dutifully returned a while later with some "chicken soup" for her mentor.

Stalker did not have such linguistic challenges, but lacked experience at the time of his appointment. He had graduated with a bachelor's degree just two years earlier and spent those two years as a junior engineer at Stout Engineering Laboratories, a firm merely dabbling at the fringes of aircraft design at its operations in Dearborn. At the University of Michigan, however, he soon developed his interest in aeronautics, engaging in further study and specialized research in addition to his teaching duties, and earning his own M.S.E. in 1923.[113]

The young associate professor Stalker was on track to full professor status when Elsie was at Michigan; in time, he would become a noted authority, respected as the author of an enduring, internationally accessed college text on the principles of flight.[114] While Elsie was studying under him at Michigan, Stalker was trying out new material for his text and also conducting significant research projects on the fundamentals of aircraft aerodynamics and areas of special interest to Elsie. One such project was a groundbreaking study of the thin layer of air at the surface of a wing known as the "boundary layer". This research led to Stalker's early-1929 discovery that "wing stalling" could be effectively delayed by controlling the boundary layer air in flight.

Like others in the aeronautics department, Stalker was impressed by Elsie's academic work and was also said to have been among those who "appreciated" her as "a person" as well as a student. The now "old man" Pawlowski (he was in his early fifties) was also impressed and personally proud of his female student. He considered her skills in aircraft design and experimental research to be remarkable by any standards, and was convinced, based on his international connections and broad knowledge of aeronautics in the United States, that she would be the first woman in the world to complete the academic and technical work necessary for qualification as an aeronautical engineer. Pawlowski was aware of a couple of women doing "work in the physics and mathematics of aerodynamics"[115] in Europe, but he distinguished between their work and that of an aeronautical engineer because the latter has benefited from studies of both aircraft design and the entire system. Elsie was not just trained and skilled, he said, but talented in it.

Pawlowski was not alone in this definition of an aeronautical engineer. Other leaders in the profession also believed that to truly qualify as an aeronautical engineer, one had to have an engineering degree, experience in the aeronautics industry or a lab, and at least "one year's post-graduate study".[116] Elsie was in the process of meeting all these criteria.

There was no doubt that she was the only woman to have enrolled in such studies in North America, and with his recent personal review of activities overseas, Pawlowski was well placed and credible when he suggested that Elsie would likely be the first woman anywhere to earn full credentials as a graduate aeronautical engineer. The professor, who would work many more years, travel internationally, receive many honours, and publish a great many respected papers, would still remember Elsie MacGill years later and brand her as "the only one in the world"[117] at the time of her graduation from Michigan in 1929.

As the final weeks of Elsie's M.S.E. program in the spring of 1929 approached, Pawlowski's confidence in her abilities and Elsie's self confidence were about to be tested in an unforeseen and dreadful way.

Paralysis

Elsie's 24th birthday had passed, a crucial set of final exams was just completed, and the process ahead seemed perfunctory. Convocation was the next day.[118] Other students were in a similar stage in their school year, and they felt comfortable enough to drive to Windsor for a night out.[119] Elsie had been fighting a cold-like flu, but decided to go along. She felt a little stiff and uncomfortable during the ride, but may not have linked those feelings to the cold since she had been sitting long hours in lecture halls and libraries, fully expecting her back and bottom to feel the strain at times.

Any pain Elsie noticed that evening was slight, more like a tickling and tingling. Her dress seemed to scrape her skin, and she felt a chill. Yet these strange feelings did not deter her from celebrating with friends even when the sensations ebbed into a light burning and prickling that reached down to grab at her toes.[120] When the pain shifted and momentarily faded around her lower back and legs, she felt relief, and after coming back to her room on North State Street, just a few blocks from the Ann Arbor campus,[121] she went to bed as usual without thinking there was anything worth mentioning to anyone.

The next morning, when she woke and touched those troublesome spots on her back and legs with the tips of her fingers, a slow cascade of queasiness washed down her body. No matter how hard she pressed or pinched, she felt nothing.

Her legs were worse than weak; she could not get out of bed. Something was undoubtedly wrong, but at this point Elsie was not sure whether her loss of strength and the nausea were solely the function of genuine physical illness or her own fear of what it meant. It was a bit of both. Within one night, Elsie's legs had become frozen.

The University of Michigan medical school had excellent facilities: a hospital, and research programs that would one day play a pivotal role in defeating the disease that may have been afflicting Elsie. Members of the university medical team recognized immediately that they could be looking at something permanent and serious. They took X-rays and samples of her spinal fluid. The results were negative, leaving them to conclude she had fallen victim to a viral infection.[122]

Throughout her life Elsie would recite their formal diagnosis as acute infectious myelitis even though many others, including those close to her, often called it "poliomyelitis"[123] or just "polio". The medical staff at University Hospital, whom Elsie had learned to respect during her time in Ann Arbor, told her that she was likely to "never walk again", and some people even feared she would die.

Elsie never used the word "polio" to describe her affliction. Perhaps at the time she was trying to fend off alarm in family, friends, and strangers, although the terrorizing polio outbreaks of the 1940s and 1950s were over a decade ahead for the United States, and there was no sign of a polio epidemic in Michigan. "There was no case reported in Windsor; and none of her companions was taken ill".[124] In any case, her official diagnosis remained vague.

But in May 1929, people were still traumatized by the Spanish flu pandemic, which had taken over half a million American lives and killed over 25 million, perhaps as many as 100 million people around the world a scant 10 years earlier. At the University of Michigan, many students still remembered attending classes with colleagues and professors trying to communicate through their "flu masques". Minor flu outbreaks in the subsequent years kept people on edge, wary of anyone ill, and capable of the irrational. Stories of vigilantes burning down the homes of polio victims would emphasize the point in later years.

Elsie did not want to consider herself a polio patient. By whatever name, she had been hit by a neurological disorder that seemed to originate with inflammation of the spinal cord, presumably driven by the seemingly mundane, cold-like virus she was suffering from the night before, on the drive to Windsor.

The diagnosis suggested an inflammation that attacks myelin, the fatty insulating substance that covers nerve fibres. The damage it causes creates scars that, in turn, interrupt communication between the nerves within the spinal cord and then ultimately between those nerves and the rest of the body. The pain can be initially severe, and for a while affected patients lose control over their bladders and bowels. Elsie needed help to urinate, had to fight spasms, and took antiseptics. Because she remained paralysed from the waist down, her persistent concern, as the days passed into weeks, was of course walking. In those first days, Elsie did not focus on the life sentence before her. She would only acknowledge that she was seriously sick, and worried about missing the opportunity to attend graduation.

She was far away from home and family, but her doctor, John Garvey, was kind and encouraging, her university friends carried her about in their arms those first difficult days, and her professors tried to help, eventually finding a way to confer the M.S.E. degree on her in hospital. Although some later accounts suggested that she wrote exams in bed to finish off her program, she had already completed the requirements for graduation. She was sincerely appreciative of all the help, but her spirits picked up most when her beloved sister Helen and her sister's husband Everett Hughes, now a professor of sociology at McGill University in Montréal, arrived, having cancelled a working trip to Europe to be with Elsie.[125]

Elsie was still engaged to be married to a young man from Vancouver, and she might also have looked to her fiancé for support. He and his family in B.C. were concerned and compassionate, initially assuring the

Elsie while attending the University of Michigan in Ann Arbor in 1928. Possibly, the last photo of her standing upright without support. (*Courtesy of Elizabeth Schneewind.*)

MacGills that Elsie's illness would not affect plans for marriage.[126] But the wedding never took place, and for the rest of her life, Elsie rarely spoke of this relationship, one that was apparently already starting to fade before the bad news of May 1929. She would give future friends few hints about the weight she placed on this particular consequence of her illness. Many of those close to her do not recall her speaking of any special boyfriend other than sporadic, unrelated references to the ham-radio-based romance, which did not last.

Instead of dwelling on this lost love, Elsie would focus her future recollections of this period on the care and support she received from her sister and her brother-in-law. The couple stayed with Elsie in Ann Arbor for a month and then took the new aeronautical engineering grad back to Vancouver and the care of her parents' familiar home. In this confusing and distressing time, Elsie left Ann Arbor without taking care of her outstanding bills or settling her affairs. She even left her once-precious gold mesh bracelet behind in a safety deposit box at the State Savings Bank where it was to remain for many years before she eventually claimed it from a distance.

Elsie was now returning to the city of her birth with a body that had been humbled but a spirit that, although wounded, was not crushed. She was now a professional engineer, a researcher, and a woman who had managed in a male environment with success — a very different person from the one who had left Vancouver six years earlier.

Elsie MacGill was beginning a new chapter in a life that had previously been invigorating and relatively unmarred. It would be a challenging, complex, and unexpected phase, but ultimately one filled with achievements based on her training. Those experiences to come would cause her to look back at her University of Michigan days with "great pleasure",[127] to see Michigan as a springboard rather than an end, and to cherish her memories, hanging onto her U. of M. class notes and project files until the day she died. Indeed, the other events of her life, those before and after, would come to dwarf the significance of those sad, disorienting last days of May and June 1929 in Ann Arbor.

Chapter IV

Roots and Wings

"Aviation and women are taking each other seriously"[128]

For Elsie, Vancouver was still, in 1929, a pleasant place to be: a vibrant city encircled by mountains, ocean, and greenery. She was returning to the West End streets of her childhood, to the beloved "mustard-coloured house", which the family had repurchased a few years earlier. Her grandmother's cousin Sarah, though aged, was still there, as were both of Elsie's parents and Yip, the most recent in the line of Chinese servants.

Elsie had reasons to feel comforted upon her arrival back home. But the atmosphere had changed. The house, now painted a darker colour, saw fewer smiles, and the conversations within its walls were driven by unanticipated and unfortunate events. Elsie's paralysis was now being measured in months, and the prognosis of "never walk again" echoed off everyone's minds if not their lips.

This was a persistent concern, but not the only cause for upset within the house. Earlier in the year, a change in the British Columbia provincial government in Victoria had precipitated shifts in the jurisdictions and appointments of juvenile court judges in Vancouver. At 65 and after 12 years as a high-profile and influential figure in the community, Elsie's mother Helen was out of a job.

The new Conservative administration had several official explanations for the changes and for ousting Judge MacGill, ranging from the growth of the city to the formal legal training of Helen's female replacement. But Helen's many and varied supporters saw it as crass politics and an effort to quash the Liberal-style reforms her work on the bench had promoted. While Helen excused herself from the public debate around her dismissal, newspaper columns, petitions, and speeches in the legislature over her worth and the merits of her apparent firing kept the subject a raw and throbbing undercurrent to daily life in the MacGill home.

The loss of her judge's salary was felt in many ways. It had been an element of Helen's sense of independence and achievement, but Jim and Helen had also come to rely on the money and could have used it, especially given Elsie's new physical circumstance. Helen had paid into a city pension plan while working as a judge, but was precluded from receiving a pension from the city since a judge's pension was deemed to be a federal responsibility. The incongruity of this and other aspects of the situation fed the protests over her dismissal, and they evolved into an organized, province-wide campaign for her reinstatement. Helen was torn because it was just the kind of campaign she might have championed had the issue involved anyone but herself.

Having learned of her mother's dismissal while still in Michigan, Elsie had been frustrated by distance, and her concern over the situation had built up in the midst of other emotions and events. The visceral support from her invalid daughter was a comfort to Helen, and Helen would, in turn, comfort and care for her daughter for years to follow.

Elsie was completely bedridden that first summer after her illness. The accepted wisdom of the time deemed that the affected limbs of a victim of paralysis be immobilized. The treatment, it was presumed, would prevent the spread of the debilitating infection. Elsie's legs were, as a consequence, placed in cast-like forms. She thus had tremendous difficulty moving for reasons beyond the damage inflicted on her weakened nervous system. Although others would recall Elsie as being exceptionally brave during this period and although she did little to dissuade them, she did allow in later life that there were times when she wished she would die.

It was a gloomy time, but Elsie had the encouragement of her sister as well as her parents. Young Helen and her husband Everett Hughes, who had both spent a month with Elsie in Ann Arbor and had accompanied her back home, stayed on in Vancouver all summer. Two years earlier, they had come to the city for their wedding at St. Paul's and the reception in the garden at the family home. There in the garden, Elsie stood at her sister's side as bridesmaid, posing for photos.

As September 1929 approached, Everett's new position at McGill University compelled the couple to prepare for the return trip to Montréal. Young Helen, now calling herself Helen MacGill Hughes, was anxious. Then, just days before the couple's departure, as if to give a signal that it was time for her sister to go home, Elsie yelled excitedly from the bedroom. When Young Helen looked into her younger sister's room, Elsie, prone on the bed with casts, was pointing down at her toe. The toe was, very slightly, twitching. This was the dawn of Elsie's recovery and allowed her sister some comfort as she and her husband headed back to their lives and careers in the east.

As Elsie moved from the bed into a wheelchair over the next year, her world opened up a little and her spirits revived. The clunky wooden wheelchairs of 1930 were cumbersome, awkward devices with little resemblance to the light, folding aluminum chairs developed a few years later but not widely available until after World War II. It was not easy to move Elsie's chair from floor to floor or, especially, to take it in the car. Still, it was a step toward freedom for Elsie, made useful in large part because her family was ready and willing to help her make the most of the chair. Among those now frequenting the MacGill's Vancouver home were Elsie's half-brother Freddy and his first wife Rosel, a hard-working woman whom Freddy had met while serving with the U.S. Army in Europe in the wake of World War I. Elsie was fond of her German-born sister-in-law, a close friend who was a bridesmaid alongside Elsie at Young Helen's wedding. At times, Rosel served almost as a full-time housekeeper at the MacGill home in part to help the family confront its varied personal and professional demands, but also to limit the self-reproach she and her husband Freddy felt over their occasional need for support.

Now freed of her court obligations, Elsie's mother Helen vigorously engaged herself in community work even though, as an out-of-favour and well-known face, she was compelled to act behind the scenes when supporting political initiatives. Helen took her invalid daughter along to meetings and made sure that Elsie got out of the house every day. Jim MacGill pitched in more than ever before with grocery shopping, work around the house, and other errands.

The increase in activity and outlook contrasted strangely with Helen's physical appearance and energy. In the early months of 1930, Elsie's mother became drawn and slow. Medical tests and then surgery showed she had cancer. Still in her mid-sixties, Helen had reason to feel robbed by her personal prospects, but her announced concern was for Elsie and the loss of her daughter's daily car rides. Through her letters, Helen asked her other children not to worry, but her reflective tone and doth-protest-too-much bravery effected the opposite.

Happily, however, radiation therapy proved sufficient, and Helen would return to her old self faster than expected, to live many years more and to give her younger daughter another example of fight and fortitude to absorb. In fact, Elsie's mother demonstrated a tough fighting spirit by battling health problems on more than one occasion. Helen suffered three broken legs over the course of her life. The first happened during the typhoon on the way to Japan in 1890; the others were the result of car accidents. The one in 1926 brought the MacGills almost $3000 in insurance money, a windfall that allowed them to regain the mustard-coloured house. Even with her leg raised and in a cast, the judge would continue to work, handling cases in her hospital room.[129]

Aside from witnessing her mother's spirited battles with illness and injury, Elsie also watched as Helen responded to the disruption in her judicial career by resurrecting her skill as a professional journalist. Helen's little book on the B.C. laws affecting women and children was selling for 25 cents per copy, and the royalties provided a little money. While it did not replace her lost judge's salary, Helen's other writing earned some money and gave her a place to express her views on the social issues of greatest concern to her. Her articles appeared in local, national, and international publications. Helen found her voice as a feminist and social reformer once again, showing a special passion for the increasing number of unemployed arriving in Vancouver in those early Depression years.

With her aspirations for an engineering career restricted by her physical condition, Elsie thought about her mother the journalist and her interrupted legal career while she herself searched for ways to keep busy and maintain her hope. Over the next few years, as she struggled to regain the ability to walk, she read aeronautical engineering trade magazines and journals voraciously devouring anything related to aviation — from features about designer clothing for female pilots to technical reports on flight testing. Working at her desk and sitting in her wheelchair, she also doodled, dreamed, and drafted her own aircraft design ideas, including a well-developed concept for a new type of seaplane that would, like other so-called "flying boats"[130] of the era, use its fuselage rather than pontoons to take off from and land on water.

Still in her mid-twenties, separated from active engineering work, and confined to a wheelchair, Elsie mustered enough confidence in her writing, her experience, and the originality of her ideas to start drafting articles for publication and to move to establish herself as a thoughtful writer. While her mother was clutched by social concerns in her works, Elsie and her writings were focused primarily on aviation, aeronautics, and engineering. Notwithstanding her personal circumstances and the economic hardships around her, Elsie's words conveyed a general feeling of optimism about the aviation industry and sometimes specifically about the role of women in it.

She was not always successful in finding a publisher for her work. Still, she steadily developed a knack for technically informed popular writing and saw some of her pieces used in fashionable magazines such as *Vanity Fair* as well as the specialized publications aimed at engineers and aviation experts. Because her articles were often distributed nationally and were widely read, many people assumed that Elsie MacGill's writing income was substantial and that she had managed to earn her keep during the worst of her illness. This perception was later added to the embellished catalogue others drew on to celebrate her achievements.

The work was evidence of her spirit and determination, but the financial benefits were likely limited. Her writing and research work instead brought other dividends. It welled her pride, emboldened her self-image, and maintained some contact with the profession she had worked so hard to understand and enter while in Toronto and Ann Arbor. It also kept her dreams alive. One dream was to fly. Although she had not yet learned to pilot a plane and was now seriously disabled, Elsie was still planning to be a pilot some day in order to better design planes and, for a long time, blamed her lack of a pilot's license on "the expense"[131] rather than her physical condition.

She was passionate about flight, knew all of the tasks involved in flying a plane, and wanted to apply this knowledge in the cockpit of a plane herself. Her 1931 *Chatelaine* article "Women on the Wing", ostensibly an essay advocating a greater role for women pilots in commercial aviation, devoted most of its attention to an analysis of the strength required to pilot a plane and a deconstruction of the physical aspects of flying. Noting that a few pounds of pressure was all that was needed to move the stick, the rudder bar, and pedals, she argued that it was "unreasonable to suggest limiting women's flying activities"[132] on the issue of physical strength. It is difficult to believe that she did not contemplate her own ability to move her legs and body as she wrote those words.

Ninety-Nines and Sevens

Just a few years earlier, in 1928 near Hamilton, Ontario, Eileen Vollick had become the first Canadian woman to earn a pilot's license.[133] Yet Elsie had known of many women pilots while living in the States; indeed, an American woman, Alys Bryant, made news in 1913 when she became the first woman to fly a plane in Canada at the air show for the Vancouver Exhibition. Elsie was only eight years old at the time.

By 1929, the year Elsie fell ill in Michigan, there were already 117 licensed women pilots in the United States. They had competed in air races, staged demonstrations, and started to organize. Unlike those involved in the suffrage movement of earlier decades, these women were organizing for professional rather than political reasons: to network, learn about their industry, and hear about jobs. All but 18 of the 117 accepted the invitation to establish a women's pilots' association, and a core group held its first meeting on the second of November of that year at an airfield on Long Island, New York. They took the name "Ninety-Nines" to honour those who agreed to join, and Amelia Earhart was later named president in recognition of her leadership and example. Within a few years, Canadian women followed suit with a much smaller group, "The Flying Seven", again in Vancouver.[134]

During those years of recovery in Vancouver, Elsie enthused about the accomplishments of women like "Miss Amelia Earhart" and the prospects for women in the aviation industry. She said, with some relief, that "Aviation and women are taking each other seriously" even though women were still being barred from commercial piloting duties involving large aircraft or heavy loads. Later historians deemed Elsie's positive comments as overly "optimistic".[135] Such optimism was also evident, of course, in her persistent, personal aspiration to be a pilot, an ambition that would endure for many years. Despite the residue of her illness and her changing financial situation, she continued to cite her plan to be a pilot as a complement to her research and engineering career.

Her desire to fly was given a boost in July 1931 when the official open-ing of the Vancouver Airport was combined with a four-day open house and mini-festival of flying demonstrations staged as part of the Trans-Canada Air Pageant,[136] a coast-to-coast demonstration event organized by flying club enthusiasts in an effort to maintain interest in aviation amidst the darkening atmosphere of retrenchment during the first years of the Depression. The pilots took paying passengers for flights and showed them the workings of their aircraft.[137]

A wide variety of aircraft were used in the pageant, including one of the most unusual and seemingly unstable planes of the time, the "autogiro", which combined a helicopter-style rotor lift system with the propeller propulsion of a fixed airplane. Elsie, frail and still unable to walk without support, talked her parents into paying for a flight and allowing her to take a ride over South Vancouver in this very odd plane. It would be the first, but far from the last time she would ride along for a demonstration flight in a machine that made others uneasy just looking up from the ground.

As her reading and research steadily expanded, Elsie's legs also slowly gained sensation and strength, allowing her to stand and then take small steps with supports. In the years ahead, she would often hear others label-ling her as "lame", and would never be completely free of canes and other supports. But in 1931, Elsie was sure enough of her evolving recovery to begin planning her return to the study of aeronautical engineering and writing letters of inquiry to this end. [138]

In early 1932, the MacGills "sold the wheelchair"[139] and Elsie and her canes headed back east, where she still had friends and relatives and where she hoped to resume a career sidelined by infection three years earlier.[140]

Massachusetts Institute of Technology

At first, Elsie did not specifically think about returning to school. Instead, she spoke of getting back into engineering and working in the aviation industry. She had viewed her research for magazine articles merely as a means of keeping current and sharp. When she determined that the best way of transitioning back into her field would be more research and study, Elsie first considered an opportunity at New York University. Perhaps inevitably, however, Elsie's investigations led her into correspondence with the Massachusetts Institute of Technology (MIT) near Boston, the only institution besides Michigan that had showed any interest when, in 1910, Elsie's former professor Felix Pawlowski sent out his proposal to establish university programs in aeronautical engineering in the United States.

By 1932, MIT was offering unique graduate courses in aeronautical engineering in addition to its strong undergraduate program, in place for many years. Women were present in most of the university's programs, women had graduated in some engineering disciplines,[141] and a few were even doing postgraduate work in fields such as chemistry. The institution was evolving into a place that was particularly interesting to motivated graduate aeronautical engineers like Elsie MacGill, and she applied to pursue further studies. She was pleased when she was admitted to MIT, but also anxious. Aware of her parents' financial stresses and her limited contribution to the family income during her incapacitation, Elsie reluctantly accepted the money needed to resume her academic career, calling it "a loan".

MIT in 1932: "Simply the Best"

Spawned in the context of the U.S. Civil War, MIT was a well-established, highly regarded technical school when Elsie arrived on its Cambridge, Massachusetts, campus for doctoral studies in the 1932 school year.[142] Elsie's former machine design professor at Toronto had always said that when it came to study in aeronautical engineering, MIT was "simply the best".[143] She also knew that the institute had a new president, Karl T. Compton, who had recruited new staff and was taking steps toward the day when MIT would be better known as a centre for scientific and engineering research. The MIT engineering faculty at the time included people like Vannevar Bush, a scientist and future U.S. national research administrator, engaged in pioneering work in the development of analog computers and other devices that intrigued the electrical engineer in Elsie.

The Massachusetts Institute of Technology began breaking out of its technician and trades image in the early 1930s with achievements like the construction of the world's first Van de Graaff particle accelerator, a device that set the standard for decades as a critical piece of equipment in atomic and medical research. Robert Van de Graaff had joined MIT in 1931 as one of the bright lights recruited after Compton's arrival.

For Elsie, a particular attraction when she enrolled in graduate studies at MIT in 1932 was the staff of the aeronautical engineering program. Within a year, the program was to be bolstered in a dramatic way by another of Compton's recruits, Dr. Jerome Clarke Hunsaker, a legendary American aircraft designer who returned to the institution, the place where he had earned his doctorate two decades earlier, specifically to take charge of the aeronautical engineering program and turn it into an academic and research power.[144] Hunsaker was not only an MIT graduate; he had also planted the seeds of the MIT aeronautics program in 1914 when he and the future Douglas Aircraft founder Donald Douglas built the institution's first research wind tunnel. A 1917 visit to those Hunsaker-built MIT facilities had inspired Elsie's old engineering professor J.H. Parkin to push for construction of the first aeronautical engineering wind tunnel at the University of Toronto.[145]

Hunsaker had also established MIT's first courses in the field of aeronautics around the time of that first wind tunnel. The courses were started just slightly later than Felix Pawlowski's more tentative and informal aeronautical engineering classes at Michigan. However, because they were introduced as part of the regular program, MIT could claim to be the first American university to offer courses specifically devoted to "aerodynamics and aircraft design".[146]

MIT's Hunsaker and the Business of Aviation

In the years between 1914 and Elsie MacGill's arrival at MIT, Jerome Hunsaker had gained some fame as head of aircraft design for the U.S. Navy. In this post, he designed the NC4, the seaplane that, in 1919, made the first transatlantic flight, skipping across the ocean and reaching Portugal a few months before the more celebrated non-stop flight of Alcock and Brown between Newfoundland and Ireland. Hunsaker also designed the Shenandoah, the first airship to use helium instead of hydrogen, and championed many other novel aviation systems.

More than just technical expertise, Hunsaker's presence at MIT meant a strong link to American industry and sensitivity to the business of aircraft design and engineering. Before the end of his 98-year-long life, Hunsaker would add senior jobs at Chrysler and other U.S. business enterprises to his resumé. In 1933, when he was only 47, he could already boast a vice-presidency at the Goodyear Zeppelin Corporation and a senior spot at the bustling Bell Telephone Laboratories. His government connections extended far beyond the navy and included the National Advisory Committee on Aeronautics, a forerunner of NASA. Being a graduate student in Hunsaker's program meant that Elsie would have a window on both the full range of opportunity and ideas in aeronautical engineering and the technical side of the aviation industry.

Most of all it meant science. Hunsaker was devoted to the belief that "the future development of aircraft depends on scientific research and engineering experiment applied to design".[147] In fact, Hunsaker was a driving force in the creation of the first American professional organization specifically committed to the promotion of research in aeronautics, the Institute of Aeronautical Sciences. The New York-based institute, which was established in 1932 around the time of Elsie's move to the United States, was an instantly prestigious body, with Orville Wright and Ludwig Prandtl, the father of modern fluid dynamics, among its founding honorary fellows. This devotion to engineering and scientific research was soon expressed in a toughening of the standards for MIT engineering students, who were expected to have mastered both mechanical issues and theoretical fields such as thermodynamics and electrical engineering. This naturally suited Elsie, the graduate electrical engineer, as did the ambiance of a commitment to research. She was excited about the opportunities at MIT and the institution made her feel special even though other women had broken down walls in other engineering disciplines before her arrival.

Recognized as an unusual student from the start, Elsie was invited to tea as a special guest of the president's wife. Taking note of Elsie's physical condition, Mrs. Compton asked if there was anything that would make the new student's life easier on campus. Elsie replied by noting her great difficulty surmounting the grand steps at the entrance of MIT. Shortly thereafter, a handrail was added to the steps, soon becoming one of the notable features of the entrance.

In class, Elsie enjoyed the support of others. Hunsaker was not the only or even the most visible figure at MIT for Elsie. There were many talented and skilled members in the aeronautical engineering faculty, men who had been recruited to the institution through Hunsaker's "many connections in business, government, and academe" as well as those who preceded his arrival. The one who specialized in Elsie's main field of interest, aircraft design, was Otto C. Koppen, an educator and scientist whose background included the army as well as private industry and whose career at MIT predated Hunsaker's return.

"At the graduate level, Koppen's class on airplane design reflected some of the new thinking that emphasized the airplane as part of a larger technological system".[148] His approach built on the romantic image of an airplane as more than a collection of mechanical parts, a holistic way of thinking that to some drew strength from the feminine perspective and that appealed to Elsie, who called it a "creative or conceptual ability... fundamental" to solving many problems and addressing challenges in many fields, not just technical ones.

"This is the ability to see a concept or an enterprise in the round, to recognize the significant elements in its functions and relationships, and to envision and evaluate the effects of changes", Elsie would say years later in mustering others to take on big political and social challenges. "It is the essential ingredient to all invention".[149]

Students like Elsie who were inspired by Koppen took note when they learned that their professor had developed this creative approach to aircraft design and aeronautics while working for Fairchild, a rapidly growing American company created after World War I by the academically inclined son of a founder of IBM. Elsie was also intrigued by the research under way in new MIT facilities such as the illustrious "I-Lab" because they were linked to the aviation industry in a special way. The MIT labs were, for example, developing the aeronautical and meteorological research instruments and survey equipment that would underpin the formation and growth of many major U.S. high-tech companies as well as aviation firms like Fairchild.

Then, as today, the combination of business creation and scientific discovery was an obvious feature of the MIT labs. Even during the Depression they were active centres for both academic and commercial research. Graduate-level students like Elsie came in constant contact with energetic entrepreneurs, innovative companies, and job opportunities. The Depression had devastated some industries and evaporated jobs in many parts of the United States and Canada, but the aviation sector, a novel undertaking with unexploited potential, continued to offer opportunity to skilled people.

Elsie was thought to be enjoying her studies at MIT, doing well personally, and moving along the path toward a D.Sc. in engineering. Years later, when recognition added honorary doctorates to her name, many people assumed that she had completed the D.Sc. degree during those Depression-era months at MIT. But instead, she dropped out before finishing her program.

In 1934, Elsie was staring at her 30th birthday on the calendar, her parents were facing financial challenges, and her salary-earning days had been cut short by illness and impairment. Although it was not something she ever mentioned, the possibility that her physical capacity to work and earn might suddenly decline again also hung over her. At MIT, the real world of work was celebrated in tandem with science, and Elsie may have seen no shame in abandoning university life if it allowed her to get more directly involved in the work and profession she was finding increasingly exciting. Indeed, she looked at MIT courses on air currents and design as a type of "refresher course" to reconnect her with her profession.

Elsie could have been persuaded to stay at MIT and finish her doctorate had she found ways to earn money while studying and working on challenging projects. She might have hoped this to be a possibility earlier in the year, when Hunsaker introduced what was described as his "biggest change in the graduate program": a shift toward more scientific research. To advance this strategy, Hunsaker decided that, for the first time in its history, the university would appoint the top aeronautical engineering "graduate students as [paid] research assistants".[150] He took this step not merely to conscript cheap labour for his research projects, although this would have been consistent with his style, but also to reward his best aeronautical engineering grad students with some real-world experience and a modest income. Elsie, who could have used the money and who had already conducted graduate-level research as a top student at Michigan five years earlier, was not included in this select group. The group was all male.

It is uncertain to what extent her personal pride and opinion of MIT were damaged, for in later years she never mentioned this event in connection with her decision to drop out. But when, a few months later, her thoughts and influences encountered an opportunity for paid work with Professor Koppen's one-time employer Fairchild, which had a new plant in Longueuil, Quebec, a place not far from her sister Helen's home in Montréal, Elsie took it and left the academic world and the United States behind.[151] It would be decades before MIT would see its first woman doctoral graduate in aeronautical engineering, and Elsie would never again consider the United States her home base.[152]

Elsie, sitting on right, while on a break from doctoral studies at the Massachusetts Institute of Technology visiting her Aunt Jennie (centre with umbrella) and her sister Helen in Toronto (1933). (*Courtesy of Elizabeth Schneewind.*)

Fairchild and Longueuil in 1934

Elsie was hired by Fairchild to work with the formal title of Assistant Aeronautical Engineer in a plant that was a modest facility, not much more than a large hangar, but nevertheless an exciting and active blend of modern technology, daring exploration, and stories of the development of northern Canada. Despite the times, the air transport business was growing rapidly in North America as the bush plane came into its own as an important economic force. With its immense geography and highly concentrated ground transportation systems, Canada had a special need for the kind of planes that characterized the era, and Elsie's new employer Fairchild was at the forefront of responding to this opportunity.

Fairchild had made itself an important part of early Canadian aviation and won a unique place in the country's history by introducing winter bush flying to Canada. From the beginning, the American inventor and entrepreneur Sherman Fairchild saw great opportunities in Canada for his aerial photography business and later for the specialized planes his firm built to conduct aerial surveys for government agencies as well as forestry and mining firms. By the late 1920s, Fairchild had subdivisions that included engine plants and equipment manufacturing sites in different parts of the United States. But because a major market for all of its products was in Canada, Fairchild wanted to have a manufacturing presence there as well. In fact, the company had built its success upon its close working relationship with Canadian clients and a deep understanding of their needs.

In the late 1920s, the firm began Canadian operations under the name Fairchild Aircraft Ltd. and opened its plant outside of Montréal to refurbish its existing U.S. products for Canadian use. Its planes already featured enclosed cockpits that could be heated and undercarriages that could be converted to floats or skis. Longueuil, the Montréal suburb along the south shore of the St. Lawrence River destined to become an aviation industry hotbed, had the combined advantage of an airport and easy access to the floatplane runways of the river. Fairchild was not alone in seeing this as an ideal site for a Canadian base.

The refurbishment and overhaul work undertaken at Fairchild's new Canadian plant was popular with Canadian pilots, and the operation expanded quickly. Within a few years, the company was ready to build entire planes at its Canadian plant beginning, of course, with American-designed models, notably the Fairchild 71,[153] a monoplane modelled on other Fairchild aircraft and, like the others, designed for accurate aerial photography, few passengers, and light transport. This American-designed aircraft was to be recognized as "Canada's finest bushplane"[154] of its time. Despite this success, some of the company's Canadian clients wanted something even bigger and stronger. The project to respond to this demand for something tougher and larger was the backdrop to Elsie's job offer and arrival in Longueuil in late 1934.

Montréal was well established as Canada's biggest and most dynamic city at the time of Elsie's move to Fairchild. Its regional population had passed the one million mark a year earlier, and almost 400 years had passed since French explorer Jacques Cartier arrived at the native village of Hochelaga at this site. Unlike Cambridge, Massachusetts, and Ann Arbor, Michigan, this city was too big to be dominated by its universities, but it did have substantial English and French educational institutions, including the esteemed McGill and the Université de Montréal, which was founded in 1878 as an arm of Québec's Université Laval. In the 21st century, the Université de Montréal is the second largest university in Canada after Toronto. Its successes include engineering programs at its affiliated school, the École Polytechnique. But in the 1930s, the entire university was struggling to survive under the weight of difficult financial times. The university had dreams for a modern new campus and buildings, but the lack of money kept these plans from being realized for many years.

Montréal was one of the Canadian cities hardest hit by the Depression. Tens of thousands of people had flocked to the city in the decade after World War I to find jobs, and thus tens of thousands were unemployed when Elsie arrived in Montréal.

When Elsie began work at Fairchild, she was thrilled to finally start a paying, full-time job in her field and in an established and respected company. Her feelings were naturally magnified by the difficult economic circumstances, which made everyone with any kind of job grateful, and the opportunity to pursue, at last, her passion for aircraft design.

From Elsie's days at the University of Michigan, she had had an intense interest in design work, an exercise that involved as much imagination as technical calculation and that appealed to Elsie's creative instincts. It was challenging. Even in the mid-1930s, the design of Fairchild's Canadian products had become a complex technical enterprise with the aviation industry moving out of its craftsman era of "stick and string" into a full-fledged science. Fairchild was engaging Ph.D. scientists in research on its novel designs and Elsie's engineering colleagues, like those at other firms, were developing precise, sophisticated, detailed models to make predictions of wind resistance affecting individual components and their positioning as well as the full aircraft.[155]

The fortunes of an entire aircraft and the consequent budget for proto-type development and production would not, therefore, be bestowed on a new young assistant engineer, no matter how talented she was — at least until that person had proven herself in the trenches of detailed mathematical study and sometimes tedious testing. Elsie was thus tasked with stress analysis calculations on designs produced by others, such as her kindly boss and new mentor, Fairchild's chief engineer Francis Percival ("F.P." or "Frank") Hyde-Beadle. Hyde-Beadle was a genial man and an experienced, innovative aircraft designer who readily took Elsie under his wing and guided her into the field of stress analysis as her entry into the world of aircraft design.

Stressful Work

Stress analysis was an important and valued aspect of aeronautical engineering. From the first flights of the Wright Brothers and Alexander Graham Bell's Aerial Experimental Association, aircraft makers recognized that flying machines and their individual components would need to endure previously unknown stresses, stresses that made their planes vulnerable to excessive deformation and fracture. Stress analysis is an attempt to avoid these problems by estimating, at the design stage, how much stress should be expected in operations in the real world of bouncing on the ground and buffeting in the sky. When the testing and calculating is done, the job then turns to proposing the materials and the means of meeting the challenges. This was Elsie's first engineering job, and even though she would recall the calculations and arithmetic as less enjoyable features of her engineering work, stress analysis led her into some of the most intriguing and important engineering challenges of her time and a major role in significant Canadian aviation firsts.

Indeed, Hyde-Beadle would involve Elsie in many rewarding projects and would do everything he could to share his skills with her. Grateful, she thrived on the opportunity and the environment. The Fairchild shops were said to have fostered a high esprit de corps as well as great individual pride in workmanship during this period, and Elsie would look back on her time there with warm feelings if not complete satisfaction.

As Elsie's recruitment and hiring by Fairchild coincided with the Canadian plant's launch of plans to develop and produce aircraft and aircraft components of its own design, Elsie would, therefore, participate in all of the firm's pioneering Canadian projects. They ranged from the design of floats and other components to development of the Fairchild 82, a sturdy, no-frills, low-priced bush plane. Working on the various versions of the 82 would be recalled by Elsie as one of her most gratifying experiences at "Fairchild's". The 82 was a great vehicle for moving freight and passengers and was exported and used in many countries. Although the total Fairchild 82 output was measured only in the dozens, the plane was better than their other models and proved successful enough commercially to allow the Canadian arm of "Fairchild to survive the Depression".[156]

At the same time, the Fairchild spirit of adventure meant that Elsie and her colleagues took chances on projects that did not fare as well and ended up blemishing their records as engineers and designers. One such project was that effort to build a plane bigger and stronger than the 71, the American-designed model that had done so well in northern Canada. This project was under way when Elsie arrived at the Fairchild plant in 1934. The goal was to design and build an all-metal bush plane specifically for the Canadian market, to be christened the Super 71.

In the early 1930s, aircraft companies, the military, and the aeronautical engineering profession in both Canada and the United States were still struggling with the concept of all-metal aircraft. A practical, safe, and financially viable design eluded them, even though the visionary Europeans Anthony Fokker and Hugo Junkers had produced successful designs, first using sheet iron and later aluminum alloys, for the German side during World War I. Leaders in the U.S. aviation industry had enthused throughout the early 1920s about the durability of metal materials, but the concept did not take hold in North America until the 1930s.

Many people worked on the problems throughout the late 1920s and early 1930s, with some progress. Nevertheless, when Elsie MacGill joined the Fairchild team confronting the challenge, only a very small fraction of the planes in the air were all metal, and the technical issues still seemed confusing and daunting. The major technical issues involved were the tendency for metal to buckle under stress and the corrosion problems experienced by the aluminum alloys then available. Both problems had the potential to manifest unexpectedly in failure during flight, and they did.

Fairchild felt up to the challenge. As early as 1932, some managers with the company had enough confidence in their experience and the abilities of the Canadian factory to start thinking seriously about building truly original, Canadian-designed planes.[157] Their confidence underpinned that first effort, the Super 71. As well as having an all-metal design, the plane was to be a single-engine bush plane capable of carrying eight people and a relatively heavy load.

Unlike its inspiration, the Fairchild 71, the Super 71 was to be conceived specifically for Canadian conditions, thinking that led the Longueuil engineers to attempt to create the first all-metal aircraft to be designed and built in Canada. Although a prototype of the aircraft (registered as CF-AUJ) was already in the works before her arrival at Fairchild, 29-year-old assistant engineer Elsie MacGill eventually played a key role in assessing the issues around the use of metal, the design of components, and the refinement of what was to be a landmark plane.

Because the project had been initiated as a personal priority of the Canadian Fairchild general manager Hubert Passmore, he had an ongoing interest in it and encouraged his teams to continue research and testing in an effort to perfect the design. There were many elements to the ensuing work, including wind tunnel testing on model wings, fuselages, engine cowlings, undercarriages, tails, struts, and, of course, all of them together in a variety of arrangements.[158] Elsie participated in most of it.

It was demanding work on many fronts. Within a few years, governments gearing up for war and working with the forerunners of the big aluminum companies, such as Alcoa and the Quebec-based operations of Alcan, combined forces to develop new lighter, stronger, and more durable alloys. These innovative materials would solve many of the problems Elsie and her colleagues faced in the design of their all-metal aircraft, but at the time of the development of the Super 71, the aircraft industry had only a limited material, duralumin, at their disposal.

Because of duralumin's limitations, the designers still needed to find creative solutions to the buckling problem and to use complex metal structures that would reinforce the metal surface while maintaining the aerodynamic curves of the exterior of the plane. The Super 71, like some other metal planes of its generation, employed a stressed-skin fuselage, a streamlined tube that drew some of its support from the metal skin itself. The technique, however, also demanded intricate and complicated thinking and new ideas to combat the stresses caused by bending the metal into shape. Elsie and the Fairchild team found a system that worked to a certain degree, enough to at least allow the Super 71 to take flight as the first all-metal aircraft designed and built in Canada and as the first in Canada to use a stressed-skin fuselage to such a degree.

Before the Super 71 project was over, Elsie would find many reasons — some uplifting and some crushingly bad — to consider her association with it as memorable, but her greatest, enduring memory may have come at the beginning of its operational phase.

When Elsie arrived at Fairchild, it was, of course, fun for her to see a fully constructed aircraft designed, at least in part, by her new colleagues, and an honour to be invited to participate in its refinement and evaluation. But she was most thrilled when advised that to do this work, she would have to perform a task she had fantasized about since hearing of Alys Bryant's demonstration flight at the Vancouver Exhibition over 20 years earlier. She got into the plane and went for a ride, not the inaugural flight, but one of the early test flights for this model. Elsie's legs were still too weak for her to consider piloting the plane, but on this day, she began a convention that would earn the respect of many pilots and recognition as a true aviation pioneer: to always accompany the pilots in any of the planes she had helped design as "the participating 'observer' on all test flights".[159]

The Super 71's 520-horsepower Pratt and Whitney Wasp motor fired up, exhaust kicked out of the plane's innovative new tailpipe, and the plane took off toward its 240 km (150 miles) per hour top speed, circled through the early winter Canadian skies, and landed. During its test flights that first year, the plane not only met the test pilot's criterion for success (allowing all on board to walk away unhurt); it also performed "in close agreement"[160] with what was predicted in development and in calculations based on the design. In many ways, this was the engineer's own definition of victory.

But meeting technical performance expectations does not equal commercial success, and the pilots and potential purchasers of the aircraft were not impressed by the data since, from a practical point of view, the design had many flaws. A serious concern was the obstructed view resulting from the location of the cockpit, which had been set far back on the fuselage in an effort to distribute weight more effectively; another problem was the lack of planning for aerial photography equipment.

Although some assessments were kinder — saying "it was a good freighter" that did not find a market simply "because its all-metal fuselage made it more expensive than its contemporaries"[161] — the plane had more critics than fans. In the end, only one Super 71 was ever made: the prototype CF-AUJ.

This lone plane stayed in service for a number of years with Canadian Airways and even made news when it showed off its large cargo bays and transport power by flying two live oxen (one at a time) into a remote northern mining camp. One of the animals weighed over 700 kilograms (over 1500 lb). Still, problems persisted, and when CF-AUJ crashed and sank in 1940 after hitting a log during take-off from a remote lake, it was written off. The company might not even have made the effort to salvage the plane and take it out of service officially were it not for its cargo of gold bullion.

This is not, however, the end of the story or even the complete description of Elsie MacGill's work on the Super 71 project. Possibly to encourage Canadian manufacturing and aircraft design, the Canadian military decided to overlook the problems with the lone prototype Super 71 and agreed to buy a couple of modified versions of the aircraft on the condition that they be adapted to serve as aerial photography planes. Specifically, the RCAF wanted the cockpit moved forward.

These two planes were to be known as the Super 71P. By the time the order was made, Elsie was a fully inaugurated member of the engineering staff. She thus had a lot more input into this version of the airplane and actively participated in its design improvements, including work to shift the cockpit position and to respond to other concerns expressed by pilots of the inaugural Super 71. The two Super 71P's had some impressive qualities. They, too, could hold a ton of freight as well as eight passengers and were, for a few years at least and despite some mishaps, a welcome sight over remote northern campsites and military bases.[162]

Yet the aircraft struggled with performance problems and required ongoing design work throughout their early service life.[163] The needed tests, adjustments, and reassessments provided the young assistant engineer Elsie MacGill with lots of valuable experience and challenging opportunities to add to her knowledge of aircraft design. They did not, however, provide her with much to brag about. One of the Super 71P planes crashed on a Manitoba lake in 1937 just a few years after being made, and the other was ignominiously taken out of service by the RCAF in 1940, around the same time as the original Super 71 crashed.

Ultimately, the Super 71 and 71P projects were to be logged, for the most part, as just another entry in the file of "learning experiences" for both Fairchild and Elsie MacGill. In a positive way, the knowledge gained from building and testing the planes influenced Fairchild's work in Longueuil for many years to come, positioned it to manufacture other products, notably the successful 82, and marked another milestone in the evolution of Montréal's aerospace industry.

The experience, for Elsie, marked the start of her paid professional career, and it was personally rewarding in many indirect ways. At Fairchild, she made contact with experts in many aspects of the aeronautics industry and learned about the innovative work under way at her company's U.S. plants. She had many opportunities to share ideas with her U.S. colleagues and to dig into the Canadian plant's ongoing experimentation with new designs. Her work included contributions and minor improvements to the firm's existing aircraft and many successful subcomponent designs.

She shared in many minor achievements. But the special knowledge and skill that would turn her into a stronger, more capable engineer was gained at Fairchild through other hard experiences and, often, through learning what did not work rather than what did.

Another such "hard experience" was the Sekani. The Fairchild F-45 Sekani was to be a general utility aeroplane, this time with twin Wasp engines, a capacity for one-ton loads, and a cruising speed of just under 200 km (125 miles) per hour.

When tests began on models of the plane in early 1937, Elsie MacGill had established herself as a competent assistant through the Super 71P work, and although she was not ready to be made a lead engineer, she was given a greater role in the engineering work and recognized by experts as a Fairchild "aircraft designer" and the first female to ever do this work professionally in Canada and possibly anywhere. During development of the Sekani, she made use of the new wind tunnel facilities at the National Research Council of Canada (NRC) in Ottawa, working with NRC researchers to test the Fairchild designs, take measurements, try different ideas, and make adjustments.[164] There, she saw familiar faces from the University of Toronto, such as her second-year machine design professor, John Hamilton Parkin, who was by then Director of Mechanical Engineering at NRC. She also made new friends, including highly trained and internationally recognized researchers like Dr. John J. Green, an expert in the science of aerodynamics who would be a source of support to Elsie for the rest of her career.

Elsie had more responsibility now. Within a few months, this translated into more of the blame. The Sekani never really made it out of the prototype stage, for only two versions based on the initial design were ever made. It was even less successful than the Super 71.

It became clear early in the research and development stages that the Sekani's basic design problems included both longitudinal and lateral instability, and despite multiple attempts by Elsie and her colleagues to address them, these issues persisted into the prototype stage and eventually convinced Fairchild to abandon the plane. A second model was built for the Mackenzie Air Service, a long-time Fairchild customer serving the remote north, with the hope — given its ability to easily transform its wheels with strapped-on skis — that it would be useful in winter conditions. With the Mackenzie colours and lightning bolt markings, it was considered a "fine looking" machine, but ultimately it was not purchased, labelled dangerous to fly, and deemed "one of the few badly designed aircraft produced in Canada".[165]

The Sekani would not find a prominent spot in Elsie's curriculum vitae and future biographical sketches. Yet it was an archetype of the notion that appropriate education and real-world training can turn enthusiasm and talent into expertise. One feature of the project was Elsie's persistence and doggedness in trying to find answers and to make things work. She felt that Fairchild had given up too easily on the Sekani; with more testing and adjustments, she believed, the plane may well have proved effective. Whether she was right or not, her position on the Sekani was

Planes Elsie helped develop and design at Fairchild — Canada's first all metal bush plane Super 71 delivering oxen to North (left) and the modified Super 71P (bottom). (*Canada Aviation Museum Library and Archives.*)

The Fairchild 45-80 Sekani — Elsie conducted wind tunnel testing and design work for it at national laboratories in Ottawa (bottom). (*Canada Aviation Museum Library and Archives.*)

Fairchild's most successful project of Elsie's time at the firm, the celebrated Fairchild 82 (right). (*Canada Aviation Museum Library and Archives.*)

consistent with her tendency to persevere beyond what others considered reasonable.

In any case, Elsie had done her job, evaluating the Sekani design and trying everything she could think of to make it viable. "She thought nothing of night-driving... from Longueuil to Ottawa in the depth of winter", lifting her bad leg onto the clutch and steering through snow in order to test out another idea several hours away in the national aeronautics laboratories. Those who watched her working in the wind tunnel labs during this period recognized that there was someone different in their midst, a professional with a perfectionist's bent that could be irritating at times but must be counted among the qualities suggesting that a successful career in aeronautical engineering was in the making: "a woman with a keen and bright mind, dedicated to a professional career in the aircraft industry"[166].

Just as others were coming to like and admire her, Elsie in turn respected and enjoyed many of the people she had met since arriving in Longueuil, and she started making friends beyond the walls of the Fairchild factory. Her new acquaintances included Helen Soulsby, a woman with a familiar first name, and her family. Elsie and this new "Helen" became good friends. They were about the same age, and Helen's husband Eric James Soulsby (also known as E.J. and most often as "Bill") worked as a manager at Fairchild. This Helen's voice floated over a light Yorkshire accent that reminded Elsie of the talk she had heard so often during her childhood in British Columbia. The two women also shared a special perspective on life, having both been impaired by serious illness while still young.

Helen Soulsby had suffered a bout of rheumatic fever back in Britain while still a teenager just after World War I.[167] Doctors knew that the collection of symptoms labelled "the fever" was likely the product of an infection, and in the midst of a world-wide epidemic, the flu was assumed to be the root cause of her illness. Years later the medical profession would recognize the fever as a rare consequence of a streptococcal bacterial infection, strep throat, that sometimes does not appear until days and even weeks later. In the 1930s, the resulting damage was evident, but the link had yet to be made to an autoimmune reaction in which a person's antibodies attack not only the bacteria, but also one's own tissues.

Rheumatic fever, an inflammatory disease, can damage the joints, skin, and even the central nervous system. For Elsie's friend, the main, enduring effect was on her heart. When it hits, the fever can cause a rapid heartbeat, the end result for many being an enlarged heart and lasting impairment of the heart muscles, valves, and supporting structures, and finally a reduced life expectancy.

Aside from acknowledging some fatigue, Helen Soulsby never talked about the prospect of an early death with her friend. Elsie, for her part, treated her own handicap "as little more than a minor annoyance which was not to be either an obstacle or a deterrent to any of her intended activities" even though her "lameness struck [others] as an appalling affliction". The two had much in common.[168]

For the most part, the two women chatted and laughed about other things, and Elsie's visits to the Soulsby home for dinner were a time away from work to relax. She enjoyed the children, and they thought her visits were great fun, pushing her to take them for a ride in the new Ford Roadster she had bought with her engineer's pay. The car was unheated and had an open-air rumble seat, but this did not deter the Soulsby children or prevent Elsie from agreeing with enthusiasm, despite the need to manoeuvre her weaker leg more often on the rolling roads of the Quebec countryside.

It was thus with mixed emotions that Elsie learned in 1937 that the Soulsbys would be moving to the far end of Lake Superior. Bill had landed a job as a senior manager with Canadian Car and Foundry (Can-Car),[169] a large company with headquarters in Montréal and manufacturing operations in many Canadian locations. One was in Fort William, Ontario, the place where Soulsby had lived, worked, and started a family years before, and the site of the Can-Car plant where he would be working in the future. Elsie was happy that her friends were going to prosper and that her friend Helen Soulsby's husband Bill was moving up the corporate ladder, but was personally sad to see the family go.

Although Fairchild was a dynamic, well-established international aviation enterprise, Can-Car represented bigger opportunities for Soulsby as a manager and an individual. As its name suggests, Canadian Car and Foundry was a Canadian company formed through a 1909 merger of two companies involved respectively in rail cars and heavy industry. The firm had built its reputation manufacturing railway boxcars, ships, and their components at Fort William and saw itself in the late 1930s as an integrated, dependable, financially viable, and all-purpose transportation equipment company.

Before he joined the Fort William plant, Bill Soulsby knew that Can-Car was working hard to be better established in the aircraft business and that it needed additional engineering expertise. This need was magnified when the firm's chief aeronautical engineer Michael Gregor announced his intention to leave the firm to pursue opportunities in the United States. Recognizing that Can-Car would want a particularly skilled and innovative engineer to replace Gregor, Soulsby and his wife thought of Elsie, who was bright, talented, dedicated, and underutilized in Longueuil.

Doing well at Fairchild and learning in a creative environment, Elsie might have had reason to be reluctant to consider a new job and a move to Fort William when she first heard about the opening at Can-Car. Even though her friend and mentor Frank Hyde-Beadle had left Fairchild by then and even though his replacement, the new General Manager and Chief Engineer Nathan Vanderlipp, was a largely unpopular taskmaster, Elsie was not particularly uncomfortable at Fairchild. She respected Vanderlipp's skill and his no-nonsense approach. More importantly, Fairchild's Canadian operations, unlike the embryonic Can-Car aviation line, had a secure future, having just negotiated a major long-term contract for the construction of Bristol Bolingbroke reconnaissance aircraft for the RCAF. Engineers working for Fairchild's Canadian arm knew there would be work and incomes for some time, a significant consideration in the latter years of the lingering Great Depression.

Elsie had had other opportunities to change jobs and had even been under pressure to apply for a post as a junior engineer with the Aeronautical Engineering Division of the Department of National Defence in Ottawa. The invitation came because she had earlier complained in person to the administrators in charge that such jobs were restricted to males, and it was this intervention by Elsie that compelled the federal civil service to open aeronautical engineering positions to women for the first time. In fact, the position, ostensibly posted for competition in accordance with government rules, had been unofficially all but promised to her. Although she did not apply for the position, she saved, as a kind of trophy, a copy of the December 27, 1937, government job posting with its highlighted, explicit, and italicized reference to the eligibility of female applicants.[170]

There were certainly other reasons for anyone to pause when thinking about life in Fort William. Elsie knew from her conversations with the Soulsbys that it was a cold, tough place and very different from Montréal.

Named in 1807 for William McGillivray, a superintendent of the North West Company, Fort William rose out of fortifications built to support the early fur traders on the western shores of Lake Superior. Over its first century, the town and its nearby sister community of Port Arthur developed around facilities for the western terminus of the Great Lakes and the starting point of rail transport to and from the west. In 1970, the two towns and other lands were merged into the present-day city of Thunder Bay, a bustling place that warrants its association with the mythical Thunderbird of Ojibwa legend. But as Elsie considered her future in 1938, Fort William was still forming and on the fringe of the wilderness.

As it turned out, these features would make it a good location for an aircraft maker. Exploration of the resource-rich north had provided the prime market for Canadian-built airplanes since the end of World War I, and any plane designed and built for Canadian clients would benefit if it reflected the rugged, remote reality of the north. In any case, Fort William was a cost-effective place to build, repair, and maintain rail cars since it erased the need for the expensive transport of equipment by water from bigger centres down the Great Lakes. Such forces had led Canadian Car and Foundry to establish its large manufacturing operation in the town. Now the threat of another world war was turning real and being felt in many countries. As the military build-up in Europe progressed, it occurred to Can-Car that its remote plant in northern Ontario might make an attractive location for the manufacture of military aircraft. Definitely a difficult spot for enemy bombers to reach, it had also established supply links and the foundations for manufacturing on a large scale.

With the Soulsbys' encouragement, Elsie made up her mind to consider the job and, at 33 years of age, she was soon formally offered the responsibility of Chief Aeronautical Engineer at the newly energized Can-Car plant at Fort William. Because the company had already started work in the aircraft industry, had built modern planes, and conducted some experimental design, Elsie concluded that the firm meant business and that if she accepted, she might be playing a key role in its aviation expansion. It would also mean a lot more money and prestige than any of the other job possibilities before her. This suited her needs and her pride.

Up to this point, she might have had strong personal reasons to hesitate before accepting such an offer. But her personal circumstances were evolving as well. In Montréal, of course, she had strong professional connections and a home. Aside from the Soulsby family and her friends at work in Longueuil, there was the anchor of regular contact with her sister Helen and Helen's husband, the rising sociology star at McGill University, Everett Cherrington Hughes. Young Helen and Elsie visited each other often, shared shopping excursions, laughed at each other's jokes, and went on occasional road trips together. In early 1938, it also looked as if this particular tie to Montréal might be strengthened with a new addition. Elsie's sister was pregnant.

By now, 33-year-old Elsie may well have wondered whether the combination of disability and a busy career had permanently impaired her prospects of having a family of her own. The thought of a nephew or niece nearby was comforting, and a reason to celebrate.

Helen MacGill Hughes would give birth in Montréal that summer. The baby, the first of two girls, was named Helen in honour of her mother and grandmother. With three Helens in the immediate family, it is not surprising that the baby girl soon picked up a differentiating nickname: "Chérie", pronounced by some as "Sherry", an expression of the French Canadian ambiance of her birth and early life exposure to Montréal-area relatives. This nickname, like those carried by other MacGill family members, was a nearly inevitable by-product of a family determined to repeatedly re-use names like Helen and Elizabeth generation after generation.

Indeed, the second MacGill Hughes girl, born two years later in 1940, would be labelled "Elizabeth" in honour of her aunt, the engineer. Little Elizabeth Hughes, later Schneewind, would eventually assume the mantle of "Elsie" as well, but not before trying out life with nicknames like "Bitty", a name evolved from "Elsiebits" and distinguishing her, a little bit of an Elsie, from her aunt, big Elsie. As she grew older, Elizabeth Hughes pleaded with her father to stop using the childlike Elsiebits nickname, as a teenager sometimes scolding him ferociously, until he finally retreated to the more acceptable "Bitty", although still managing to offend with the seemingly "sloppy American pronunciation [of] Biddy".

To add to the disorder, Elsie and her sister called each other "bonks" or "bonksy" all the time. Elsie's nieces knew her best as "Aunt Bonksy" even though their aunt would use the same name in reference to their mother. It was confusing for outsiders and not always clear who was referring to whom. The tradition of honouring each other with names and then the ensuing tenderness of nicknames illustrated the warmth, joviality, and

Elsie MacGill while still at Fairchild in Longueuil in 1938. (*Library and Archives Canada PA-148380.*)

persistent closeness of the family, anchored as always by the loving bond between Elsie and her sister. But in the late 1930s, the two women were also building independent careers, and lives intertwined with others. As it turned out, Elsie's little nieces would not see as much of their aunt as they would have liked during their first years of life.

In 1938, "after eleven years at McGill [University], Everett was invited to join the Chicago department" of sociology,[171] which was highly respected internationally and growing. It was also the place where he had first met Elsie's sister. The now 35-year-old "Helen fair", as she was called at McGill, and her husband had many friends and a strong social network in Montréal, but the proposition from Chicago was just too good, and they did not waver long. They accepted the offer, determining to return to the United States by the commencement of classes that fall for what would turn out to be the rest of their lives. They were thus preparing to move to Chicago in the spring of 1938,[172] at the same time as Elsie had career decisions of her own to make.

Fairchild was strong, but changing; her friends had moved away; and now her sister and her family had resolved to leave Montréal. Can-Car beckoned with an offer that was looking better and better. Within this swirl, the blend of opportunity and change helped make the decision for Elsie. On Saturday, May 28, 1938, barely nine years since the day she was struck by paralysis in Ann Arbor, Elsie Gregory MacGill packed her belongings and once again boarded a train for another place, another enterprise, and another step in what was shaping up to be a remarkable career and life.[173]

Chapter V

The Maple Leaf of Mexico

*"... it has been flown by a number of civil pilots,
who have enthused over its performance"[174]
"— a record-breaking performance"[175]*

When Elsie MacGill landed in Fort William to take up her new position in the summer of 1938, the remote northern Ontario town was already accustomed to the racket from fighter aircraft overhead. Watching the heavy, armoured planes take off from the Bishopsfield airport[176] and move across the sky in formation, some residents sensed the looming war even though the threat was half a continent and an ocean away. These sights and sounds also brought a paradoxical feeling of relief to the town, for activity at the Can-Car factory meant jobs and a boost for the strained local economy. Many considered the spectacle of the planes overhead to be "quite inspiring",[177] and in some circles, Can-Car could do no wrong.

In 1938, the Canadian Car and Foundry's operation was regarded as a concern that helped define the fortunes of the Lakehead region around Fort William even though the plant had been dormant for years. In its early, pre-World War I days, Canadian Car and Foundry was known as a national rail-car and metal components maker, but WWI also brought dribbles of specialized military work to the firm's Fort William subsidiary plant, specifically contracts to build minesweepers for France. Some of those ships disappeared during maiden-voyage encounters with stormy Lake Superior. Other problems led to the shutdown of the Fort William plant in the early 1920s, and it sat inactive for over a decade before it was purposely resurrected to help the company make a leap into the aircraft manufacturing business in 1937. The reopening to target the aviation business was part of the company's broader strategy for survival during the hard times of the Depression and was welcome news in the Lakehead region.

The CBY-3 Loadmaster — built in the 1940s, using the Burnelli design evaluated by Elsie when first arriving at Can-Car. (*Canada Aviation Museum Library and Archives.*)

Elsie's appointment as the plant's second chief aeronautical engineer was another step in the deliberate, ongoing determination to move the firm onto another level and to give new purpose to the Fort William plant. It would also help position the firm for the economic benefits of another overseas war.

Her arrival confirmed an existing trend as much as it launched a new era; she was stepping into an operation that had already produced planes, had others in the works, and was facing some special challenges. Through its Montréal-based head office and other factories, the firm was already involved in the development of novel aircraft engines, doing aircraft repair work, and even investing in a little research aligned to aviation.[178] While Can-Car executives were clearly determined to get into the aircraft industry in a significant way, they knew they had strong competition and that time was tight. They were willing, therefore, to take chances in order to make an aviation name for the company.

Can-Car had gone out on a limb as early as 1936, announcing plans for large-scale production of bizarre-looking new planes known as

One of the Grumman G-23 Goblins crated, as they were for the illegal shipment to Spain. (*Canada Aviation Museum Library and Archives.*)

Burnelli flying wings. The innovative and slightly eccentric American designer Vincent Burnelli believed that if the fuselage of an aircraft was constructed in the shape of a thick, wing-like airfoil, it would increase the overall lift of the machine and make the plane sturdier and safer, presumably by decreasing the take-off and landing speeds. Burnelli tried to promote his ideas throughout the 1920s and 1930s, engaging the famous pilot Clyde "Upside Down" Panghorn (the stunt flyer who had made the first trans-Pacific crossing) in demonstrations that eventually came to Montréal and caught Can-Car's attention. Can-Car obtained the rights to manufacture versions of Burnelli's design, and one of Elsie's first tasks after she settled into her office at Can-Car was to review the aeronautical reports and layout drawings of the Burnelli plane.[179]

Elsie's assessment was largely a neutral recounting of data, but this and other considerations led the company to shelve its plans to use its Burnelli licenses and instead to focus on other opportunities. Seeing the Burnelli proposal, other young engineers could have been unsettled by a new employer's unorthodox ideas about what might work in the aviation industry. But Elsie had become accustomed during her time at Fairchild to open-mindedness, innovation, and daring, and was comforted when she saw the same attitude at Can-Car. In addition, the Soulsbys had assured her that Can-Car was a serious company with lots of potential.

Elsie and Can-Car would have their confidence tested in many ways over the next few years, yet neither would lose their capacity for daring. Remarkably, after a stream of great aeronautical advances during WWII had made most 1930s' ideas obsolete, Can-Car returned to the Burnelli flying wing design and finally built a plane based on it. Only one model, the CBY-3 Loadmaster, was ever made. Odd and unpopular in many quarters, but nonetheless unforgettable, the plane carved out a unique place in Canadian aviation history as a symbol of the enduring willingness to take chances that surrounded Elsie during her first years with the firm.[180]

The Burnelli flying wing experiment was only one of the company's unusual adventures during its early aviation era. Well before Elsie's arrival, Can-Car had also undertaken an energetic and unorthodox drive to get into the fighter aircraft business. As the firm did not have the capacity to begin from scratch with its own design and development work, it shopped around for an existing model, like the Burnelli design, that it could produce under a licensing agreement with an established aircraft builder. Perhaps unwisely, Can-Car settled on a biplane fighter developed by a businessman and one-time American naval pilot, Leroy Randle Grumman, for his former bosses in the United States Navy. The Grumman FF-1 fighter, whose Canadian model would be identified as the G-23 (also GE-23) "Goblin", was a respectable aircraft in terms of range, speed, and power. But the clumsy-looking biplane had the appearance and aura of a passing era, and American military demand for such planes was waning.

Can-Car might have been naive in thinking it could tap into unexploited markets with the Grumman G-23 design, or it may simply have decided that it could build the plane easily, cheaply, and efficiently at the Fort William plant. In any event, Can-Car managers were desperate for a product they could use to demonstrate their plant's ability to build planes. They may not have thoroughly considered its commercial marketing potential.

To be safe, the firm's fledgling northern Ontario plant, which began the G-23 project well before it hired Elsie MacGill as chief engineer, adhered closely to Grumman's specifications and direction and relied on the U.S.

company for most of the components. Over the next few years, Can-Car would make over 50 of the machines. They performed as expected, but the chubby, odd-looking biplanes appealed as little to the Canadian armed forces as they did to the U.S. Navy, and Can-Car was compelled to look abroad for sales.

In the end, most of the Canadian-made G-23 Goblins were exported. The trial product, the only one of these planes to survive into the 21st century, was sent to Nicaragua in 1938.[181] Another one went to Japan around the same time. The late-1930s export sale of an American-designed fighter plane to the militaristic and aggressive Japanese government was somehow allowed even though it made many heads shake at the time. It later became clear that the Japanese, who in 1938 were engaged in the development of their own aircraft including the Mitsubishi Zero fighter plane, wanted only to disassemble the Can-Car aircraft and study it for intelligence purposes.

This was, however, a modest transgression in the context of the firm's other G-23 business activities. The vast majority of the planes, 40 in all, were built under a convoluted and highly illegal arrangement to supply fighter aircraft to the left-leaning Republican side in the tragic and twisted Spanish Civil War.

The United States, Canada, and other nations had tried to stay out of the Spanish conflict and in 1937 imposed an arms embargo on the country, believing that an influx of weapons and equipment to support the Republicans would prod Hitler and Mussolini into even greater support for their fascist friend General Franco and his right-wing Nationalists. Consequently, Can-Car broke off negotiations with representatives of the Spanish government, and the planned sale of 40 planes was ostensibly scrapped.

When agents purporting to represent the Government of Turkey approached Can-Car a short time later with an identical order for 40 planes and with identical shipping instructions, it might have seemed too much of a coincidence. But Can-Car did not ask many questions, or perhaps any, and set to work filling the "new" order from the Fort William plant. Thirty-four of the planes in whole or in part were shipped to France and then "unofficially" to the Spanish government. Despite the illegal nature of the transaction, the project helped establish Can-Car's reputation for technical competency. Some of those illegally shipped planes were

The Maple Leaf Trainer I, and the FDB-1 with test pilot George Adye, Manager David Boyd, and Elsie's predecessor Michael Gregor, December 1938. (*Canada Aviation Museum Library and Archives.*)

used for close to two decades in Spain, where they were known as Delfins (Dolphins) or Pedros Ricos (Fat Petes).

More such roundabout shipments were in the works when the scam (which had been facilitated by stolen and forged Turkish government documents) was uncovered by the American government. Although Can-Car managers were never prosecuted, some of those involved on the other side of the deal were imprisoned, and when the affair became known, it was embarrassing and potentially damaging for the company and indeed for the entire Canadian aircraft industry because American technology had been involved. The U.S. government complained vociferously to Ottawa.[182]

Thus, as Elsie was getting established at Can-Car, her new company was still smarting from the effects of the scandal and needed to find another buyer for its first production-model plane. This led the firm to contact the Government of Mexico, which had received one of the Goblins as a demonstrator and agreed to buy more if Can-Car would build them at its air force workshops near Mexico City. The Mexicans sent a high-level delegation to Fort William in late 1938 to initiate the negotiations. During their visit, Mexican military engineers met Elsie MacGill and set the stage for a separate project, one that would soon consume much of her time and energy.

The awkward, ongoing struggle to unload the remaining Goblins would be the business backdrop to Elsie's work at Can-Car over the next few years. But she did not appear too concerned, and the business frustrations did not impact her technical work other than as an ongoing irritation for some of her new colleagues. Eventually, 15 other Goblins, including new ones made after Elsie's arrival at Can-Car, were sold to the Canadian military. They were all but donated to the RCAF, perhaps as part of the firm's efforts to build a business relationship with the Canadian government.[183] If Can-Car hoped the gesture would dramatically enhance its reputation, it would be disappointed.

Called "Pregnant Frogs",[184] the 15 Goblins were ridiculed by the Canadian media, and RCAF pilots would end up making limited use of them in training around the Rockcliffe air base in Ottawa and, latterly, in a few patrols off the East Coast. The Canadian Air Force scrapped them a few years later when alternative, more modern patrol aircraft came available. Elsie's role as a designer in the project was limited, as the G-23 design was already well defined and restricted by Grumman requirements. But she did make a contribution as chief engineer for that last, small production run in the summer and fall of 1939. Once again, she assessed the aircraft's airworthiness and, in what was becoming the expected norm for Elsie, flew along as observer with the test pilots during the inaugural flight of each and every aircraft.[185]

Fortunately for Elsie, her firm and her reputation were unscathed by the experience. Can-Car continued to take chances. The decision to appoint as Chief Aeronautical Engineer a young woman with less than five years in the field, little management experience, and a serious disability was made in this same spirit of seemingly audacious confidence. Elsie's recruitment was a gamble that would pay off, although not immediately and not before a few other experiments proved less productive.

Because aircraft work was already well under way when Elsie came to Can-Car, she stepped into a very active operation when she arrived, and her first tasks involved helping out as much as leading or experimenting. In fact, if she envisioned a more exalted role with her prestigious new job title, she might have been disappointed in her first weeks at the Can-Car plant in 1938. Not only was she entering an operation tarnished by the Spanish sale scandal and diverted by the Burnelli flying wing proposition, she was being tasked with seemingly routine "stress analysis and performance calculations",[186] work similar to what she had been doing at Fairchild as a junior engineering assistant right out of university five years earlier.

The object of her studies was another odd, fat biplane fighter, a successor of sorts to the Grumman G-23 Goblin. This one, however, Can-Car had been developing and building on its own, concurrent with its production of the Goblins. The plane was the Gregor Fighter, destined to be the first all-metal fighter designed and built in Canada. It was the brainchild of Elsie's predecessor as Chief Aeronautical Engineer, Michael Gregor, a passionate and driven Russian-born designer who was well known and highly regarded within some parts of the U.S. aviation community, and it was this reputation and the associated contacts that made it possible for him to eventually leave Can-Car and to set up shop as a consultant in the United States. Gregor was still in Fort William when Elsie arrived, however, and would remain for several months,[187] although anxious to leave. He wanted to pursue his vision of a new generation of biplanes with a business focused on the booming aviation industry developing around airfields on Long Island, New York.

As Grumman, the U.S. Navy, Elsie, and many others had realized by 1938, biplanes, even new ones like the Goblins, were starting to take on the feel of museum artefacts from a quainter era. The faster, sleeker monoplanes were all the buzz. But the enthusiastic Gregor managed to convince Can-Car that he could combine the best of the new designs, such as an all-metal fuselage, clean aerodynamics, and gull wing style, with the advantages of "manoeuvrability, rate of climb, and greater ceiling" inherent in the biplane. Long after the evidence seemed to confirm the contrary, Gregor truly believed that he could produce a mixed-design military aircraft that could "outfight" the competition.[188]

For Elsie, on a personal level, her assignment to conduct data analysis on the Gregor was, although routine, a familiar task and an easy introduction to her new company, and it was a simple way for her to demonstrate her basic skills and understanding of aeronautical engineering. The plane's design had undergone stress analysis and testing against U.S. regulations known to Michael Gregor, but not sufficient for approval in Canada, which at the time relied upon British standards. Elsie, who was required to redo the testing on the plane, was happy she had scraped up the money to purchase her own set of manuals and reference texts before leaving Montréal. As she suspected, she needed these tools for her job in Fort William.

It was as a result, therefore, of Elsie's analysis work that the plane, Canada's first all-metal fighter, was eventually deemed airworthy by the Government of Canada and put into service.[189] The prototype Gregor was rolled out and unveiled for the first time on December 17, 1938, with light snow around the Fort William airport. The shiny, "modernistic",[190] and unique plane suggested no problems, at least that day — a good day at Can-Car, for despite the purpose of their product, the prospect of war still seemed limited and unreal to those who celebrated the achievement. Reality would close in around everyone present for the photo op when the plane's colourful English test pilot George Adye was recalled to Britain to serve in the Royal Air Force (RAF) a year later. Elsie's friend Adye was shot down and killed in aerial combat with German fighters, crashing off the coast of Britain shortly thereafter.

Meanwhile, despite its initial promise, the Gregor Fighter started heading down the path toward failure when it came to moving on to the sales and production level. Elsie's heart sank, and she shared the pain when an unfortunate and embarrassing loss of oil pressure on the way to the highly publicized New York to Miami Air Race in January 1940 helped to seal the plane's fate. Any possibility that the Gregor Fighter might be mass-produced for Canadian or U.S. clients was sunk by this and other mishaps. A hoped-for transfer of the prototype to Can-Car's operations in Mexico was derailed by Defence Department concerns and new export restrictions introduced when war broke out in 1939.

Production plans were cancelled, and the lone Gregor FDB-1 (Fighter Dive Bomber-1), Canada's first domestically designed modern fighter plane, was put in storage in a hangar at St. Hubert, Quebec, where it sat until it was destroyed in a fire a few years later. Nothing has survived of the historic aircraft that Elsie MacGill helped launch. It was, perhaps, the last breath of the era of biplane fighters.

Nevertheless, despite the commercial failure, Elsie had done her job and her technical skills had impressed Can-Car's executives and production team. Her job seemed secure, and she was even starting to build a reputation within the wider industry and, most gratifyingly, within the field of aeronautical engineering. She was becoming a familiar face in research laboratories and engineering facilities in Ottawa and Montréal and recognized, most importantly, as a full member of the club that was her profession of engineering.

Just days before her departure from Fairchild and Longueuil, in the spring of 1938, she was accepted as the first woman to be a full corporate member of the Engineering Institute of Canada (EIC), the leading national professional organization. Although she was made to feel welcome and her admittance was announced in an affirmative way, her gender was still a big deal and disturbing for some. When this unique "lady was accepted as a member",[191] it marked a traumatic break with a half century of tradition, and certain senior members of the previously all-male institution were "shaken to the foundations" by the mere prospect of the election of a female member.[192] But the agitated old boys were calmed by their more amenable colleagues, and the Montréal branch, which had previously only admitted a few women as "Student Members", trumpeted Elsie's election in a press release and held a special reception. At the event, the media and other guests were particularly struck by the new EIC member's light-hearted manner and youthful appearance. Elsie stirred the pot by coming with what she called a "giddy hat" and the look of "not a woman — but a girl!"[193]

Although everyone in the room could see the beaming smile on Elsie's face and may have noticed her "giddy" demeanour, few would have known how especially sweet and personally important the recognition was, an exhilarating contrast to the baffling and bureaucratic rejection letters she received from another professional body just a few years earlier. She had tried in vain to join the newly founded organization Professor Hunsaker

Elsie being honored by the Engineering Institute of Canada — she became its first
female member in 1938. (*Library and Archives Canada PA-204364.*)

had touted to the students at MIT: the Institute of the Aeronautical Sciences (IAS) in New York. Elsie was told that the institute was postponing
the admission of women until their numbers warranted and the associated
special arrangements could be made, blaming, for example, the rules of
the chosen venue for its dinner meetings. Elsie found the response both
convoluted and personally galling since her former classmates, males with
the same credentials and sometimes less experience, had already been
accepted to IAS and even honoured by it. Since she intended to travel
internationally and planned to work a lot in the United States, she believed
that exclusion would be damaging to her career and her reputation.

Frustrated by the inability of this particular old-boys club to deal with
the novelty of her achievements within its smoking rooms and dusty procedures, Elsie was exposed to the stiffer, chauvinistic side of a profession
she had, to this time, somehow regarded as unscathed by gender bias.
She painstakingly pointed out the contradictions and flaws in the IAS's
position, and its amiable secretary, Lester Gardner, subsequently acknowl-

edged the merits of her case — its "logic", her "convincing" reasoning, and her "rational point of view"[194] — and, perhaps embarrassed by his club's position, suggested that she might buttress her future applications by first seeking admittance to the Royal Aeronautical Society and to Canada's own engineering institutions.

She took personal offence at the response to her 1936 application letters. But it was not personal. Elsie was not the first woman to be rejected by the organization; after a formal vote at its founding meeting in 1932, one of the names on the proposed membership list was scratched off with the notation "a woman" written beside it. The name was "Amelia Earhart".[195]

In 1939, three years after Elsie's failed attempt to join the organization, officials of the Institute for Aeronautical Sciences in New York formally changed their position and invited an Ohio aeronautical engineer and MIT graduate named Elsa Gardner to join their organization. Elsie and many other women would, decades later, join incarnations of the institute, but Elsa Gardner, who was the editor of the *Technical Data Digest* at Wright Field in Ohio at the time of her admittance and who would later work for the U.S. Navy, remained the U.S.-based institute's sole woman member for many years.

In a peculiar way, that institute's odd, contorted 1936 rejection of Elsie's application for membership and its weak response to her subsequent "firmly and persistently challenging"[196] pleas for reconsideration could be taken as a compliment. They were further evidence of Elsie's exceptional status as a female aeronautical engineer and position at the head of the line of her gender at the time. Elsie consoled herself in 1936, saying that "it was not a matter of if, but when"[197] and by moving on to seek a place within other networks and engineering bodies. The irony of her attempts to seek validation from a male-only institution may only have become fully apparent years later when women formed more and more of their own organizations and decided for themselves who deserved recognition from within their ranks.

As Elsie moved ahead in her profession, the Canadian aircraft industry was also progressing. The Gregor fighter plane's failure to find a market did not dissuade Can-Car from its strategy. Somehow Can-Car managers knew that they had to keep trying and that difficulties, even with the legal authorities, were not a reason to abandon their company's quest to be a leader in aircraft manufacturing. As a result of these persistent ambitions and the new female chief aeronautical engineer's evident skill, Elsie MacGill was rewarded in January 1939 with a new assignment, one that gave her a great deal of autonomy, creative freedom, and power. She was asked to prepare the complete design, from nose to tail, of an all-Canadian biplane that Can-Car hoped would be used as a primary trainer by the armed forces of many countries.

This was a tremendous vote of confidence in Elsie. She knew it was not an easy decision for Can-Car; the firm had, after all, had a very unpleasant experience with an early attempt to build a biplane trainer of original design. This previous effort was widely known as "the Wallace Trainer", named for its American designer Leland Wallace even though Can-Car had officially dubbed it "the Maple Leaf Trainer". The plane, completed in Fort William in early 1938, was plagued with performance problems from the beginning, and Can-Car eventually decided to abandon it as "unsatisfactory" despite serious expressions of interest from Nicaragua.[198]

When Mexican officials came to Fort William later in the year to negotiate for the manufacture of Can-Car Goblins in their country, they let it be known that they would also be interested in the Wallace Trainer if it could be modified for their specific high-altitude needs. Because of the earlier problems and the Mexican requirements, the firm chose to start virtually from scratch with a completely new design to be crafted under Elsie's leadership. The company liked the name "Maple Leaf" and still wanted to use it, so to distinguish the new larger, more powerful plane and its associated cost accounting from the flawed predecessor, it named Elsie's project "Maple Leaf Trainer II" or more often "Maple Leaf II".

It was a new kind of challenge for Elsie, different from the armament-equipped fighter plane and complex in its own way. A trainer is an aircraft specifically constructed, as its name suggests, to train pilots, navigators, and flight crews. A trainer must, therefore, have at least two seats and be versatile. Versatility in the 1930s usually meant that the plane needed to be lightweight, yet sturdy; highly manoeuvrable, yet stable at slow speeds. Although a pilot trainee would not normally be asked to conduct aerobatic feats, a good trainer aircraft had, almost by definition, to also be a good stunt plane. For example, Snowbird squadron, the Canadian forces flight demonstration team of later years, chose CF-114 Tutor jet trainers precisely because they are also well suited to formation flying and stunts.

A well-designed trainer, therefore, would need to meet the same technical qualifications as an aerobatic plane.

Can-Car and other aircraft makers knew there would be an urgent demand for trainer aircraft if the world entered into another all-out war. Even though the agreements that would later turn Canada into a pilot factory and what F.D. Roosevelt called "the Aerodrome of Democracy" were not in place in 1938, many people assumed that Canadians would be called upon, once again, to train and supply aircraft pilots as they had during World War I.

In fact, as Elsie started work on her design for a new trainer, the Government of Canada was furtively negotiating with Great Britain for a mandate to establish a massive network of air training bases and facilities across Canada. The prime minister, William Lyon Mackenzie King, was hunting for a politically acceptable way to contribute to the defence of Britain, a way clear and substantive enough to please Canadians with strong ties to Britain but also free of forced conscription or other measures that would draw on the blood of young Quebecers. Pilot training met these criteria.

The invasion of Poland and the declarations of war in September 1939 would thus prompt King to suggest a deal that led to the creation of the British Commonwealth Air Training Plan (BCATP). The agreement gave Canada control over the training of pilots from many countries against standards set by the British. Canada also bore the cost, which would eventually run into many hundreds of millions of dollars.

A Massive Air Training Program

Even though training would not begin in Canada until April 1940 and did not really take off until the fall of France a few months later, over 100 flight training schools were soon established with units at hundreds of sites across the country. By the end of the war, a total of 131 553 pilots, navigators, bomb aimers, wireless operators, air gunners and flight engineers from throughout the British Commonwealth, the United States, and countries of occupied Europe were trained in Canada. Almost half the total aircrew employed on British and Commonwealth flying operations were trained in the BCATP. Canadian graduates alone numbered 72 835, providing crews for 40 RCAF home defence and 45 overseas RCAF squadrons, as well as constituting about 25 percent of the overall strength of Royal Air Force (RAF) squadrons.[199]

Even though no one could have predicted the magnitude of this enterprise early in 1939, Canadian Car and Foundry, just glimpsing the possibility, knew that the need for trainer aircraft would be enormous. The firm knew that it would need an excellent product to break into this market and may have pushed consideration of the specific Mexican requirements to the side in order to take a shot at the larger opportunity.

Elsie MacGill had been entrusted with more and more responsibility and given more and more say in the design of aircraft at Fairchild and now she had a senior position at Canadian Car and Foundry. Yet never before had she been given the complete freedom and resources to pull all of her knowledge and data together into one project.

She was ready with a portfolio of ideas developed over a decade, and she was enthusiastic. Her attitude was contagious. From the beginning, the engineering team at Can-Car felt they were participating in something exciting and special. For this reason, they tried to keep many of the novel ideas and designs secret. The Maple Leaf II plane became "something of a mystery plane"[200] within the aviation industry.

For those involved in aeronautical engineering and design, however, some of the problems that Elsie's team faced would have been predictable. As a trainer, the plane would not only need two seats, but two fully outfitted cockpits, each equipped with an airspeed indicator, altimeter, compass, engine gauge unit, tachometer, turn and bank indicator, and ignition switch. Elsie insisted that her plane also had to have emergency equipment repeated in both front and rear cockpits. Other features that would become noteworthy included ball bearing mounts for all the surface controls, adjustable pedals, seats that could be moved into three different height positions, and other devices allowing the plane to adapt to a variety of occupants, from heavy males to delicate females, with a range of experience and skills. She might be rightly accused of consciously or unconsciously designing a plane that she herself would fly.

Although the principal goal of the project was the invention and creation of a new flying machine capable of manoeuvring easily through the skies, Elsie's work was marked by the unusual amount of attention she paid to design features affecting how her plane behaved on the ground. She devised ways to ensure it was easy to handle while taxiing in different wind conditions and heading down the runway at varied take-off speeds.

Shock absorbers and special braking systems smoothed out the plane's performance on the ground to an uncommon degree.

Finally, although Elsie's trainer aircraft was developed to respond to interests generated in Mexico, it was also clearly designed to meet Canadian needs. It had an attachable canopy that could be easily added in cold Canadian winters, components of durable new materials such as chrome molybdenum steel spars, aluminum alloy ribbing, and, finally, an undercarriage that allowed the wheels to be quickly and easily replaced with skis on the same chassis.

For her part, Elsie saw the plane's greatest innovation as "the system of inter-plane wires… designed so that the breakage of a single wire would not change the loading distribution throughout the wing cellule".[201] Extra experiments were conducted on the wing struts to complement this innovation. As a consequence, the wings of the plane did not need reinforcements to cover this contingency, the end result being a lighter wing.

"The Maple Leaf II", a plane suitable for Canadian conditions, was worthy of its name and its association with her country's most recognized national symbol. Elsie MacGill's two-seat trainer took its first test flight on October 31, 1939. Like many other flights around the Fort William airport, it was made in cold winds and frosty air,[202] and like many flights to come, the slender young designer and her cane were on board. Given the problems with the plane's predecessor, the Wallace Maple Leaf I Trainer, one might have argued to limit the risks of the test flight to the pilot alone. But Elsie was absolutely insistent that she had earned the right to be on board. The flight was smooth, and with the test flight's safe landing, Elsie MacGill had become what many have suggested is "rightly considered the first woman to have designed an aircraft"[203] and, perhaps more specifically, the "first woman to design, build, and test her own airplane" in the world.[204]

Elsie had thrown herself whole-heartedly into the project, and the resulting unique design was a function of her ingenuity. She exploited the technical and engineering freedom that her position as Chief Engineer had given her and the result was a novel invention. Yet the assertion that this marked a world first can only be judged by reviewing possible contenders for the title as well as the substance of Elsie's own work.

Elsie with Bill Soulsby and Maple Leaf Trainer II in photo with the shadow on her leg. (*Courtesy of Ann Soulsby.*)

In the early days of aviation when almost every plane was a tinkered and handcrafted personal product of those who were to fly it, some women pilots helped introduce new ideas and clearly contributed to aircraft design. E. Lillian Todd, a woman living in New York in the first decade of the last century, is said not only to have designed many large-scale model airplanes as a passion, but also to have had a hand in the design of an aircraft that flew in an event witnessed and reported in 1910. Bessica Raiche, touted by some to be the "First Woman Aviator in America", also worked with her husband to build a plane as early as 1910, introducing materials such as silk and piano wire that were genuine innovations in aircraft design. But Raiche (who eventually returned to school to become a medical doctor) and others of her era neither pursued aircraft design as a profession nor were they able to undertake the study of aeronautical engineering as a science. When she designed the Maple Leaf Trainer II, Elsie MacGill was both a graduate aeronautical engineer and a professional researcher of aircraft systems.

Even in the late 1930s, when more and more North American universities were introducing and developing aeronautical engineering programs, few were able to point to women among their graduates. By the time

Elsie was completing her work on the Maple Leaf II, her alma mater the University of Michigan could still boast only two other women graduates, both at the bachelor's level, from its aeronautics programs, and in the years leading up to the war there were typically just a few female students enrolled at the various levels of the undergraduate program. Elsie remained apart, almost a decade after her graduation, as the university's lone female graduate researcher and recipient of a master's degree in a related field.

Some of the early women aeronautical engineering students at the Massachusetts Institute of Technology (MIT) went on to graduate studies in the 1930s, but most often their grad work was pursued in basic sciences, not in advanced aircraft design and aeronautical research like Elsie.

One woman who might be counted as Elsie's equal in both the academic and industrial aspects of aeronautical engineering was Rose Lunn, who received a Bachelor of Science degree in the aeronautical engineering department of the University of Washington in Seattle in 1937. Lunn was the first female to earn the degree at that university and did it in style, coming first in her class.[205] Not surprisingly, she continued her studies, moving to MIT where she not only earned her master's degree in aeronautical engineering, but also, like Elsie, took courses in the doctorate program.[206] Lunn worked at Curtiss-Wright and North American Aviation after finishing school, eventually establishing herself as an expert in vibration and flutter.

But, despite her unique achievements, Lunn was not involved in aircraft design work to the same degree as Elsie. With apparent gender prejudice stalling her career, much of Lunn's technical successes were realized after Elsie's breakthroughs in aircraft design. In fact, "when Lunn was first hired, she was assigned secretarial duties. It took quite some effort on her part to convince her supervisors that she was capable of a lot more than typing!"[207]

United States and Canadian commentators and colleagues appeared confident in asserting that Elsie's work was unique for a woman in a North American context, and some international sources noted her achievements and the praise they had attracted. While it is possible that some unheralded professional woman in another country might have preceded Elsie in the design of a complete aircraft, it seems unlikely, given the nascent nature of the field, the degree to which Elsie's work was celebrated in the years that followed, and the fact that similar and even greater levels of gender bias existed elsewhere. These forces had combined with the worldwide economic depression to stifle such opportunities for breakthroughs and magnified the exceptional nature of Elsie's work.

"In most countries, with the possible exception of Nazi Germany, the 1930s were not good times for a woman to get a job in engineering".[208]

Nazi Germany publicly proclaimed stereotypes of all kinds, including those with respect to the role of women in society, and for the most part this posture diminished the chances for German women to succeed as engineers in the 1930s. But despite purges and patriarchal systems, some women were able to pursue advanced studies in engineering and even participate in advanced research projects thanks to the Kaiser Wilhelm Institutes, which were mandated to promote industrial development through technology. Senior male scientists were powerful figures within the institutes, and this power allowed them to override the otherwise prejudiced, rigid system and hire talented women into key positions if it served their personal research needs.

One of the women to benefit from this crack in the system was Irmgard Lotz (later Flügge-Lotz), a scientist who built upon her academic credentials in mathematics and applied mechanics to pursue an impressive career in aeronautical science that began under the aeronautics giant Ludwig Prandtl at the Kaiser Wilhelm Institute for Fluid Mechanics in Göttingen and ended in the United States decades afterward.

"Lotz later wrote in her curriculum vitae, that from 1929 to 1934 she was an assistant at the Aeronautical Research Laboratory"[209] of the institute, placing the initiation of her career at just the same time as Elsie was completing her aeronautical engineering research and study at the University of Michigan. Lotz may, in fact, have been among the women on Professor Pawlowski's mind when he mentioned female Europeans working in the physics and math of aeronautics around the time of Elsie's graduation in aeronautical engineering. While impressive and important, this work would be different from that of the professional engineer and designer like Elsie.

Finally, any review of Elsie's credentials as the first woman aeronautical engineer and professional aircraft designer would also have to acknowledge the moving and impressive career of American engineer Elsa Gardner, the woman who had succeeded where Elsie MacGill had failed by breaking into the venerated New York-based Institute for Aeronautical Sciences. Gardner began studying and working on the mechanical aspects of airplanes as an aircraft inspector during World War I, almost a decade before Elsie entered her first formal aeronautical engineering program at Michigan.

Like Elsie, Gardner's inspiring life was marked by both "physical lameness"[210] and a struggle to overcome gender-based barriers. But to a much greater degree than Elsie, Gardner had also faced significant financial difficulties that prevented her from pursuing aeronautical engineering studies full-time for almost a decade and a half after realizing this was to be her field. Not until she was awarded a scholarship to MIT in 1932 was Gardner able to devote herself to the credentials that would allow her to work in the aviation industry, the U.S. Army, and the U.S. Navy in a variety of aeronautics functions.

A linguist as well as an engineer, Elsa Gardner understood Latin, Greek, French, German, and Italian as well as English and could draw on foreign language sources in writing for U.S. publications such as *The Aero Digest* and *The American Machinist* and in editing *The Army Air Corps Technical Digest.* Gardner generally saw her male engineering colleagues as supportive and encouraging. Yet, at least for a time, she was not allowed to sign her name to professional articles because it might disturb a publication's male readership.

There were undoubtedly other women of achievement in the early years of aeronautical engineering. Yet the fact that Gardner, Lunn, Lotz, and the other women most often cited as pioneers in aeronautical engineering acquired their qualifications at least a few years later than Elsie MacGill reinforces the notion that Elsie might have been the world's first woman aircraft designer and aeronautical engineer. Considering her leadership and control of the unique Maple Leaf Trainer II project, and her milestone academic work at Michigan in the 1920s, the assertion seems reasonable.

Still, the lives of other women aviators and engineers match the drama and struggles of Elsie's story in many ways, implying that it is folly to try to compare these amazing women on the basis of a specifically defined superlative or original. For some authorities, the exercise recalls the absurdity of publicity around early aviation "when so many aeronautical laurels [hung] on the interpretation of a phrase and the insertion of a conditional clause".[211]

Nevertheless, there is no doubt that Elsie was very happy with the design and construction of the Maple Leaf II. When in late 1939 she posed for a picture in front of the plane, with the plant manager Bill Soulsby by her side, she beamed with pride. As the photo was being taken, Elsie knew it was one she would come to cherish and to share widely. The importance she attached to it was clear when later she expressed distress over shadows in the picture that made her bad leg look abnormally thin, "like a peg leg".[212]

Concerned that the photograph might suggest that there was even more wrong with her legs than the significant reality, Elsie hinted that she might sue the photographer. It was a joke, but it did betray a concern for such things. Although Elsie was not known as particularly vain, she did take photographs seriously, at least for much of her early life. She took care, for example, to hide a crooked tooth with closed-mouth, thin-lipped expressions. As a result, her formal, official pictures often seemed serious and even grim. Candid photos, on the other hand, almost invariably caught her smiling broadly or laughing.

Such thoughts and concern about shadows, however, did not stop Elsie from making and sharing many copies of the official photo of her Maple Leaf II and her boss, the long-time friend she still called "Mr. Soulsby".

For a while, her pride seemed justified. Just eight months from the day Elsie began her design work, her prototype plane (registered as CF-BPU) received its Certificate of Airworthiness, Acrobatic Category. It was a "record breaking"[213] achievement, and the plane soon started drawing attention from the Canadian aviation industry. This interest was magnified when the story circulated of "the attractive young lady" behind the "very attractive"[214]machine. But the real interest came as a result of the plane's remarkable operation and easy handling. Pilots who used it "enthused over its performance"[215], and Canadian Car and Foundry officials promoted it robustly in the trade media and with demonstration flights for the military and civilian market. But again, their new product, like the Gregor Fighter and the Goblins, struggled to find a market in Canada.

Others Were There First

When Canadian Car and Foundry began its quest for a position within the growing aircraft industry, other manufacturers were already there, acting to fill the needs Can-Car was only then recognizing. In addition to Elsie's first employer, Fairchild, the other great aircraft maker wise enough to plant itself in Canada to be near the market of northern exploration and development was the British firm de Havilland. It established a sales office and branch plant near Toronto in the late 1920s to build planes based on its highly popular Moth series design, initially importing its components from Britain. Many Canadians were comfortable with de Havilland products. Some had flown them in World War I overseas, and as early as 1917 Canadians had already built one de Havilland plane at the Canadian Aeroplanes Ltd. plant in Toronto. Another company to begin Canadian manufacturing operations before 1930 was Fleet Aircraft in Fort Erie, Ontario. The planes that de Havilland, Fleet, and other firms turned out were initially aimed at foreign markets and based upon foreign designs, but slowly the Canadian teams added their own design features and embellishments. Eventually, they added Canadian customers.

At de Havilland, a Canadian WWI fighter pilot turned company test pilot and promoter named Phil Garrett was appointed manager of the Toronto plant. He had worked hard to keep his operation going during the Depression, and his efforts paid off in 1937 when he sold 25 Tiger Moth trainers to the RCAF. This sale, in turn, stimulated Canadian production, which soon numbered in the hundreds. Fleet had meanwhile developed and sold its own trainer aircraft, the Finch and the Fawn, to the Canadian Defence Department. Thus when in 1939 Canadian Car and Foundry came knocking with its novel new machine, designed and developed by Elsie MacGill, the military had already committed itself in a big way to these other aircraft.

Notwithstanding the Maple Leaf Trainer II's outstanding performance and novel design features, it proved impossible to break into the military market despite the escalating growth in demand under the air training program. The British had started using Tiger Moths and other de Havilland products as trainers almost a decade earlier, and it was the British who, at first, set policy and standards for the BCATP even though the training took place in Canada.

To make matters worse, "rumours [were] circulated about the machine [the Maple Leaf Trainer II]… [implying] that it was not up to Commonwealth Air Training Plan requirements"[216] by individuals in the Canadian government who needed to defend earlier decisions to invest in other aircraft to the exclusion of a Canadian innovation that seemed to be gaining popularity and reputation.

Ironically, another rationale cited for not buying the Maple Leaf Trainer II was that "it was too easy to fly".[217] Pilot trainees, said the military, needed a more challenging aircraft to prepare them properly for the exigencies of war. Over the next five years, thousands of young men from around the world would die crashing into Canadian soil being "challenged" by trainer aircraft in the BCATP.[218] This "Battle of Canada" cost more lives than most battles overseas and accounted for most Canadian deaths during the early years of the war. Some lives would have undoubtedly been saved had their training been in machines that were more stable and easy to pilot.

The criticism frustrated Elsie in many ways. It was irritating to think that official circles might prefer the comfort of a familiar aircraft to a superior one, and easy for her to conclude that the Maple Leaf Trainer II had been rejected by the BCATP out of hand. This magnified her feeling that the prevailing system for making such decisions and for comparing the performance of new aircraft was flawed, and she often felt frustration over her inability to address these weaknesses in the system.

Elsie knew by now that her dream of becoming a pilot had been stalled, perhaps permanently, by her weakened legs, the passage of time, and other constraints. Still, she could not help slipping her mind into the pilot's viewpoint each time she flew as a passenger on a test flight. She was typically identified as the official "observer" of these flights and had a clear idea of what her job was. Yet Elsie also knew full well that the people with their hands on the controls were the only ones who could really understand and judge the more subtle features of a new plane's performance in flight.

The aeronautical engineering and aircraft design profession had not yet come to grips with the need to integrate and balance all aspects of flight testing in official, repeatable processes. Perhaps because of these personal frustrations, Elsie decided to take on the challenge and developed her own system for evaluating aircraft designs.

Since she was not a pilot, she sought to guide the pilots of her planes by extension, creating a set of standard forms for use in flight tests not only to record the technical information from the perspective of the technically trained observer, but also to document the more subjective and imaginative experience of the pilot. Her new Standardized Flight Test Reporting Forms were powerful reflections of her many real-world experiences both in and out of planes at Fairchild and Can-Car.[219]

Reflecting an inspired designer's bent as well as scientific thinking, her system was crafted to support creativity as well as encouraging less bias and more consistency in the evaluation of an aircraft's performance in test flights. To allow for later comparison tests, her system covered, for example, the need to provide a formal description of the aircraft, including such details as propeller size and wheel type. Her forms also prescribed the parameters for quantitative tests such as calibration of airspeeds in level flight and stall, and, more interestingly, sought to standardize reporting on qualitative issues such as controllability and feel in take-off and landing. She soon realized that her approach might have wider benefit.

In February 1940, she had a unique opportunity to pursue this insight at the Engineering Institute of Canada's General Professional Meeting in Toronto, where she set out her ideas in a presentation that cogently merged her early interests in design with her new preoccupation with organization and planning. Her paper did not overtly bemoan the lack of standards for test flight reporting or belabour the impact of poor and inconsistent reporting; instead, it laid out the positive case for a professional and dependable assessment covering all the features involved in testing new products and designs.

Through this proposal, she was sharing her personal belief that test flights constituted as much of a professional engineering and scientific undertaking as did any other phase of the process of aircraft design, and that they should be treated as such. Elsie was also revealing and documenting the personal importance she placed on riding along on test flights herself and on observing the performance of her aircraft first-hand, actions she saw as a necessary expansion of her role as aeronautical engineer and designer.

Yet despite her underlying passion and personal feelings about the role of the engineer, the only editorial-type commentary Elsie made in her short, to-the-point paper was not about designers and engineers. Rather, she emphasized the important role played by test pilots, particularly those flying prototype planes, in the design and development of aircraft. In this regard, while arguing that her standard forms would be appropriate for testing production models, she noted that the purpose of such tests was merely to confirm anticipated performance. Test flights on prototype planes, on the other hand, were undertaken to experiment, to learn, and to create something new, and this is the process she wanted to encourage most.

Elsie thus regarded her test pilots as "close collaborator(s)" in the process of perfecting new designs, saying that test pilots and designers like herself should work together and try to keep an "open mind" when conducting tests on a new airplane. Designers, she suggested, need to be open to independent assessments and criticism of their brainchildren, while pilots must avoid preconceptions and pay careful attention to how a plane actually behaves in tests.

Her comments and ideas, which were later published and shared widely by the EIC, reflected her commitment to continuous improvement and a passion for both the mechanics and the conceptual side of engineering research. They were used by others and may have influenced the design of other aircraft in the years to come.

The well-received paper was a small by-product of Elsie's work on the Maple Leaf Trainer II, and while gratifying, it was not a substitute for the hoped-for manufacturing and sales in Canada. Can-Car managers continued to be supportive of the project, but there was a limit to the firm's commitment. The company vigorously denied rumours maligning the plane's design and had strong evidence to the contrary. Nevertheless, by the summer of 1940, it had set aside hopes of selling its unique Canadian product in Canada and focused instead on other business lines.

It did not discard the plane entirely.

Can-Car was still clinging to its option of building Maple Leaf II trainers for the Mexican air force. It now had shops established partly for this purpose at the *Balbuena* airfield near Mexico City, and even though Mexico was officially neutral, the ambiance of a growing global war magnified the country's interest in military training aircraft. Although its air force was humble in an international context that included the mighty Luftwaffe, the RAF, and the U.S. Air Force, Mexico was an aviation nation and accustomed to investing in its military.[220] It had, in fact, seen military aircraft in its skies more than 20 years before it investigated the purchase of Elsie's Maple Leaf II, and in 1940 Mexico was reeling from decades of rebellion, domestic uprisings, and bandit raids. It still wanted the planes even though several years had passed since it first contacted Can-Car about building the new trainer.

Mexico was not bound to British-designed planes, as were Canada and the Commonwealth, and in the late 1930s, an era of nationalization of oil companies and other industries, Can-Car's offer to have the planes built on Mexican soil made it easier for the Mexican government to buy into the new trainer model from Canada.

Yet by mid-1940, the Mexican government would have had reason to be frustrated with Can-Car. The company's Balbuena shops, which were established primarily to build Grumman G-23s, had yet to produce a single plane of any kind, and Mexico's attempt to bring the Gregor FBD-1 Fighter prototype directly from Canada was blocked by Canadian government export controls that reflected concern over officially neutral Mexico's connections with Germany.

The accounts of what happened next vary. To the end of her life, Elsie always told those who asked that her prototype and "two half-finished aircraft" as well as "all accessories, spare parts, jigs and tools and fixtures, tracings and blueprints" were transferred in 1940, presumably along with license rights for the manufacture of others, to what was then a new U.S. firm, Republic Aviation.[221] Elsie was later told of photographic evidence suggesting that Republic transferred her aircraft to the U.S. Navy.[222] Other authoritative accounts contend that another Long Island, N.Y., firm received the prototype in October 1940 and that the Mexican air force later ended up with those parts and with tools to build others.[223]

The final chapter of the Maple Leaf Trainer II's story was probably a blend of all these reminiscences, made purposefully confusing by Can-Car's willingness to disregard the finer points of federal export regulations. A Canadian Civil Aircraft Registry records her prototype plane, CF-BPU Can-Car Maple Leaf II, as having been approved for export to "Columbia A/C Corp, Port Washington, Long Island, New York" in the fall of 1940,[224] and her plane was actually photographed on a Long Island airfield near the Columbia plant around this time. If this aircraft, the first Maple Leaf Trainer II, was sold off separately from the spare parts and rights for manufacture, it would explain some of the conflicts in records and recollections.

Maple Leaf Trainer II in flight in 1940 and under construction in Fort William in 1939.
(*Canada Aviation Museum Library and Archives.*)

Columbia Aircraft had close ties to the US Navy, the key customer for an amphibious biplane, the Grumman J2F Duck, built by Columbia as a subcontractor during the war. The firm's Long Island factory was near a U.S. Naval Reserve training base. If Columbia had a trainer aircraft in its possession, it is hard to imagine it would not have made it available for navy training purposes. But if Columbia once owned the prototype Maple Leaf Trainer II, as the records imply, it did not keep it very long, and it definitely did not produce others.[225] Elsie's memory about who was initially given manufacturing materials, therefore, may be correct. Republic Aviation's later connections with the Mexican air force,[226] and its status as a newly restructured business in 1940, are consistent with the ultimate arrangements for the development and manufacture of the Maple Leaf Trainer II.

Elsie's specific recollections notwithstanding, others aware of Can-Car's activities understood that, through such roundabout and probably illicit business deals and the intermediary of a firm or firms in the then-neutral United States, the rights, equipment and original parts for other planes of Elsie's design did end up in Mexico, where they were assembled and used by La Fuerza Aérea Mexicana, the aviation arm of the Mexican armed forces.

By April 1941, the frustrated Mexicans had decided to cancel their business arrangement with Can-Car and negotiate to take over the further development and final production of the Maple Leaf II trainer themselves. Engineers and other representatives of the Mexican government were sent north to wrap up the contract with Can-Car and take parts, equipment, and possibly Elsie's prototype plane back with them. They travelled not to Montréal or to Fort William to deal with the Canadians, but to "la cuidad de Nueva York"![227]

One of the Mexicans who went to New York to conclude these negotiations was a celebrated young engineer named Roberto de la Barreda, whom Elsie had met years earlier. On his return home from New York, de la Barreda soon went to work developing his own modified version of the Maple Leaf II. Miraculously, he and his team had a plane in the air that summer. The aircraft caused quite a stir, and not only in Mexico.

Before Mexico's decision to officially support the Allies in the war, the country was riddled with German spies, and other countries, besides Canada, were uneasy about shipping military equipment to it. U.S. intelligence officers kept a close watch on the Mexican military and reported back on anything significant.

U. S. Intelligence Spots a Maple Leaf in Mexico

On August 8, 1941, a U.S. military attaché based in Mexico City filed Report No.75 stating:

"The first training plane constructed entirely in Mexico was tried out on August 6 [1941] by pilot Captain Luis Noriega Medrano, who put the plane through the most rigid tests, from which it came out alright. Mexican experts will state whether or not more machines of this type will be constructed... The ship is a primary trainer whose construction was started by the Canadian Car and Foundry's shops at Balbuena...

When [the Can-Car contract] with the Mexican Army was cancelled [see Report 9854 dated May 23, 1941] General Fierro decided to complete manufacture with his own [army] personnel. The plane is a two-place, dual control trainer with high lift but low speed... Its cruising speed is between 100 and 110 mph. General Fierro states that he has all the parts, including engines, for 10 more planes of this type and design".[228]

Although U.S. Military Intelligence Report No. 75 identifies a new plane as being built entirely in Mexico, there are reasons to believe that it may instead have been Elsie's Fort William-built prototype, perhaps flown or shipped in parts unofficially to Mexico, to be either reassembled or merely enhanced with Mexican modifications under de la Barreda's supervision. Just over three months earlier (in April 1941), the Can-Car Balbuena shops had still not been able to produce a single plane, not even one based upon the well-defined and proven Grumman G-23 design. More damning, it took the Mexican team two more years to produce a second such plane even though it had "*all the parts, including engines, for 10 more*" at the time of that August 1941 flight.

Considering the times, the likely circumvention of Canadian export rules, and the grander business considerations, all parties — Canadian, Mexican, and American — would have reason to go along with the ruse. By her own admission, Elsie had little interest in such things and probably based her story about Republic Aviation on second-hand information or an assumption drawn from former Can-Car engineer Michael Gregor's connections with the firm. Whether Elsie was purposely misled by Can-Car officials or not, the firm's management would have less and less motivation to share such information with her in the years to come.

In any case, having gone through "rigid tests" and having done "alright", that initial prototype "Maple Leaf of Mexico" impressed La Fuerza Aérea Mexicana enough to prompt them to produce others. It took anther two years of serious technical challenges, but 10 fully Mexican-made aircraft were eventually produced using Can-Car parts, Elsie's basic design, and Roberto de la Barreda's innovations drawn from studies aimed at making the design "more economical".[229] These planes modelled on Elsie's trainer were known as Ares models,[230] celebrating the mythical Greek god of war and reflecting the new ambiance of the project. Published photographs of the second plane in the Ares series, the Ares 2, later led some historians to conclude erroneously that all the Mexican planes had been named Ares 2, echoing the Maple Leaf Trainer II number and name. They were, in fact, numbered and named Ares 01 to Ares 10.

These Mexican-built trainers had slightly more powerful 165-horsepower engines as well as other alterations designed to make them functional as patrol aircraft capable, as hoped, of reaching unexpectedly high altitudes of as much as "7,000 feet above sea level".[231] Such performance would have been useful to the Mexicans, who had experienced trouble in mountain flying with other aircraft in the 1930s.

Given that the Mexican air force was still using some of its other WWII trainers decades later, it is possible that the Ares aircraft gave their country years of solid service even though the 10 Mexican-built planes had serious problems with their propellers and were grounded for a while shortly after being produced.[232] None of these planes, including the Maple Leaf II prototype, survive in whole or in part today.[233]

It is hard to measure the direct impact this aircraft had on the Mexican air force, which anyway was working on other designs and was soon to be flooded by new equipment from the United States. But the training program supported by the Can-Car Maple Leaf Trainer II and design was certainly effective. That prototype plane, possibly Elsie's own aircraft, was eventually transferred to the Mexican air force's flying school (La Escuela Militar de Aviacion) in Monterrey, but was also used at the Balbuena airfield where the other Ares planes were built and tested.

Mexico officially entered World War II on the side of the Allies on May 22, 1942, after a variety of run-ins with Axis powers including the sinking of two Mexican tanker ships by German subs.[234] Thousands of Mexican nationals subsequently enlisted in the U.S. and other Allied armed forces, and the Government of Mexico supported the Allies with supplies and many other forms of assistance throughout the war. But when it came time to participate militarily, all concerned, the Mexicans and the other allied nations, pointed to the country's small but well-trained and respected air force as the best resource to call upon.[235]

About 300 members of the Mexican air force's El Escuadron 201, which included dozens of pilots as well as mechanics, support crews, and engineers, took part in fighting in the Pacific theatre, supporting the drive to liberate the island of Luzon in the Philippines in 1945. They used Republic Aviation's P-47 Thunderbolts in the attack, having relied on Republic in the United States for training support before deployment. Dubbed "the Aztec Eagles", the pilots were still celebrated into the 21st century as national heroes in both Mexico and the Philippines. They were also honoured by the United States for their skill and bravery in the Luzon bombing runs and other fighting in the last year of WWII.

While most of their advanced training took place in the United States, some of these heroes were initially trained at La Escuela Militar de Aviacion and at the Balbuena airfield, developing their skills and love of flying in the cockpit of a biplane conceived by a young woman engineer who lived far away midst the snow and forests of northern Canada. At least one of them, the Maple Leaf II test pilot, Captain Noriega Medrano, went on to play a key role in Mexico's entry into the war.

By the time German U-boats began their attack on Mexican shipping in May 1942, Noriega Medrano, the man who had been celebrated for piloting the trainer designed by Elsie MacGill, was now Major Noriega[236] and in command of a select group of Mexican pilots chosen to be the first to take specialized training in the United States in the use of North American AT-6 aircraft, which they did in early June 1942. Upon his return to the Balbuena airfield that month, Noriega Medrano was conscripted by President Avila Camacho to conduct public dive-bombing demonstrations at the airstrip as part of the effort to stir up domestic enthusiasm for Mexican participation in the war. The demonstration was a success, and Noriega Medrano became a celebrity. His star took on an even brighter glow the next month, when he took his squadron to the Gulf of Mexico to begin patrols. At the end of June, Germany's U-129 attacked two more Mexican tankers, amplifying the importance of the air patrols and the seriousness of the air training program.

Elsie's prototype Maple Leaf Trainer II at Long Island, New York, in late 1940, likely on its way to Mexico. (*Canada Aviation Museum Library and Archives.*)

On July 7, 1942, Major Noriega spotted the infamous U-129 about 30 km (19 miles) off the coast and hit it with two "one-hundred-pound" bombs, seriously damaging but not sinking the German sub. This action established the Mexican air force's presence and utility in the defence of North America and paved the way to formation of the Aztec Eagles. This contribution to the Allied effort is also said to have brought Mexico many direct and indirect benefits, including "new fighter aircraft and a better trained, combat experienced air corps" and, perhaps more importantly, a new role on the world stage with an invitation after the war "to join the United Nations and... [receive] an initial non-permanent seat on the Security Council".[237]

Those Mexican pilots are also credited with building a school. On July 20, 1944, the pilots, air crews and mechanics who were to form Escuadron 201 were assembled at the Balbuena base to hear a speech from President Avila Camacho before shipping out to the States for further training and then combat assignments in the Pacific. He ended his rousing speech with an invitation to the airmen "to petition me with whatever you may desire". A soldier in the rear ranks took two steps forward, smartly saluted, and said in a loud, clear voice, "*Mi Presidente*, I am Angel Cabo Bocanegra del Castillo, and, Sir, I request that a school be built in my home town of Tepoztlan, Morelos".[238]

The school was built and served the community for many decades.

Any inference that the Mexican Maple Leaf Trainer II might have had a major influence on these developments would almost surely be an overstatement, but as its use is exemplary of the innovations, the military interests, and business dealings of the times, the plane clearly made a contribution and was developed, sold, and used in the context of much grander shifts in international politics and technology.

If Elsie was oblivious to these events, the real needs of her Mexican clients, and the multi-party, multi-nation business deals and military intrigue that swirled around her aircraft, it would have been consistent with her customary focus on the scientific and technical challenges and on the pursuit of design excellence in the task at hand. While this focus may have blinded her to some of the realities of the wartime business world, it also led Elsie to develop and build a unique and innovative aircraft in its entirety. This, in turn, made her the first woman professional engineer and aircraft designer in the world to have done so.

Based upon the plane's early airworthiness successes, its effective per-formance in prototype demonstrations, and its use in the United States and Mexico, Canadian Car and Foundry, its partners, and Elsie MacGill might have been justified in trying again in 1941 to convince Canadian and Commonwealth military planners to reconsider their "neat little primary trainer"[239] for the BCATP. Elsie had an obvious emotional attachment to her brainchild that would endure for decades, and Can-Car's Fort William plant, which would finish off its aviation days making other trainer aircraft,[240] was certainly capable.

But during the war years, no one at Can-Car, including Elsie, bothered to pursue the fortunes of the Maple Leaf Trainer II, its design, and the trainer market any further. From 1939 on, they had something much more important and pressing to do.

Chapter VI

The Ice Queen of the Hurricanes

*"The speed with which Canadian production of Hurricanes
got under way was remarkable by any standards
and was achieved through extraordinary feats of organization..."*[241]

In late 1939, as the war in Europe slowly unfolded, the entire world was sliding under a dark shadow. Elsie MacGill had to deal not only with this widespread tension, but also with personal sadness and concerns. In January, within 12 days of a cancer diagnosis, her father Jim MacGill, the lawyer, one-time reporter, and sometime businessman, died in Vancouver in his 70th year. Elsie had been put off, at times, by what she saw as her father's stiff approach to life and his prickly demeanour. Yet she truly loved him and was always quick to point out that both Jim and his suffragette wife had been there to support and encourage their daughter's pursuit of engineering studies and her unorthodox career.

Soon, however, Elsie's mind turned to the survivor. Although her mother had been reinstated as a judge after another shift in B.C. politics in 1934 and thus had the preoccupation of her job and a modest income, there was no estate, and age was catching up with the now very alone Helen. The judge's eyesight was weakening, and her dependence on others was growing. Elsie's sister and half-brothers were doing well and could help a bit, but were, like Elsie, busy and living elsewhere. Eric's logging business (Flesher and Richardson Logging Company) in Phillips Arm, up the coast in British Columbia, was booming; Freddy, who had divorced and remarried in 1934, was "set up in real estate in Portland [Oregon]" with his new wife Margaret Andrews; and "Young Helen [in Chicago with Everett and the first of two baby girls] had to her credit a Ph.D. in sociology" and rigorous, steady work in her field.[242]

Elsie and colleagues (David Boyd on left) watch Hurricane fly past at Canadian Car and Foundry airfield in Fort William early in World War II. (*Library and Archives Canada PA-148465.*)

In any case, Elsie felt a unique responsibility to her mother, who had cared for her invalid daughter more than anyone else during those years of recuperation. Elsie had used her new salary to help buy her parents a home on Cardero Street in the West End of Vancouver, and after Jim's death had her mother come to Fort William by train for a visit. But Helen did not stay long at the Lakehead. She was determined to muddle along in her job, living in Vancouver in smaller quarters that eventually took the form of an apartment and semi-solitude.

Although Elsie had been earning what she considered a healthy salary at Can-Car ($350 a month to start, many times more than what her mother ever made as a judge),[243] it was more costly to live in Fort William, and she fussed at times over paying her parents' mortgage back in Vancouver. Elsie's situation was such that she found an unexpected income tax bill of $16 upsetting and something to fight. In the 1938 tax year, government officials had based their calculation of her income tax on her status as a resident of both Ontario and Quebec. Elsie responded with formal appeals and railed only half-jokingly against "taxation without representation"[244] since she was being double taxed by Ontario for money she had earned while living in Quebec. The protests were made mostly upon principle and with a smirk, but money was an issue at times and there were limits to what she could do for her mother from a distance.

For more than a decade, Elsie had been able to find distraction from such worries and personal challenges by focusing on her studies and career. She would do so once again in 1939 by following up on the Goblin and Gregor projects, completing the Maple Leaf Trainer design, and finally by submerging herself in a daunting new assignment from abroad that would dominate her thoughts for most of the next four years and come to define much of her career as an engineer.

The task arrived at a point when someone in Elsie's position could easily have been discouraged by engineering work. There had certainly been times when it might have appeared that her professional life would never have much of an impact. Despite her seeming steady advancement and some professional recognition, she had been constrained in her design work to "perfecting the past", retracing the steps of others and sometimes failing. While the work was often enjoyable and interesting, her total output was not supremely impressive.

Elsie had been powered all along by her natural curiosity, the stimulus of technical challenges, and the energy she drew from working with creative people. Her achievements had been personally rewarding, yet Elsie later acknowledged that had her aeronautical engineering career ended at this point, it would not have had the special shine her next big project provided. She knew that her contributions at Fairchild had been characterized by one plane, the Super 71P, that was deemed a tremendous commercial failure, and another, the Sekani, that was already being maligned as "one of the few poorly designed" Canadian aircraft of the era. Now at Canadian Car and Foundry, despite an imposing title and lots of work, she was, for the most part, absorbed in developing, refining, and testing aircraft later cited as the last gasp of the biplane era. Even the highly praised Maple Leaf Trainer II, which embodied her design dreams come true, had yet to find a market or a path to large-scale manufacturing.

At the same time, through journals, her engineering networks, and the media, she learned that other aeronautical engineers and aircraft designers of the time were enjoying high-profile success with completely different approaches and ideas. These different approaches produced aircraft that were to be pivotal to both sides throughout World War II. It is fortunate for Elsie MacGill and for the world that these aeronautical engineering heroes included two determined, creative Brits.

One was Reginald Joseph Mitchell. In 1939 Mitchell's name was known to Elsie and others in the aircraft industry for two reasons:[245] his sad death in 1937 from cancer at the age of 42 and the seeming pinnacle of his career, and his role in the development of the Supermarine Spitfire, a fast, extremely maneuverable single-seat fighter that entered service with the Royal Air Force following an order for 300 aircraft placed just prior to his death. The Spitfire, which was destined to become one of the best-known fighters in World War II, had not yet had an opportunity to prove itself in combat. It was, however, already causing excitement within the British military as a new kind of airplane and a source of hope for a country facing a formidable enemy.

The plane was, to be sure, quite different from the ones Elsie MacGill had been working on in Canada, and Mitchell was a different type as well. Portrayed as a brave genius in films and books, he would set the stage for later efforts to lionize the Allied aeronautical engineers.

Born a decade earlier than Elsie, Mitchell was the product of the rougher pioneer phase of aviation, when some high school, an apprentice-ship, and a few night-school classes would suffice as technical training for a designer at the Supermarine Aviation Works in Southhampton, U.K. Mitchell's unique insights were a function, not so much of academic study and research, but rather of his two decades of on-the-job experience and his passion, as a young man, for racing seaplanes such as his Supermarine S6B, which set a world speed mark in 1931.

His Spitfire was a monocoque monoplane. A monoplane, as distinct from a biplane, has one support surface or one set of wings, an obvious streamlining adaptation dating from the earliest days of powered flight but ignored because multiple support surfaces were generally considered essential. Although civilian aircraft, including the Fairchild Super 71 that Elsie helped design, had used monocoque styling before, it was still considered innovative as a fuselage structure for fighter planes in the late 1930s.

Rather than a square, truss-type fuselage, the monocoque fuselage used a tapered tube built around hoop-shaped supports. The components and overall integrity of the design presented many challenges for aircraft builders. As Elsie knew well, the ultimately successful versions benefited from the numerous little innovations, learning experiences, and improvements that began well before Mitchell's work on the Spitfire. Mitchell, however, used the monocoque concept to maximum effect by combining it with technical changes including such features as thin wings, a slick nose cowling, and a carburetor concealed in a way that increased streamlining. In appearance and performance, it was a dramatic contrast to the square, snub-nosed, radial engine biplanes typified by Can-Car's Gregor Fighter and Elsie's Maple Leaf Trainer II.

Because of its look and legend, in many minds the Spitfire came to typify the new age of military aircraft. Yet it was far from being the only monoplane design to express the technological blending of speed and manoeuvrability. In Japan, Mitsubishi Heavy Industries was developing the "Zero", a single-seat, low-wing monoplane that was a source of terror in the horrific early Pacific war. Germany was well ahead of the Allies' aircraft industry thanks to the visionary designer Willy Messerschmitt, whose Bf 109 fighter had been tested in brutal and bloody combat in the Spanish Civil War and, by mid-1939, had set a world speed record of 775 km (481 miles) per hour[246] and was in full production.

Even in Britain, the Spitfire was playing catch-up to a less glamorous and slightly different fighter. This other British monoplane flowed from the mind of Sydney Camm, another of the great aeronautical engineering personalities admired by young engineers like Elsie MacGill. Since 1925, Camm had been thinking about monoplane fighters in his job as chief designer at Hawker Engineering, a firm created out of the post-World War I residue of the Sopwith Aviation Company. Sopwith Aviation had made a name building biplane fighters such as the famed Camel during WWI, and Hawker continued the tradition under the influence of Australian Harry Hawker and others. Hawker died early in the 1920s, and the firm fell under the influence of people like Camm, whose daring design and development work culminated in the early 1930s in the successful Hawker Fury. Although a biplane, the Fury was considered one of the most advanced fighter aircraft of its day and provided a strategic advantage to the RAF at the time. This success gave Camm the credibility and confidence to start work on his own monoplane design ideas, incorporating new technologies and novel approaches long before the Royal Air Force or even his own firm had officially sanctioned the project.

In the beginning, Camm worked on his plane design at his home at night on his own authority. As a consequence, he could present Hawker with basic design plans for an advanced, high-speed monoplane fighter when, a few years later, talk about the new technological innovations made the concept interesting to the British military.

One of those other new innovations was an advanced, water-cooled, 12-cylinder V-engine developed by engineers at Rolls Royce. With its special supercharger, injection system, and high-octane fuels, the engine was exceptionally powerful, outperforming all other aircraft engines when first tested in the early 1930s. The engine's name — "the Merlin" — recalled the legendary Arthurian wizard but was, in fact, chosen to honour a bird: the small, fast falcon. As soon as he heard about the Merlin, the astute Camm readjusted his designs and positioned his aircraft to become the first to use the new Rolls Royce engine, doing so before Mitchell's Spitfire despite the fact that Mitchell, Supermarine, and Rolls-Royce had a close relationship, having collaborated earlier in developing those record-setting seaplanes. Camm's design work, the Merlin, and the political forces churning around them would soon come together to change the course of Elsie MacGill's career.

In another move, eventually to impact Elsie and her Can-Car colleagues in a big way, Camm took a chance by designing his new aircraft to carry the lighter, U.S.-produced Browning machine guns. Other British aircraft had been wedded to their own country's heavy, undependable Vickers armaments. The Vickers guns were so prone to jamming that aircraft designs had to allow for easy pilot access to repair them in flight. So when Camm heard that an English company, Birmingham Small Arms, had recently acquired a license to develop and adapt the American Browning technologies, he moved quickly to redesign his fighter, placing a number of the lighter guns inside the wings and thus increasing both firepower and aerodynamic advantage.

When the prototype of this new Hawker fighter flew in November 1935, it was deemed a technical triumph and ready for production. Hawker was ready to get to work. Yet, even though the threat of war had by now made it clear that increased aircraft purchases and production would be needed in Britain, the danger was still weak enough in late 1935 to allow the British military and government room to hesitate before placing a large scale order for the new Hawker fighter plane.

Fortunately, Camm, the designer, had a kindred spirit in the executive offices of his company. Thomas Octave Murdoch Sopwith, later Sir Thomas, the daring pilot and aircraft designer who had founded Hawker's predecessor to provide planes for the defence of his country in WWI, had now assumed the position of chairman of a conglomerated aviation interest renamed and reconstituted as Hawker Siddeley. Despite some business challenges over the years, Sopwith had apparently not lost any of the courage that made him famous as a young man. In early 1936, Sopwith and his board of directors ignored the government's dithering and ordered their firm to start retooling, hiring, and building space for the manufacture of as many as a thousand of the new Hawker fighters, without the endorsement of the British government or a single plane order and in the belief that the RAF would soon come to realize the need for and the merits of the new monoplane designs.[247]

He was right. Within a few months, the British Air Ministry came through with a request for 600 of the aircraft. It was the largest single order it had ever placed for combat aircraft in peacetime.

In the midst of war, aircraft production orders and design characteristics would be cloaked in secrecy. But in the mid-1930s, the British government was seeking to reassure as well as defend its population. It thus publicized the purchase with fanfare and celebrated the plane as a revolutionary machine capable of tremendous airspeed. In the context of this hype, the British Air Ministry announced in June 1936 that the new fighter would be christened with a name that was soon to be firmly intertwined with that of Elsie MacGill: the "Hurricane".

The plane had, in fact, achieved speeds far times greater than winds classified as hurricane force.[248] It was the first RAF plane of any kind to exceed a speed of 300 miles (483 km) per hour in level flight and would soon clock much faster speeds in strong tail winds and during dives. Each of the monoplane fighters of the era had unique strengths resulting from their own design features. The Messerschmitts were faster, but had limited range. The Spitfires and the Japanese Zeros would have greater speed and range, but were still under development and encountering design hitches while the Hawker Hurricane was ready for production.

The Hurricane's power can be explained simply: it was the right plane at the right time. As a result of the ingenuity, foresight, and courage of people like Sopwith and Camm, a man also destined for knighthood, in September 1939, when their country entered World War II, the people of Britain had a dependable air force equipped with hundreds of modern fighters and many more in production. On that day, "there were 315 Hurricanes in operational squadrons, with 107 in reserve".[249]

Hawker Siddeley's modest head start was enough to allow it to endure some hiccups in gearing up for production, to learn from its mistakes, and to standardize its specifications with confidence. The Hurricane's basic, stable, and comparatively simple design also made it easier for the company to transfer the manufacturing techniques and process knowledge to additional plants and to train new workers, and to contemplate entrusting its designs and production needs to a firm relatively new to aircraft manufacturing and located in the bush of northern Canada.

Can-Car and the Hurricane

As early as 1938, components for Hurricanes had been shipped to Canada for assembly in Vancouver. Some of these British-made/Canadian-assembled Hurricanes were to be used, appropriately, by the Royal Canadian Air Force (RCAF) to escort the King and his Queen on their tour of Canada in 1939. Canadian Car and Foundry, anxious to establish a relationship with the military market and exploit the investments it had made in Fort William, was quick to see a special opportunity in the Hurricane. It lobbied for the right to produce a few more Hurricanes at Elsie's plant, primarily to show off what the Fort William factory could do.

The timing was right, and Can-Car had key support from C.D. Howe, Fort William's local member of parliament and a powerful federal cabinet minister, and from Max Aitken, the man known as Lord Beaverbrook, the British Minister of Aircraft Production. The Canadian-born Beaverbrook had been a founder of Can-Car decades earlier and was brother-in-law to the man who was the company's president in the late 1930s.[250]

Howe, Beaverbrook, and others may have encountered difficulty in some quarters selling the idea of producing advanced aircraft in the forests at the far end of northern Ontario. Yet despite the commercial failure of the Goblins, the Gregor, and the Maple Leaf Trainers in the Canadian context, Elsie MacGill and Can-Car had proven through these projects that they understood the challenges of aircraft production, could produce reliable machines, and were truly committed to the industry. In recognition of such achievements and with the support of the RCAF, in 1938 Hawker Siddeley agreed to send fuselages, wings, Merlin engines, and other components to permit the assembly of a few Hurricanes to be used in Canada by the RCAF as demonstrators. By the end of the year, a deal was reached with Canadian Car and Foundry to produce its own Hurricanes in quantity; Elsie's plant received its first large order, for 40 aircraft, on December 5, 1938.

Other components were duly shipped to the Lakehead along with the data, directives, and all the information needed for full-scale manufacturing of complete planes; indeed, the instructions even allowed for the possibility of using North American-made parts. Eventually, a tremendous organizational effort would unfold, requiring great coordination between British and Canadian industry across a troubled ocean and "involving, for instance, the committing to microfilm of the drawing of every jig, tool and component... a total of 82,000 items".[251] Elsie MacGill was often the conduit for this flood of technical information.

Now surrounded by piles of blueprints and specification sheets, Elsie, along with colleagues like her eventual successor and carpool buddy Jim Carmichael, began the engineering work needed to support the assembly of materials, machinery, and workers. Before the first plane was produced, Can-Car's production capacity had become clear enough for the British and Canadian government officials to move from an order for 40 planes to licensing, contracts and further orders for many more Hurricane aircraft to be used by both the RCAF in Canada and the RAF in Britain.

Not everyone involved would have appreciated it at first, but the success of Can-Car in attracting new business was as much a function of Elsie's skills and her company's daring as it was a consequence of the dramatic events overseas and the imagination and drive of British engineers such as Sydney Camm. It would have been easy for others to regard the Can-Car Hurricane production contract as a routine assignment based upon someone else's creativity and engineering talents. Yet had Can-Car not taken chances, it would not have been in a position to contribute during the war in a vital way and to be, like the Hurricane itself, at the right place, at the right time, and at the ready. C.D. Howe and Lord Beaverbrook would not regret their confidence in Elsie's factory at the end of Lake Superior.

Nearly seven decades later, full knowledge of the preparations and intent of the Axis powers makes the development of the Canadian aircraft industry seem like an obvious measure for the late 1930s. But many Canadians, including the country's leaders, were in a state of denial or at least of desperate hope that full-scale conflict could be avoided. Both the major national parties were opposed to conscription, and Prime Minister Mackenzie King emphasized both his country's lack of enthusiasm for the conflict and independence, delaying Canada's declaration of war until September 9, 1939, a week after Britain and France had announced their response to the invasion of Poland.

In the fall and winter of 1939, the war seemed less than real to many people as Germany considered its options and made only tentative attacks on its other declared enemies in western Europe. Elsie was, in fact, most disturbed that winter by reports of the fighting between Russia and Finland, not by the German threat to Britain. British Hurricanes participated in minor skirmishes, but the need for massive aircraft production was not yet obvious. Fortunately, aircraft manufacture was well under way, and output increased at Hawker's British plants while Elsie and her friends at the Can-Car plant in Fort William worked to perfect the first Canadian-made Hurricane and to lay the foundation for the manufacture of many others to follow.

By the beginning of 1940, the first Can-Car Hurricane was in the air. The successful test flight of the company's premier monoplane fighter took place in January. As the Canadian Hurricane was, like all others at the time, a single-seater, Elsie had to stay grounded. She and her friends looked up and watched anxiously as Can-Car pilot Shorty Hatten took off, cut across the sky around Lake Superior, and finally landed.[252] The rumbling of the Merlin engine would become a familiar, comforting sound around Fort William over the next few years.

To this point, Elsie MacGill and her Can-Car colleagues, like plant manager Bill Soulsby, were preoccupied with the basics of expanding plant facilities, hiring workers, training skilled staff, and managing operations. Elsie had to put aside her ambitions as an aircraft designer and her inclination to follow and promote the Maple Leaf Trainer as she applied her engineering skills and knowledge to supporting the organizational and administrative tasks related to the Hurricane.

Elsie was not, as some reports would later suggest, overseeing everything at Can-Car or even in charge of manufacturing or plant operations. Instead, her job remained focused on running the engineering office, which meant direct supervision of fewer than 30 people. Regardless, it was not easy. Elsie's team were fully responsible for managing the increasingly technical and complex paper flow that underpinned the factory work and for translating the engineering information from England into instruments and instructions that could be implemented effectively in Canada.

For the young engineer, previously confined to the drafting room and wind tunnel research, it was a daunting challenge and would have been "a colossal job" for anyone. As chief engineer, Elsie was faced with "no less than 3600 drawings from which to work". She not only had to orchestrate support for the assembly of hundreds of main components requiring thousands of subtasks, such as the installation of the "14,500 rivets [that went]… into each wing;" she also had to oversee engineering specifications in support of the manufacture of some 1500 parts and even, in many cases, the tools to make them. There were some "eight hundred distinct operations [involved] in making and assembling the parts in one aircraft".[253] Elsie carried a lot on her shoulders during this time, but those who worked with her closely do not recall her showing any stress.

At the same time, new buildings were being erected and new suppliers recruited. It was a dynamic and engrossing time undoubtedly complicated by technical and logistical issues, but also by powerful human concerns and social change driven by the influx of hundreds of new faces. In the early 1940s the Can-Car plant, which started with a team of just over 100 workers at the beginning of the Hurricane era, was adding hundreds more workers to its payroll each month.

Elsie was surrounded by men. Even though a quarter century earlier, in WWI, Canadian women had proven themselves more than capable in nontraditional factory work, women were once again few and far between on the factory floors of 1940. Some women had been hired early on at Can-Car to sew and iron fabric for the aircraft wings and to fill a few administrative jobs around the plant,[254] but the riveting, wiring, and engine work were still considered male endeavours in the early months of Elsie's time at Can-Car. Elsie had, of course, already worked her way through very male classroom settings at four universities and in another male-dominated aircraft company. The issue of gender hardly seemed noteworthy to her at the time, and she was comfortable. Others did, however, see her position as unusual and found it startling that as chief aeronautical engineer she might have input into reviewing "the qualification of every man hired to work in any part of the plant".[255]

In any case, if she encountered any initial awkwardness in dealing with the men at the plant or in sitting at the centre of gender-based change, it was soon subsumed by an atmosphere of urgency and by obligations vital to everyone's interests. Furthermore, these pressures helped clarify the value of workers of both sexes, and Elsie and her male colleagues at Can-Car were joined by more and more women factory workers.[256] Many adjustments had to be made around the plant, not all of them of the mechanical kind.

Somehow, the Fort William plant, its managers and staff rose to the occasion and met the varied, mushrooming challenges of gearing up for production in what was later viewed as an incredibly quick process and a triumph of organization. If Elsie had worried beforehand over whether her earlier engineering work was making a real contribution or having an enduring impact, she would not have to concern herself with such questions much longer. The need for the Can-Car Hurricanes became clear and acute.

By the summer of 1940, the crisis was magnified by Hitler's late-spring sweep through Belgium and the Netherlands to capture France. The rapid defeat of the formidable French forces precipitated the evacuation of Allied troops at Dunkirk. Hundreds of Hurricanes, transferred to the continent for its defence in the previous months, were left behind, in many cases after being set on fire by the British to keep their new planes from enemy hands. The immediate impact of these events, which left Britain vulnerable and anxious, was to induce an escalation of both aircraft construction and thus pressure on manufacturers such as Can-Car.

Equipped with an estimated 2000 planes, including hundreds of the feared Messerschmitt Bf. 109s, Hitler planned a two-stage assault based on his assumption that with the surrender of its mainland Allies, Britain would be unable to mount a sustained resistance against the massive German forces. Elsie and her friends listened to radio reports with apprehension as Winston Churchill, now prime minister, warned his countrymen that they would have to "brace" themselves and strive to make the looming struggle "their finest hour".

When, as predicted, Germany began its July 1940 Luftwaffe attacks, which aimed to destroy the Royal Air Force, establish air superiority, and pave the way for an invasion, it was in for a shock. Thanks to the Hurricanes and, to a lesser extent, some Spitfires in the hands of the RAF, the Nazi bombers were confronted by an unanticipated and extremely effective response.[257] Over those few months, the people of Britain lived with increasing terror, destruction, and death. But the Luftwaffe pilots suffered astonishingly heavy losses, which confounded their superiors and eventually led to Germany's abandonment of the air assault on Britain.

This confrontation, "the Battle of Britain", was a clear Allied victory and a turning point in history. The many reasons for its success — beyond the obvious skill of daring British pilots and the performance of their aircraft — included the inherent range limitations of the Messerschmitts and the foresight involved in the invention, development, and installation of early radar systems along the south coast of England.

Among the factors most often celebrated on this list was British industry's capacity to build and resupply its pilots with Spitfires and Hawker Hurricanes at a rate unmatched by its enemy. Lord Beaverbrook had made the construction and maintenance of fighter planes a national priority in Britain, and, as a Canadian, had been keen to develop Canadian suppliers, identifying many capable of making unique contributions as the war unfolded. Yet the one to first highlight Canada's capacity to help out was the company Beaverbrook had endorsed a year before war was declared, a company prepared to play a role in the summer and early fall of 1940, when help was needed most: the Can-Car plant in Fort William.

The Canadian-built Hurricanes, which were among the RAF aircraft flown in "the Battle", were the only machines available to the Royal Canadian Air Force (RCAF) Number One Squadron (later the 401) when it arrived in England to join the fight in August 1940. Elsie MacGill was well aware of this fact, and she followed the Battle of Britain "with a strong feeling of participation".[258]

Canadians made a critical contribution to the Battle of Britain in many ways. Over a hundred Canadians piloted fighter aircraft on missions, many more flew in bombers and patrol aircraft, and many, many more served in ground crews and technical positions with both the RAF and the RCAF. They won medals and were celebrated along with the British pilots and aircrews from other countries.[259] The RCAF pilots and their Canadian

Hurricanes, however, could celebrate a unique accomplishment of their own. Through their participation in the Battle of Britain, they established a foundation for the RCAF and effectively launched it as an impressive and effective entity. For many, it marked the true beginning of Canada's Air Force.

In World War I, Canadians had flown for Britain's Royal Flying Corps and the air forces of other countries, but not their own. Canada's RCAF was not formally established until 1924, and in the beginning it was assigned only a few modest old planes for training. Its ranks were reduced during the Depression, and no modern military aircraft were purchased for it throughout the decade of the 1930s. When World War II began, the RCAF would have been without any relevant modern planes if it were not for the Hurricanes and the connections made for assembly and construction in Canada at the plant in Fort William

When these Hurricanes and the RCAF pilots headed into action over the skies of Britain in August 1940, therefore, they made history in several ways. One was by participating in "the first occasion in which Canadian airmen flew in Canadian units [and Canadian-made planes] in a sustained battle".[260]

Forty of the Canadian Hurricanes that Elsie helped get off the ground in 1940 had been crated up and sent across the Atlantic to get there in time to support the fight in the looming air war. Ten were lost at sea on the way to the conflict. The remaining 30 could be considered a largely symbolic contribution to the Battle of Britain. Still, this symbolism in conjunction with the bravery of the RCAF pilots was a powerful force, laying the foundation of credibility that helped draw attention to "the Canadian voice"[261] in planning for the air war and the expansion of international aviation that followed it.

The Can-Car work on the Hawker Hurricane, even its modest contribution to the Battle of Britain, would be cited as one of the company's greatest achievements and one of Canada's great industrial contributions to World War II. Elsie MacGill also referenced her personal role with pride, and others commended her for it.

Although she was fully aware of what her team and factory had accomplished, the reality of the experience was not always gratifying, nor was the outcome always certain. The likelihood of success was not consistently

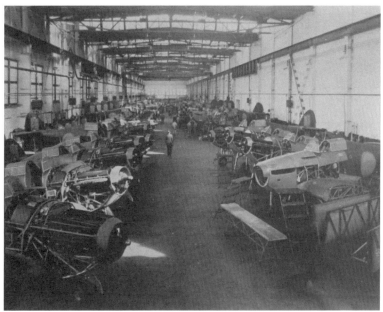

Hurricanes at Bishopsfield Airport in Fort William and under construction at the Can-Car Plant in 1941. (*Canada Aviation Museum Library and Archives.*)

evident to her or to those around her, and during those war years they often feared business failure as well as technical defeats. Stories about the Canadian-built Hurricanes usually mention a final total of well over 1400 aircraft produced. But this number conceals the fact that the orders for these planes arrived in a sputtering and tentative way: sometimes, like the initial order, for as few as 40 planes. Considering that Elsie and the teams at the Can-Car plant proved capable of completing 25 planes a week during the height of the Hurricane years, there was little employment security to be derived from such small orders.

This situation created the paradox of a large and often-growing workforce on the one hand, and on the other lots of down time and even layoffs. It was often not clear when another order for planes might come, and Elsie and the other managers at the plant shouldered much of this stress, struggling with the implications for the thousands of lives inside the plant as well as the community at large.

The escalation of the war impacted on Elsie MacGill's life and her company's aircraft operations in many other ways. While it certainly increased pressure to produce airplanes, it simultaneously increased the complications involved in making them.

Aircraft construction needed two things: people and parts. People, especially males, were increasingly drawn into military service by the development of the air training bases across Canada. Those with skills were also in demand in other industries, government service, and laboratory research. Elsie and the other managers at Canadian Car and Foundry soon realized that, in order to survive and meet the terms of their contracts, the company had to change; specifically, it had to expand on the example of its engineering office by recruiting even more women to work in those positions previously reserved for men.

Despite the need and even though the plant already had many more women employees than it did at the time of Elsie's hiring, some residual resistance to women working in machinist-style factory jobs had persisted. Possibly a holdover from the Depression, when jobs were scarce, the notion persisted that each family deserved only one well-paying adult job and that the male of the house was the seemingly obvious choice to hold it.

But the increasing grimness and horror of the war broke open the doors, and women were soon welcomed into equipment plants and munitions factories throughout the world. In the United States, a campaign celebrating women in these roles was launched under the brand of "Rosie the Riveter" through posters and other advertising. At Canadian Car and Foundry, thousands of women workers were recruited, trained, and put to work over the next few years, and eventually more than 40 percent of that workforce would be female. Often colourful, optimistic, and dedicated, these women and their stories, celebrated 60 years later as the "Rosies of the North", touched the core of aircraft manufacturing during the early 1940s, an experience that came to delineate Elsie's own developing career in engineering.[262] The human dynamics of a growing and changing workforce swirled around all aspects of plant life and affected Elsie's own day-to-day experience.

Managers like Elsie were not only consumed for many months in the logistics of hiring, training, and managing Hurricane production staff; they also worked endlessly to locate and secure scarce supplies.[263] In the end, most parts were either made or purchased somehow, but one key component posed a major challenge: the Merlin. The engine was the cornerstone of the Hurricane's speed and performance, and as hostilities were amplified, British factories needed all the engines they could get their hands on. At the same time, Rolls Royce was increasingly reluctant to risk its valuable product in shipments across the U-boat-filled North Atlantic. Elsie was uneasy about the situation, worried that the lack of motors would disrupt production, and feared that the disruptions would hurt her reputation as well as that of the plant.

A few years earlier, Canadian Car and Foundry in Montréal had made a wildly unsuccessful attempt to design and build its own aircraft engine, possibly intended for use in Elsie's trainer. During its trials, the pistons had seized and wrecked the engine (designated Maple Leaf, Model R500A, No. 1) after only two hours in test facilities.[264] The firm was not, therefore, anxious to try to replicate the innovative and constantly evolving Merlins. For a time, Elsie's Fort William plant kept building Hurricane airframes without engines. Some were sent to Britain, where the Merlins were then added along with navigation equipment and other components not available on Elsie's side of the Atlantic. Elsie for one did not like this approach because it seemed like a half measure and created the impression that her firm was only capable of making "half-built" planes and of working with materials and components provided by the Brits.

Elsie and others in Fort William were particularly anguished when in mid-1941 Germany overran the Island of Crete and secured a stronghold in the Mediterranean. British military leaders said that the heroic defenders had been let down by a lack of air support. As Elsie listened to these reports, over 100 completed Hurricane airframes, destined for that region of conflict, were sitting outside the plant in Fort William waiting for engines.

Fortunately for Elsie and her colleagues, the seeds of a solution to Can-Car's problems were sown around the same time, when Rolls Royce licensed the U.S. high-end automobile company Packard, in Michigan, to build its engines. The United States, which was officially neutral, had a stated policy of opposing the sale of military equipment or supplies to countries like Britain and Canada that were deemed "belligerents". But Packard had no problem with the reverse process, accepting technologies *from* a "belligerent", and it started tooling up for Merlin production at its plant in Detroit. By the time the American firm was ready to produce its Packard Merlins in quantity, Japanese planes had erased the distinction between belligerent and non-belligerent by bombing the Pearl Harbour naval base in Honolulu. Can-Car and Packard were now ready to go into business.

Almost. Because of its own design preferences, Packard made its Merlins slightly different in configuration and size. Initially, this showed up as operational problems for Can-Car as it tried to squeeze the Parkard Merlins into its planes, causing even more headaches for Elsie and her team. A bigger issue was the impact of Packard's mass production approach to engine manufacturing. Whereas the Brits acted almost like artisans and craftsmen in handling the Merlin parts, adapting each component by hand-milling when necessary to ensure a perfect fit, Packard built from design specifications, with the result that many of the "engines had to be returned to Packard for rectification".[265]

In some cases, Packard's changes demanded new blueprints and design alterations around the nose and propeller of the Can-Car Hurricanes. This unanticipated and ostensibly unwelcome requirement gave Elsie MacGill an opportunity to pick up her drafting pencil and help Can-Car adapt its planes for the new engines, creating a completely new version or Mark (Mk). In all, Can-Car made seven different versions of the Hurricane (Mk I, Mk IIB, MIIC, Mk X, M XI, Mk XII, Mk XIIA), with various combinations of weapons and engines. Elsie was always involved to some degree in making the changes.

Along with the intensity of multiple pressures and tasks at the plant, Elsie MacGill now encountered a completely different kind of complication, generated by a force from outside the aviation industry: the wartime propaganda machine. Amidst the fever of patriotic hype, the novel and inspirational image of an attractive young woman working in a highly technical domain aligned to the fighting abroad was irresistible to the media, the military, and the public relations teams engaged in stirring up support for the war effort. In those first war years, Elsie was not only featured in local news reports about the work of the Fort William plant, but also in national and international media stories. Pictures of her posing at the engineer's drafting table accompanied the stories and were even carried as magazine covers. A 1940 story in *The New York Times* highlighted the notion that she might be the only woman, anywhere,[266] working in the senior position of chief engineer in an aircraft plant. Eventually, her story would become well known in other circles, with a pumped-up version being chronicled in an American comic book under the banner "Queen of the Hurricanes", as part of the *True Comics* series on wartime heroes and heroines.[267]

While the media spotlight emphasized Elsie's achievements in a positive way, reminding her of what she had accomplished, it had other effects as well. A few of her colleagues and other employees at the Can-Car factory felt that she was claiming too much credit for the plant's work, and even ridiculed news reports implying she was building the Hurricanes almost single-handedly. Elsie, of course, recognized the overstatements as well and squirmed when she read them.

Still, some people felt she did little to correct the inflated accounts and suspected that she encouraged them even though she was often quoted as giving credit to her whole team and asserting that any qualified engineer could have done what she had done in the Hurricane production work. Elsie was rattled by the criticism and for while she recoiled. Some records suggest she may have even sought to end all publicity about herself around this time, for fear it was hurting her professional standing and would be seen as unseemly.[268]

To what extent a man might have encountered the same jealousies and scorn is hard to gauge since the publicity that came Elsie's way was clearly tied to her status as a woman.

> **Female-powered Flight before the Wright Brothers**
>
> Elsie's situation echoed the experiences of other women in aviation history, including Aida de Acosta, the woman who piloted a powered aircraft (an engine-driven dirigible) near Paris in June 1903, over five months before the Wright Brothers first flew their plane at Kitty Hawk. After a triumphal celebration and a flurry of initial publicity were deemed unladylike, de Acosta felt chastened for her exploits, sought anonymity, and kept her accomplishment secret for almost three decades.[269] At the time of her flight, those who aspired to the label of "lady" were advised to keep their names out of the papers unless it was to announce their weddings or their deaths.

As surreal as the magazine covers, comic pages, and news stories seemed, they did in a way parallel the two-sided reality of Elsie's experience at the Canadian Car and Foundry factory during this period.

Notwithstanding the ups and downs, the manufacture of the Hurricanes was a genuine success for the company, and Elsie played a significant, although not dominant, role in it. Her reputation outside the plant was helping the firm and may even have cultivated the ground for other contracts and work in years to come. But although at times she had reason to be proud, there was a flip side to Elsie's profile and recognition. Besides attracting jealousy, she also found herself responsible for defending the firm and explaining the delays, the threat of lay-offs, and the shortages that became commonplace during the bumpy Hurricane days of intermittent orders and small contracts.[270]

Elsie had some understanding supporters. As well as her family, her thoughtful colleagues recognized that the reports like *The New York Times* story and other articles could hardly have been orchestrated since they contained an equal number of patronizing references to Elsie's career and inferences dripping with condescension that would have been as hard to endure as the overstatements of her contributions. She was praised, for example, for being "all feminine" and "not severely manish" despite her profession. Sometimes described as a laudable woman who still cooks, knits, and likes afternoon teas, Elsie was portrayed in terms that would make many women cringe, regardless of the times. At the same time, despite the fascination with her professional status, her skill was subtly questioned by the media, with the surprised observation that she had "enough faith in her own creation", the trainer, to fly in it with the test pilot.[271]

Although she felt awkward at times, Elsie was generally focused on the job at hand, joking about the situation and directing the conversation back to the technical and business issues at hand when talking with other Can-Car managers, especially David Boyd of the Montréal head office and Bill Soulsy at the Lakehead. The three of them worked as an informal special projects team, hashing out tough issues, celebrating progress, and trying to laugh off the frustrations. Elsie would not have missed their discussions for anything.

Nevertheless, while the challenges of building aircraft in a remote location during wartime never really disappeared, Elsie, the Can-Car plant managers, and their colleagues assumed a kind of rhythm to their work. Gaining from experience, contacts, and confidence, they found answers to most problems quickly, continuously improved production, and shipped planes with increasing speed. The factory was, at times, humming along. The task of getting the Hurricane into full production was, of course, a technical and mental challenge for Elsie's engineering team at Can-Car; notwithstanding the plane's preordained design, it would be difficult to overstate this. Yet it was a methodical and focused exercise, different from the high-level and creative process of aircraft design that had intrigued Elsie and engaged her talents.

Through her professional contacts and networks, Elsie still had a forum to consider issues in a creative way and to maintain a scholarly style of approach to her work. She also had a way to share her ideas with others of a similar bent. By 1940, Elsie was a very involved member of the Engineering Institute of Canada (EIC), which now had a Fort William branch. Her status, gained in 1938, as the first woman corporate member of the institute, enabled her to make contacts and to raise the profile of technical and scientific issues of personal concern to her.

Beginning in 1938, even before her election as an institute member, Elsie tentatively and apprehensively began presenting papers for consideration and possible publication to the EIC meetings in Ottawa and Montréal.[272] These presentations may have played a role in her groundbreaking admission to the institute and given her a bit of a track record in her field. Now, a couple of years later, as the chief aeronautical engineer at a large manufacturing concern, she had much more experience and a confidence fuelled in part by the positive response to her proposal for standardized reporting of flight testing.

As work on the Maple Leaf Trainer II wrapped up and the issues started to become clearer on the shop floor at the Can-Car plant, Elsie's mind thus drifted again and again into the visionary sphere of engineering design. She furtively longed for a return to peacetime and the freedom to contemplate the vision of innovative bush aircraft. For the most part, she applied her energy to the challenge in front of her: the drive to mass-produce aircraft to feed the desperate needs of the European battlefront.

This mix of thoughts, ideas, and concerns crystallized into the hypothesis she advanced in another two technical papers presented that year to her local EIC branch. In them, Elsie astutely and boldly pointed out the nakedness of the emperor that was her own industry.[273] What the aircraft industry was applauding as mass production in response to the war, she charged, was not really mass production at all, but rather a simple multiplication of "one-at-a-time" manufacturing. The manufacture of 10 times more planes thus generally demanded 10 times the number of workers and 10 times the production facilities. Throughout her industry around the world, advanced aircraft like the Hawker Hurricane were being built in large hangar-like buildings holding dozens and dozens of stationary workstations and jigs, each employing the same basic processes as would be applied had only one plane been under construction.

Unlike the automobile sector — where design, standardized parts and systems had been folded into cost-effective and efficient assembly-line process taking full advantage of the scale of production — aircraft and their components were still, as the Packard Merlin experience showed, being designed for manufacture in an artisan-style mode despite the mushrooming war-time demand. Elsie's key point was the simple observation that aircraft had been primarily designed for performance and for specific operational requirements and that production had traditionally been a secondary concern, with little regard for costs and efficiency.

Her papers, which were printed and circulated widely, conveyed both an innovative way of thinking and a deep and thorough understanding of the engineering challenges faced by this 1940s aircraft manufacturing plant. While some of her critics may have been justified in disputing media reports crediting Elsie for everything going on at Fort William, any suggestion that she was not at least aware of everything at the plant would have been quite wrong.

Perhaps recalling her days close to the Michigan auto industry, she recognized that "time spent on the assembly of components is reduced by breaking down their manufacture into a number of stages" and that to maintain quality while reducing costs, "presses must supplant jigs", "differences in parts must be eliminated", and "standardization" of both semi-finished components and materials was essential.

As Elsie acknowledged at the time, it was probably too late to change things dramatically for planes currently under production in Canada, and she probably did not expect her papers to have much immediate impact. Leaders within her industry, such as Boeing, did eventually adopt such approaches to manufacturing and design, which in time would spread throughout the sector. Elsie's voice would be just one of many pointing toward reform of mass production techniques in aviation. The significance of her ideas and her 1940 papers lies instead in their worth as evidence of her ability to see issues from a global perspective and as an illustration of her inclination to espouse unconventional approaches to problems, a style that would serve her well in other arenas and would soon bring gratifying recognition from her peers.

Her engineering colleagues immediately saw the merit of her thoughts, and her papers also struck a chord in the manufacturing industry. A year later they would solidify her position within the profession with formal honours for "outstanding contributions to engineering". That following year, at the age of 36, she was awarded the EIC's then-highest award, the Gzowski gold medal.

The award marked clear acceptance of the young woman as a multi-talented engineer. A singular and highly symbolic honour, the medal was named for an international icon of engineering, Sir Casimir Gzowski. Gzowski, a one-time honorary aide-de-camp to Queen Victoria, designed and built foundational roads and bridges in 19th-century North America, including the challenging span between Canada and the United States over the rough waters separating Fort Erie and Buffalo. He anticipated the St. Lawrence Seaway by a half century and helped found the EIC itself. Elsie wore her association with Gzowski with pride and was emboldened by the recognition of a community, engineers, she had come to respect even though some elements continued to struggle with the notion of women within their ranks.

Elsie's capacity to step back and reflect upon her business, in spite of the escalation of the war in Europe and the pressures this brought to engineering shops around the world, was partly due to the increasing predictability and stability of the Hurricane. From early days, pilots and crews clearly recognized the Hurricane as a stable and rugged fighting platform. This relatively simple-to-build machine in turn provided imaginative designers with the basis for a number of innovations, and Elsie's work reflects their influence.

After the successes of the Battle of Britain, the flow of new Hurricane fighters was directed to other battle zones, other countries, and other duties. Hurricanes were "tropicalized" for warmer climates and adapted to use bigger armaments, carry bombs, and even to be catapulted off ships. This latter adaptation was tied to the Allied challenge of protecting shipping during the first half of the war. Fighter aircraft could not follow ships far from the coast, advanced escort ships had yet to be developed, and sensing equipment was still primitive. The solutions fomented by the military planning centres of the time included Project Habbukuk, a peculiar scheme to build massive platforms — floating air bases — on icebergs in the North Atlantic. The concept of putting Hurricanes on small rockets to sling-shot them off ships not originally intended as aircraft carriers may in contrast have seemed reasonable, even though the question of where the pilots would land on completion of their missions was never completely worked out.

A new order for 40 modified planes with stronger airframes and special attachments for the catapults (Sea Hurricanes, familiarly known as "Hurricat" planes) now put demands on Elsie MacGill and her engineering office. Elsie was also called upon during this time to lead several other specialized tinkering projects, including adjustments to accommodate the introduction of materials available in Canada, especially North American-made parts. In addition to the larger, U.S.-built Merlin engine, such parts included different propellers, meaning that most Canadian Hurricanes would no longer carry the distinctive cone-shaped spinner coverings on their nose that made them easy to identify in the field. Allowances also had to be made for the fact that "Canadian-built Hurricanes had aluminum covered wings with a metal structure"[274] whereas their earlier, British-made counterparts originally had fabric-covered wings.

Most of these adjustments were the result of deliberate decisions, external circumstances, or highly predictable developments associated with shortages caused by the conflict or distance. But one set of design and engineering changes were generated locally in response to what should, in retrospect, be a natural task for aircraft builders in northern Canada. These changes would allow Elsie to make her own distinct aircraft design contribution to the history of the Hurricane.

Although the Canadian Hurricanes built under Elsie's engineering direction were later used all around the world, a major market for them at the time was Russia. After the Nazi armies turned east and invaded Russia in 1941, first the British and later the U.S. government signed alliances that included pledges to provide the Russians with new aircraft to bolster their obsolete equipment. Hundreds of Hurricanes, again including many built with Elsie's input in Canada, were crated and shipped to the Russians to be flown with help from British pilots and crews.

The standoff between Germany and Russia turned to Russia's favour in large part because of a greater capacity to endure the country's severe winters. The importance of winterized equipment in this theatre of war was obvious in the field and was fed back to Allied planners, reaching distant suppliers like Elsie's Can-Car plant quickly. In learning of the winter challenges faced by the Allied pilots in the fighting of early 1942, Canadian military and government engineers considered the varied aspects of the problem, but focused initially on the possibility of using skis on the Hurricanes.

It was not a completely new idea. In the years prior to the outbreak of the war, Canadians had pioneered the use of skis on bush planes. A country of vast fields of snow and ice that led the world in air transport business during the period, Canada was uniquely motivated to experiment with aircraft skis and winter flying. Indeed, the very first airplane flights in Canada, in February 1909, were made from frozen Bras d'Or Lake in Nova Scotia, and the first planes made in Canada in World War I were commonly used in winter with skis. A couple of enterprising northern Ontario brothers, the Elliotts, became known internationally for their aircraft skis, which were used by Admiral Byrd in the Antarctic. Both Fairchild and Canadian Car and Foundry had experimented a little with aircraft skis in the late 1930s. Elsie's involvement in this creative work was among the reasons she was known within the aviation research community.

With the introduction of the massive British Commonwealth Air Training Plan program in Canada and the firing-up of aircraft production, casual observers might have expected the development of winterized aircraft with skis to be accelerated. But, as is often the case in science and technology, the trend was influenced by developments in another discipline. Rapid improvements in snow-clearing equipment and machinery suddenly meant that it was much easier to clear runways of snow and to pack down unpaved surfaces in winter. Planes with wheels could now operate year-round from military bases, and despite the demands of the times, most military air operations were planned with the presumption that wheeled aircraft could be used in all seasons, even in Canada.

The conflict in Russia exposed weaknesses in this strategy. There, fighter aircraft needed greater flexibility and more options than the wheeled aircraft could provide in winter.

Combat missions, including those using Hurricane fighters built in Canada, had shown that in the tumult of precarious and rapidly changing military operations, dependence upon the availability of a cleared, rolled runway was not just restrictive, but naive. Rolling and clearing took time, equipment was not always available or operable, and aircraft were concentrated into easy targets when forced to gather around runways.

Canadian scientists were asked to dust off their pre-war research and to work with Elsie and her team at Can-Car to investigate the possibility of using skis on the Hurricane.

In January 1942, the Canadian government and military brass, questioning the wisdom of a decision to abandon work on aircraft-ski development with the outbreak of the war, struck a high-level committee to attack the problem. Because many of those Canadian scientists who had been working on the aerodynamics of skis in the 1930s were now among Elsie's personal friends and colleagues, she was well aware of their studies and the years of Canadian experience with aircraft, skis, and snow.

At the federal government laboratories in Ottawa, one of its first priorities of the wind tunnel constructed in the early 1930s had aircraft-ski research. This work included novel studies driven by the versatile design engineer, inventor, and 1920s University of Toronto grad, George J. Klein, as well as laboratory research on aerodynamics involving Elsie's close friend John J. Green.[275] Klein, who had known Elsie at the U. of T., was starting research that would eventually make him the world's foremost expert on snow/ski interactions. Green's related work on skis first touched upon Elsie's career when he tested the stability, specifically the pitching moment features, of Fairchild skis for the Super 71. Later, in the 1930s, Green and others launched some of the first ski studies ever, using high-performance aircraft such as the Hawker Audax biplane,[276] and in 1938, shortly after the first Hawker Hurricane demonstrators arrived in Canada, Green initiated work on the Hurricane skis. All of this took place before Canadian Car and Foundry had its first production orders for the plane.

Based upon this research, Elsie's friend Green and another NRC scientist, G.S. Levy, filed a report in December 1939 describing their development of "streamlined skis for the fast Hurricane fighter aircraft".[277] Their ski design had "the lowest drag and best pitching characteristics of any yet tested". Designated the 72-5, this ski design was recommended for "general use" by the Government of Canada.[278] Green and Levy had taken the first steps toward preparing the Hurricane for winter use.

Regrettably, this element of the research was shelved that same year, but all was not lost. Three years later, when aircraft-ski research in Canada was resurrected as a priority at the request of the Royal Canadian Air Force, the Hurricane was once again high on the list of aircraft to be tested. Inevitably, Elsie MacGill and Can-Car were engaged to help out.

To those outside the field of aeronautical engineering, the process of adding skis to the undercarriage of an aircraft may appear simple: merely attach long strips of wood or metal to the points where the wheels normally reside. Instead, it is an exceedingly complex task, and the challenges were not well understood in 1942. Compared to the rigidity of the airframe, skis are inherently unstable appendages that can tilt or flop in the wind, bringing both volatility and drag to flight. For fighter aircraft duelling with an enemy in a lethal dance based upon manoeuvrability and speed, these issues were far from inconsequential.

The obvious solution of locking the ski in the most aerodynamically advantageous position was not an option for an airplane like the Hurricane; as a tail dragger (a three-wheeled aircraft that tilts back on its rear wheel on the ground), it needed the flexibility to allow for a slanted posture in taxiing, take-offs, and landings. Engineers like Elsie addressed the problem with trimming gear: cables, hydraulics or other equipment used to adjust the skis to maintain aerodynamics in flight while allowing the needed flexibility on the ground.

Because of the hiatus in aircraft-ski research in Canada, none of the refined 72-5 skis designed by Elsie's friend J.J. Green prior to the war were available, and the RCAF and NRC scientists were now compelled to address the issue from scratch. They first considered the possibility of developing a retractable ski undercarriage for the Hurricane.

But to speed up the process, they began their research using skis produced earlier by Noorduyn Aviation for tests on other aircraft, and now made available to the government scientists. Through the RCAF, two Canadian Hurricanes were eventually tested as part of the ski research project. Trials were conducted in Trenton, Fort William, and Ottawa, and both aircraft were modified and tested under Elsie's supervision.

In separate, earlier tests, the Noorduyn skis were reported to have had a negligible negative effect on the airspeed of Harvard aircraft, and estimates projected a loss for the Hurricane of around 3 percent. But when the flight tests were conducted in Ottawa in early 1943 on the plane outfitted by Elsie's team at Can-Car,[279] the loss of speed ranged from a surprising 10–11.5 percent, meaning a loss of over 50 km (31 miles) per hour.[280] The Noorduyn skis already having a streamlined enclosure for the trimming system, the increased drag was eventually attributed to the struts added to the special legs for the skis. Recognizing the seriousness of the issue, Elsie MacGill's team sought to minimize the impact of the skis on the Hurricane's speed by having the wheel wells covered and linking the undercarriage hydraulics to the ski trimming mechanisms.

In the end, the system worked satisfactorily though less efficiently than expected. Importantly, data collected during the research would provide the basis for ski use on planes, specifically the amount of the level of trim to use at various speeds. The Hurricanes-on-skis project also disclosed interesting and strong differences of opinion among aircraft operators regarding the best material for sliding surfaces on skis, which clearly differs according to snow conditions and geographic location.[281] This information helped fuel a new line of research that eventually led to a greater understanding of the interaction of skis on snow, snow conditions in general, and all research related to ground-cover snow.

Elsie later said that to her knowledge at least one of her two ski-equipped Hurricanes was used "somewhere in Russia", but it is more likely that her ideas were employed in the operation of other Hurricanes in Russia. Most accounts of her project state confidently that neither of the test planes was ever used by the RCAF in battle and that one crashed near Bagotville airbase within a few years of its conversion to skis. The research project added significantly to a base of knowledge on aircraft-ski design that would support winter operations not only during the war, but also in the post-war economic boom period, when Canadian-made bush planes like the de Havilland Beaver, operating on skis influenced by this wartime research guided by Elsie MacGill, opened up northern Canada to exploration and development.

Because the shiny, silver, tube-like skis were a highly visible feature of Elsie's experiments with winter-ready Hurricanes, they are the features remembered most by those who witnessed the test flights in early 1943 and the most noteworthy aspect of the photographic record of those tests. Yet they were only part of the grander experiment being conducted under Elsie's supervision that winter. Deciding skis were not enough, she undertook to use the opportunity to design and build what she and others would later cite as "the first winterized version of the Hurricane".

By renewing her relationship with the scientists in Ottawa, Elsie learned about research work on a wide range of aviation issues, including one that complemented the ski-on-snow studies and involved an even more pervasive concern to the aviation industry: ice.

Elsie knew that ice build-up on aircraft is an extreme hazard. Even in spring and fall, let alone in a Canadian winter, an aircraft cutting through the wind generates supercooled air, the result being ice formation on every exposed forward-facing part of a plane: propellers, wings, tail surfaces, windshields, and even the induction system of the engines. Elsie, like others in her industry at the time, recognized that the obvious impact icing had on aerodynamics was magnified by the threat of prop and engine failure when ice invaded these areas.

It would surprise few to hear that ice posed a formidable problem for early Canadian aviation. As late as 1950, experts were still reporting that "icing ranks second only to terminal visibility as an obstacle to regular air navigation in this country... Icing conditions may be encountered on the majority of the air lanes in Canada over ten months of the year... on the

Rocky Mountain routes even during the summer season… On the North Atlantic route, it has been estimated that the probability of encountering icing conditions from September to May at altitudes below 15,000 feet [to be]… 100 percent"![282] From the beginning, ice was clearly something Canadian aviators and engineers like Elsie had to consider, and the pilots did everything they could to avoid flying when it was a threat. But since the demands of war made it almost impossible for a flight crew to wait for ideal weather conditions, research on icing was a priority.

Thus, when the Hurricanes-on-skis project was directed to Elsie MacGill in late 1942, the Canadian National Research Council (NRC) laboratories were already engaged in the development and construction of new facilities and in testing new ideas aimed at solving the problem of de-icing aircraft. It was difficult and daring work with a variety of challenges, and the scientists were thwarted at times by the RCAF's reluctance to share aircraft and pilots for research purposes. Such reluctance was understandable, involving as it did the testing of a machine in extreme conditions. Indeed, two of the aircraft used in the research were lost in crashes.

Although justifiable and logical, the limitation on access to the experimental aircraft was a frustrating constraint on icing research. Elsie's decision to act on her own — to outfit a Can-Car-made Hurricane with special de-icing equipment as well as skis — was more than likely a consequence of the lack of other alternatives.

At least one contemporaneous report suggests that Elsie's winterized Hurricanes were equipped with a propeller de-icing system. If true, her planes would have boasted an advanced experimental design probably related to a body of research (by others) described by historians of engineering as representing "one of the major contributions to technical progress" made by Canadian scientists during the war.[283] It is possible that Elsie had access to one of the early versions of this innovative propeller system since a few prototypes were made around the time of her research and her clients in the RCAF were given some for testing. But the official post-war report on this work, which identifies seven different aircraft used in the propeller de-icing tests, does not mention a Hurricane, Can-Car, or Elsie.

In describing her winterized plane later in life, Elsie did not mention the use of a propeller de-icer. Rather, she felt her own contributions to winterizing the Hurricane were tied to the development of de-icing technologies for the wing and tail surfaces as well as the cold-weather starter system. Her winter starting system probably relied upon a new fuel injection process that was being developed and tested in several different aircraft at the time. Elsie's unique input to the development of such systems would have involved its adaptation to an operational Merlin engine and its integration with the other components unique to the Can-Car Hurricane fighters.

The problem of icing on aircraft wings was less understood. It was clear, however, that something new was needed. The pastes and liquids spread on aircraft wings and other surfaces at the time were ineffective, and experts often suggested that they were applied before winter flights

The Winterized Hawker Hurricane designed by Elsie MacGill — this plane photographed in Fort William in 1943. (*Canada Aviation Museum Library and Archives.*)

mainly for the psychological benefit of the pilots. Other attempts had been made using mechanical means such as a flexing cover material that could break off the ice in flight; nets or other fine coverings to protect from frost while on the ground; and even by directing exhaust fumes strategically. Elsie knew, however, that the exhaust scheme was found in some instances to damage airframes and cover materials.

Elsie had several options for wing de-icing at the time of her work on the winterized Hurricane. The wing de-icing technique that eventually took hold, however, was a variation of the electro-thermal mechanism developed for the propeller system that was secured with special conducting rubber pads and required new kinds of generators. In the end, the most important aspect was not the choice of specific technologies for specific purposes, but rather the package she developed, which illustrated the viability of high-performance aircraft in severe winter conditions. With her first "winterized Hurricane", Elsie earned herself a footnote in the history of the famous aircraft. Her achievement was not recorded as a major influence on the outcome of the war mostly because the design was applied through modifications made in the field and Can-Car did not manufacture a line of winterized Hurricanes. It was too late to consider such an enterprise, for by this time, the Hurricane was itself starting to be surpassed by other technologies and weapons.

However, this point touches only a fraction of the significance of such research and development work. Its true value rests in the fundamental knowledge it generates and in the development of techniques that can be applied in other, often unforeseen, ways. When, for example, the post-war jet age plunged aircraft into extreme winds and unimaginably cold temperatures, the issue of ice build-up was revived as a major challenge to the aircraft industry. Engineers and designers solved these problems in part by drawing upon the lessons learned from the early work of people like Elsie in winterizing high-speed planes, specifically the Hurricane.

During the war, Can-Car made a total of 1451 Hurricanes, almost 10 percent of the total worldwide production of the aircraft.[284] In addition to those sent into the Battle of Britain, Russia, sea battles, and other overseas fronts, Can-Car planes were used for training in Canada and for patrols off both coasts.[285] They were widely recognized as symbols of Canada's contribution to the war effort and the country's evolution as a technologically sophisticated country.

Through her combination of imagination and rigour, Elsie solidified her position not only as "Queen of the Hurricanes", as the comic books described her, but also as a designer and innovate developer playing at the outer frontier of her field. She had been at the core of a team who managed to take a small factory operation at the low end of the aircraft learning curve and transform it into one of her country's major produc-

Image from 1942 True Comics "Queen of the Hurricanes" celebrating Elsie MacGill.
(*Library and Archives Canada.*)

tion facilities, employing thousands of trained people and delivering with unanticipated speed an advanced product across half a continent and a hostile ocean.

With these accomplishments, she had played a unique role in helping solidify Canada's position within the blossoming aviation industry, in launching the country's air force, and in promoting new industrial systems. She earned herself a place in Hurricane history as the designer of the winterized plane, and was an inspiring, emblematic expression of the contribution of women to wartime industry and the unrecognized capacities of people with physical limitations.

Elsie's involvement in the Hurricane's success was, therefore, a bright spot — a clear achievement within a situation that otherwise was personally complex and professionally difficult during those first months of 1943.

When Fort William's local radio station carried reports of the December 7, 1941, Japanese bombing of the U.S. naval base at Pearl Harbour, Hawaii, the announcer's words at first conveyed a mixture of messages and induced a complex assortment of feelings in listeners like Elsie MacGill.

The initial impact of the surprise attack and devastation was lessened by the low estimates of casualties, by the acclimatization to appalling loss that more than two years of war had engendered, and by self-interest. The overall gloom of the event was lightened for many Canadians, including Elsie MacGill and staff at the Canadian Car and Foundry plant, by a feeling of relief from knowing that the U.S. would finally be compelled to enter the war. Despite a few significant successes, the Allies needed the help.

Some in the Canadian business community may also have been quick to recognize the industrial implications of the probable alliance with a deeply angry and driven American society. Elsie, as a player in the aircraft industry, noted in particular that this decisive strike, like many in the war in Europe, had come entirely from the skies.

Within days, these mixed feelings changed into dread as broadcasts and newspaper reports hinted at the true level of destruction, which would count over 2400 dead, many vessels including eight battleships damaged, and over 200 aircraft destroyed. The U.S. military presence in the Pacific had been crippled, and Pearl Harbour was only the beginning. Japanese planes had also attacked U.S. bases in the Philippines and, over the next few weeks, Japanese troops would land at points along the East

Asian coastline. Japan's rapid and forceful advancement hit home when Canadian troops were killed and captured with the fall of Hong Kong at Christmas.

As the dark image of full-scale war in the Pacific spread, one feature remained a constant: the leading role of aircraft, particularly those launched from ships at sea. The attack on Pearl Harbour had been started by planes launched from Japanese carriers over 400 km (250 miles) north of Hawaii, and notwithstanding the Japanese army's successes throughout the region, the major events of the next six months — the Battle of the Coral Sea, the Battle of Midway, and even the ground attacks — were essentially determined by the preparatory air battles. The value of aircraft engineering and design was driven home in April 1942 when the largely symbolic but morale-boosting attack on Tokyo was staged under the command of Dr. James Doolittle, an American army general, aviator, and MIT graduate in advanced engineering. Doolittle's highly publicized raid was inspired by his technical ingenuity and knowledge of aeronautical engineering. He survived the raid and the war to receive many honours and to live to 96.

After December 1941, it was obvious that success for the United States and its allies in the Pacific would depend upon the design and construction of a new generation of bombers and fighters capable of being launched quickly from ships. Although Elsie MacGill and her friends at Canadian Car and Foundry had only started work on such aircraft with the order for sea-launched Hurricanes in early 1941, many in the aviation industry had been thinking about the technical issues for decades. One was Glenn Hammond Curtiss.

An American who set records racing motorcycles and who had established a reputation making small engines in upper New York State in the first years of the 20th century, Curtiss had pursued much of his interest in aircraft design in Canada and in partnership with Canadian pioneers, such as Casey Baldwin and J.A.D. McCurdy, under the umbrella of Alexander Graham Bell's Nova Scotia-based Aerial Experiment Association (AEA). Curtiss cemented his ties to Canada in the last years of World War I, when his famous biplane trainer, the JN-4 or Jenny, was manufactured, largely in Toronto, as the JN-4D or "Canuck" version. During the post-war period, barnstormers and bush pilots using Curtiss Canucks marked many aviation firsts in Canada and the United States.

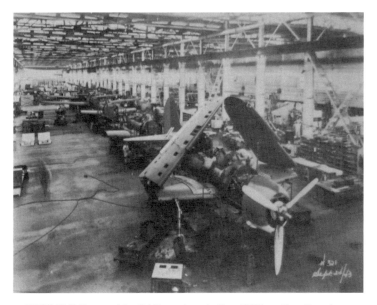

SB2C Helldiver and its folding wings in Fort William Can-Car plant.
(Canada Aviation Museum Library and Archives.)

Apart from the Jenny and his personal contributions to early Canadian aviation, Curtiss had his greatest impact on aeronautics and indirectly on the life of Elsie MacGill by designing and developing seaplanes for the U.S. Navy. In 1911, a biplane of his design became the first plane of any kind to be launched from a ship,[287] and later Curtiss was recognized for finding ways to use seaplanes, both with pontoons and with flying-boat bottoms, in conjunction with warships. But in the years leading up to World War I, Curtiss and his company were mired in patent infringement lawsuits brought by the Ohio-based Wright Brothers, a legal mess that was set aside in the national interest during WWI and finally resolved with the merger of the two companies as the Curtiss-Wright Corporation.

Curtiss-Wright built upon its co-founder's ties to the navy after his death in 1930 with the development of dive-bomber aircraft including a 1937 biplane model that sat among the U.S. machines on the ground at Pearl Harbour in December 1941.

As it mounted its response over the next year, the U.S. Navy relied upon one of the new generation of monoplane fighters: the Douglas Aircraft SBD Dauntless. For its role in the turning-point sea battles of 1942 and

1943, the Dauntless gained a reputation for dependability and effectiveness as old "Slow But Deadly" (SBD). Yet even before these battles were being waged, the U.S. Navy planners were acting on the recognized need for something new, for something with greater speed, range, and payload capacity. In 1939 the navy gave Curtiss-Wright a contract and the specifications for an upgraded version of its dive-bomber, soon dubbed "the Helldiver". Within a year, and even before a prototype had been flown, the contract was expanded into an order for 200 aircraft in response to the outbreak of war in Europe (and despite the United States' official neutrality).

This seemingly advantageous demand for its products presented Curtiss-Wright with two problems. First, its main production facilities were tied up producing other aircraft, notably the P-40 Warhawk fighters. Second, the Helldiver was encountering serious development problems: both the first two prototypes of the Helldiver had crashed within a few months of their maiden flights. One had its engine cut out; the second saw its tail and a wing collapse in a test dive. In 1942, the plane was redesigned, new prototypes were made, and the company and the U.S. Navy pressed on with plans to manufacture the plane, a project now made desperate by Pearl Harbour.

When these pressures and problems compelled the Americans to look north for additional production facilities, Elsie and Canadian Car and Foundry were ready, having established their standing in the industry with the Hawker Hurricane work. Elsie's firm was anxious in 1942 for a new challenge and a new contract. It was clear that despite its utility in the early days of the war, the Hurricane had been surpassed by new technologies flowing from the intensified atmosphere and resulting rapid innovation. No other Hurricane contracts were anticipated and layoffs were being planned at Can-Car.

Elsie MacGill was among those most pleased when her company announced in May 1942 that it had secured a contract to produce up to a thousand Helldiver bombers for the Americans at $60 000 per plane, potentially $60 million.[288] There was a sense of relief around the plant with news that there would be work for virtually everyone at Can-Car for the foreseeable future. But Elsie and the plant management, who knew about the Helldiver's development problems and the U.S. Navy's demands, were also apprehensive. The Helldiver was continuing to experience technical troubles and a suitable, stable prototype had yet to be produced. Pilots were unimpressed, and many hoped the plane would be abandoned despite the burning need. One pilot was killed when his aircraft broke up in a test flight.

But 1942 was not a time to start fresh. The United States urgently needed planes, and the navy and Curtiss-Wright pressed on, bringing the new Canadian subcontractor along with them. The following year was a messy and convoluted time for all concerned, and Elsie stood in the vortex of this different kind of hurricane.

The Helldiver was clearly an imperfect, "unstable design"[289] that, to put it mildly, needed refinement. But constantly bombarded as they were with new demands and technical considerations generated by the war, the Curtiss-Wright designers had no time to isolate problems and devise solutions. For instance, pilots and their navy commanders realized they needed more armour to protect fuel systems if they were to survive in battle, an adjustment likely to result in a 50 percent increase in the weight of an aircraft already struggling to maximize speed and range. The biggest challenge for the U.S. design team, however, flowed from the navy's fundamental insistence on the creation of an aircraft that, for doubly fast deployment, could be launched in pairs off the narrow elevator platforms of its existing aircraft carriers[290]. The Helldiver's trademark folding wings could only go so far towards solving this requirement.

Thousands of formal design changes were made to the aircraft over the next year. While some blamed Curtiss-Wright for the confusion and delays, years later others would say: "It is a tribute to Curtiss [engineers and managers] that they handled these crushing problems as well as they did."[291]

For Elsie and Canadian Car and Foundry, the problems seemed to grow exponentially because each design change had profound implications for the set-up, tooling, and training required for the manufacture not only of subcomponents but also the airframe itself. There were different models of the Helldiver, and different design changes to each. Add to this the fact that Can-Car equipment and tools were made to British standard measurements and the blueprints were made to American standard specifications, and the complete ingredients for disarray in the engineering shop and production line were quite obviously at hand.

The volume of changes made it impossible to consider drafting entirely new blueprints each time, so Elsie and her team distilled the combination of major design changes, adaptation to different standards, and tooling specifications into a series of official notes, called Engineering Work Orders (EWOs). Other EWOs came up from the States, unsorted and snarled. The resulting avalanche epitomized the confusion and frustration of that first year of gearing up for Helldiver production at Can-Car. With this and other barometers, plant staff would eventually count over 50 000 changes in the engineering design specifications for the plane.[292]

Contrasted to the production of the Hurricanes, which had been based on a simple, replicable, and proven design, the early Helldiver work was a cauldron of frustration and irritation. Elsie felt it from the beginning, but her friend from Longueuil, the plant manager Bill Soulsby, was the person who bore most of the pressure and carried most of the blame for the inevitable delays and continual adjustments. Tension built between Soulsby, his superiors in Montréal, and his American clients. He could no longer call upon his friend David Boyd, who had left the Can-Car head office to take his talents and government connections to another aircraft company.

The year 1942 was awful for the man. His wife of 17 years, Elsie's unwell friend Helen, struggled increasingly with her weakened heart. She tried a variety of treatments in her search for relief. Some did more harm than good. At 43, Helen "Nellie" Soulsby wanted to participate more in life outside the home and to spare Bill as much as possible from worrying about her and their two children, 13-year-old John and 10-year-old Ann. But she was tired almost all the time and considered an invalid. If she and Bill went out to the movies for a night, she would need three days in bed to regain her strength.

As plant manager at Canadian Car and Foundry, Bill Soulsby could afford domestic help not available to others. Still, his home was a constant concern. In addition to his wife and children, his home also provided shelter to his wife's aging parents, whom he had brought to Canada from England for safety in 1936 when the smell of another war in Europe first entered the air.

Bill tried to ease his wife's burden as much as he could. He came home at noon each day and, when possible, took Ann and John to the Can-Car plant with him. John would ride his bike around the factory, including on the airport runway, while his little sister played at the home of the purchasing agent, who lived on the site and had a big dog, a blackboard, and toys.

As their mother's health faded, the Soulsby children assumed unusual independence even beyond the freedom common for those growing up in a remote Ontario town in the 1940s. Their mother would ring a bell to let them know when dinner was served, but if they did not show up, she had no choice but to assume that John was hanging around the local car dealership and repair shop, that Ann was playing at a home in the neighbourhood, and that the two of them would come home when hungry to eat their meal cold.

In September 1942, Helen Soulsby's fight, which had begun with rheumatic fever in England over 20 years earlier, ended. She and Bill had known for years that her life would be shortened by her heart damage, and it was heart-rending but not shocking when she suffered congestive heart failure and passed away that month. Bill had his children, Helen's parents, and friends at work for support, and a pressure cooker of a job for distraction. Sadly, within five months, Helen Soulsby' elderly mother also passed away, and the family settled into a unit that included "Granddaddy" Heaps, now a widower and thousands of miles away from England and who, it was assumed, would stay with them for the rest of his life.

Soulsby was not the only one feeling pressure that year. The company's chief aeronautical engineer Elsie MacGill was pedalling as fast as she could to keep on top of the highly technical and erratic paperwork, and the plant workers could hardly fail to be unaffected by the frustration engendered by the production problems.

The normal stresses of manufacturing, common to wartime production work, were soon magnified by increased security around the factory; the company's own police force now had more than 50 officers. This security force had the power to fine, suspend, and terminate one's employment for minor infractions such as smoking outside allotted times, and would direct serious cases of theft to the authorities. It created a tense atmosphere, and whether by coincidence or by tightening procedures, the tension was amplified in the year following the Helldiver contract announcement. From a period when weeks would pass without any recorded complaints, the company police went to having over 200 reports of missing property within the year. In the early months of the war, children like John and Ann

Women working on Helldiver production in the Can-Car plant.
(*Canada Aviation Museum Library and Archives.*)

Soulsby were free to wander the plant facilities on their own, quite unnoticed. But now, everyone was watched much more closely. The women at the Can-Car factory were subject to additional supervision, and Elsie, due to her position and prominence, was being watched, it seemed, by everyone.

The women employees, now numbering in the high hundreds and heading towards thousands, were young and often away from their homes and families in eastern Canada and the prairies for the first time in their lives. Public pressure and government support compelled the company to make special provision for them with separate staff houses with a shop, cafeteria, recreational facilities, and lounge areas. The company residences for women also had dedicated female supervisors, and in the factory, a team of matrons did their best to protect the women workers, limit the influence of the men, and maintain the dress code. The concern that male and female workers might develop relationships including physical contact was an ironic result of the initial policy against hiring any married women at all and the firm's aggressive campaign to recruit young single women to fill jobs vacated by men joining the military.[293]

Whether embossed by foggy memories or based in fact, oldtimers from Can-Car later recalled many failures in the company's policing of personal contacts and workplace romances. In any case, the official company stand was that women employees should not be married and that obvious workplace romances were not welcome.

This and the Helldiver mess constituted the backdrop to the day in May 1943 when Elsie and Bill Soulsby were imperially marched to the gate of the Fort William plant and dismissed.

"my dear Mr. S" and a New Era

"a music struck… hard driving maverick".[294]

Eleven-year-old Ann Soulsby broke down and cried. Although she wasn't sure what had happened, she knew that her father had been fired from his job, and Ann had been taught that this was an embarrassing thing, akin to being suspended from school. Other people who had lost their jobs at the Fort William factory had been caught slacking off or stealing. Her brother John, two years older, was not as distressed, although he too had come to think of the Canadian Car and Foundry buildings and yards as a second home. The plant had been an anchor for the Soulsby family while it was being buffeted around by illness and death. Bill Soulsby's dismissal was upsetting for the children, as it meant the security of the aircraft plant would disappear and signalled other changes to come.

The two Soulsby children knew it was likely they would have to move away from Fort William and say goodbye to their friends. Although unsettled at first, Ann, for one, eventually came to see this as a good thing, for the weeks and months that followed brought small-town gossip and additional awkwardness to their situation. She was glad to leave this feature of the town behind.

Soulsby explained to Ann and John that there had been problems at the plant around the Helldiver bomber and told them about his conflict with the anxious U.S. Navy officers investigating the production delays. The two children also heard their father mumble about office politics and envy. Within their home, however, no link was made between the firings and their Dad's relationship with Elsie MacGill.

Others, however, did make the association. While some, including close friends, were shocked by the news of the couple's dismissal and even

Ann and John Soulsby around the time that Elsie MacGill became their stepmother in 1943. (*Courtesy of Ann Soulsby.*)

more so by word that the two were, in fact, a couple, others had been talking about Bill and Elsie's relationship for some time. In any case, the connection between their departure from Can-Car and a workplace romance was now discussed openly, particularly when, two weeks later, on June 4, 1943, Bill Soulsby and Elsie MacGill went together to Kankakee, Illinois, to be married.[295] The couple went there because it was possible to be married by a justice of the peace, albeit with some wartime paperwork for non-U.S. citizens, and both Bill and Elsie had little desire to be married in a church. Bill Soulsby called himself an atheist but did not impose his views on others: his daughter, for example, attended church regularly with her friends.

Illinois held a specific attraction as a site for the wedding because it was once again home to Elsie's sister Helen, who by then was raising two daughters, a next generation "Helen and Elizabeth" of her own, and working at the University of Chicago along with her husband Everett. Elsie's sister was glad to accommodate her now-unemployed youngest sibling, and after helping fetch the justice of the peace from a nearby tavern and seeing the ceremony completed, she celebrated the seemingly hurried nuptials with a small reception at her home near the university campus back in Chicago.[296]

Elsie's honeymoon in Chicago was short but memorable, particularly for her young nieces. It generated the first vivid memories the two little girls would have of their new stepmother, someone they came to love and enjoy. The drive to Kankakee alone was an adventure for the two girls, who seldom travelled in a car. They also remembered the wedding day well because they were ejected from the wedding chamber after causing a commotion for first stealing and then playing with their father's fedora on the floor.

The girls' memories from that week ironically also included the sight of Elsie in a wheelchair, a device she had fought hard to avoid for over a decade and would only use again with great reluctance. Possibly to make a trip to the Chicago Zoo easier for her sister and the energetic young children, Elsie, the woman who worried about the distorted image of her leg in a photo with Bill Soulsby a few years earlier, set her pride aside to use the chair to go on outings during her honeymoon.

Bill and Elsie also talked about going out west to visit Elsie's mother and to show the groom around Vancouver. But they were under pressure to return to work, earn money, and take advantage of specific opportunities back in Canada. The trip to the zoo with Young Helen and her family was about the only vacation the new couple would allow themselves in the days after their marriage. Within a week, they packed up and headed off to make a new home for themselves in Toronto.

Young Helen in 1943

It was natural for Elsie to look to her sister Helen for support when entering a new phase of her life. The two women, now on the threshold of middle age, were still intensely close friends and confidants. Young Helen had been there to support Elsie when she entered engineering studies in Toronto, when she confronted paralysis in Michigan, and when she started an aviation career at Fairchild in Montréal. Now she was on hand yet again to boost Elsie into married life.

Not merely a source of inspiration, Elsie's older sister was also a solid sounding board and a structure for Elsie to reference in making moves and taking important life decisions. Even though she was still called "Young Helen",[297] "bonks", and other nicknames, Helen Elizabeth Gregory MacGill Hughes was by then Dr. MacGill Hughes, a 1937 Ph.D. graduate,

Elsie (seated to right) and Bill Soulsby in 1949 with Elsie's sister Helen (Bill's right) and her daughters, Elsie's nieces, Elizabeth "Elsie" Hughes and Helen Hughes, with Aunt Jennie Williams in centre back. (*Courtesy of Elizabeth Schneewind.*)

professional woman, and someone who it was easy for Elsie to respect and admire. In mid-1943, Elsie's sister was a thoughtful, sturdy, hard-working person living a contented life with few regrets.

If Elsie needed encouragement to leap into matrimony and confront an unanticipated change in her career, she would have found it in her sister's cheerful face when the two women greeted each other in those first weeks of June 1943. Years later, Helen MacGill Hughes would recall this period as a time when she "felt luckier than any woman". Elsie's sister certainly loved her husband Everett and her role as a mother, and had reason to be satisfied with her professional achievements. A writer recognized for her skill and intellect, she was intensely interested in current issues in her field of study. Her Ph.D. thesis had evolved into a unique, scholarly book that would be a forerunner of modern media and communications studies. Helen Hughes' work was praised by her mentor, the sociology icon Robert E. Park, who called her writings important because they seemed "to open up to empirical investigation... the role and influence, not merely of the newspaper, but of popular literature, to contemporary life".[298] In her research, Helen MacGill Hughes was obviously drawing upon many influences, but she specifically said her work could "properly be described as the outcome of a sort of family ferment".[299] Her writings and her face suggested no great tension between her professional work and personal life in a way that likely reassured her younger sister Elsie, now stepping into her own blending of the two forces.

In 1943, Elsie could, therefore, never have guessed that her sister Helen harboured strong anxieties and would live to question her positive attitude and to declare, 30 years later, that she may have been "unalert" and even "stupid"[300] about the implications of her role as the female partner in a marriage of two sociologists. Although she enjoyed a uniquely productive working life as well as a happy home, over the years Elsie's older sister would come to realize that her career as a sociology scholar had been consistently diminished by her marriage and her sex. Only in her eighth decade of life, when Helen MacGill Hughes became an activist and organizer for women's causes, did her views change. Reflecting in the 1970s upon the lot of others, particularly younger women, she recognized the gender-based limitations that her own career had borne and the constraints on women scientists in the early decades of the 20th century. Many of those restrictions appear to have flowed directly from her marital status and, ironically, from her continuous participation in the working world.

In a peculiar way, then, Elsie's engineering career may actually have benefited from the paralysis that ostensibly interrupted it in 1929. First, the illness and consequent confinement reduced Elsie's chances of entering into an early, career-constricting marriage. Second, it compelled her to spend years in self-led study and reflection separated from the conservative, dispiriting attitudes prevalent in the sometimes hostile work settings of academe and industry in the late 1920s and early 1930s. When paralysis and illness intervened to limit Elsie's social life in 1929, she was at the same age, 22, was engaged to be married, and was at the same point in her education, graduating with a master's degree, as her sister Helen had been when, two years earlier, she entered into married life and embarked upon a career that, while successful by many measures, was quite different from Elsie's.

After homesickness and administrative mix-ups prompted her to leave Elsie in Toronto and head back to Vancouver in 1923, Helen resumed her studies at UBC with a different perspective.[301] She took a fresh look at her father's legal work with Asian immigrants and at the social forces expressed in the parade of souls passing through her mother's courtroom. This reflection and curiosity prompted her to take her first courses in sociology.[302] The field captured her imagination a year later when Robert Park, already well known as one of the leading thinkers in the discipline, passed through Vancouver to present a seminar. Elsie's sister Helen pushed herself forward to speak to the great professor. After a brief exchange, Park had heard enough to urge her "to come to us in Chicago"[303] for graduate studies. With this special encouragement and the financial assistance of a scholarship, the younger Helen MacGill left for Chicago immediately after graduation from UBC in 1925 to pursue her new interests in sociology.

Chicago was *the* place to be for aspiring sociologists in the 1920s. It was the home of the continent's first and probably the world's most solidly founded sociology department, and it included not only Park, but also many of the nascent field's other leading lights among its research stars. Elsie's sister was intelligent, well-liked, and soon recognized as one of the department's more promising students. She enjoyed her studies and from the start hoped to pursue a career in academe, and her enthusiasm might easily have led her directly into doctoral studies in Chicago.

But she also wanted to pursue a life with Everett Cherrington Hughes, another grad student and her equal as a favourite of Professor Park. Everett, who was certainly brilliant, was the first of the two to realize a substantive career opportunity. When, in 1927, he was offered an assistant professorship in the McGill University Sociology Department, Canada's first, the couple married and moved to Montréal.[304] From that point forward, Helen's scholarly career was often defined both directly and indirectly by Everett's.

Everett Hughes was a supportive husband, and his marriage to Helen was a genuine partnership and compromise in personal matters. The bride's interests were clearly primary when, for example, the "wholly American"[305] Hughes family acceded to holding the wedding in Vancouver, and when two years later Everett's plans for study and work in Europe were cancelled to respond to the traumatic illness of his wife's younger sister in Ann Arbor.[306]

Professionally, however, his career did come first. Helen had several part-time jobs at McGill University in Montréal, but could not

engage in substantial professional
work there as her doctoral studies involved residency requirements in Chicago. Everett's work
also demanded that they take trips
abroad, including a year-long stay
in Germany in 1932. Helen nevertheless persevered, obtaining her
Ph.D. from Chicago in 1937, a
decade after her wedding.

Young Helen always made the
most of her situation. She enjoyed
a lively social life with friends
and extended family in Montréal,
and even turned their stay in pro-
paganda-filled Germany into fod-
der for her doctoral thesis and
that resulting book, *News and the
Human Interest Story.* Elsie was
impressed, and when she started
work at Fairchild's Longueuil factory in the mid-1930s, she saw her
older sister, then living just across

Photo of Elsie Gregory MacGill. P.Eng.
used to publicize her consulting business in
1940s. (*Courtesy of Ann Soulsby.*)

the river in Montréal, as someone who was doing an admirable job of
balancing marriage and career. This glowing image of her sister may have
been a factor in Elsie's seeming blindness to the gender-based barriers
within her own field.

In 1938, a year after graduating with her doctorate, Helen gave birth
in Montréal to the first of her two daughters and entered a phase of life
coloured by the demands of child rearing and homemaking.[307] When
years later she was ready to resume her professional life, her husband was
by then resolutely established as a leader in the couple's shared discipline
and they were back at Chicago, where she was relegated to the role of
what she blithely termed "the Faculty Wife Employed on Campus".

Despite her self-effacement, Young Helen still strived to be academically productive, although in a different way. Elsie's Ph.D.-trained sister
worked in a number of modest administrative positions associated with

the Chicago Department of Sociology before eventually securing the post of Managing Editor of the *American Journal of Sociology*, for many years the premier U.S. publication in her field. This gave her a vehicle to remain current and knowledgeable despite being separate from active research. Over the following decades, Elsie's sister also made unique contributions outside the central path of sociological scholarship by supporting her husband's work, including studies on life in French Canada,[308] by active involvement in emerging professional groups, by writing for popular publications such as *Time*, and by independent study on topics of particular personal interest. In her later years, she was elected to leadership positions in organizations including the American Sociological Association, and worked as a visiting professor at a number of U.S. universities. Her career was impressive and influential in many ways including as a strong, continuous thread of interest in broad social issues that wove in and out of Elsie's often more technically oriented life.

Marriage, Science, Technology and Women in 1943

Nevertheless, when in the 1970s she looked back on her life from the vantage point of a new era of feminist thought and change, Elsie's sister sadly wondered whether it actually "added up to a career". She reflected upon the lot of other women and concluded that marriage was as much a factor as gender in limiting her work life.

Unmarried and "never felt discrimination"

Certainly, many of the most celebrated women working in research and science during Helen MacGill Hughes' era stayed single during key periods of their life or never married at all. One of the Hughes' exemplary single, independent female colleagues and friends was Aileen Dansken Ross, who became a full professor and eventually Professor Emeritus at McGill after a "long productive and meaningful career [during which the unmarried Professor Ross was]... never denied promotion... [and] never felt discrimination".[309] The unmarried "Ross experienced no difficulty in getting research funds, was never rejected and never perceived the granting process as one of great competition".[310]

Indeed, with only minor exceptions, the early women in science who were labelled successful were those who remained single all their lives, with "successful", most often, in this context, being defined by the assumption of positions as full professors or high-level government researchers. For much of the last century, "marriage, in most cases, was detrimental to a woman's career advancement".[311] A typical female career in early Canadian science and technology was summarized either in terms of "[she] was required to resign because of her marital status" or "her career ... progressed well. She never married".[312] Throughout much of the period, marriage often appeared a toxic ingredient when added to any female life bent upon scientific and technological excellence and recognition.

This was a specific expression of the widely held societal attitude about jobs and women evident in many circumstances, not just the Can-Car aircraft factory. In hard economic times, a family holding two full-time jobs appeared greedy, and women were simply expected upon marriage to abandon paid employment in favour of homemaking, particularly if their husbands were employed. Many of those in scientific and technical professions "remained single because, particularly during the Depression, marriage and scientific work were considered incompatible".[313] These expectations took the form of official anti-nepotism rules or outright bans when a husband and wife sought to work at the same university or other professional institution. Considering the potential for a young couple to meet at work around similar interests, it is not surprising that, in the years leading up to Elsie's marriage to colleague Bill Soulsby, a number of talented women researchers were forced to abandon career opportunities when they married a colleague.

The phenomenon was not exclusive to male-dominated disciplines. Even those scientific fields where women researchers were welcome still seemed to favour women who avoided marriage. To make matters worse, at the dawn of the last century science was still regarded as a somewhat novel profession, even for men. Women's participation in science is illustrated by data showing that "women publishing on Canadian scientific and technical topics prior to 1914... constituted [only] about 1.4 percent of all authors".[314] Since these published women were limited to the few fields traditionally associated with women scholars — such as natural history, botany, horticulture, and zoology — it was predictable that the first "successful" female scientists would come from such fields.

The Other McGill Women

When in 1912 McGill became the first university in Canada to appoint a woman as a full professor, it was in such a discipline. Carrie Derrick received the unique title of Professor of Morphological Botany as a consolation prize after being passed over for the permanent position of Professor and Chair of the Department of Botany. The way for her appointment had been cleared by a series of actions dating back almost three decades to 1884, when Lord Strathcona donated money to McGill expressly to facilitate the admission of women to the university. Nevertheless, women were still clearly constrained by marital status. In fact, Professor Derrick and all but one of the 18 other women "Officers of Instruction" at McGill in 1912 were unmarried.[315]

Also at McGill, Margaret Newton, who became her country's first woman Ph.D. in agricultural sciences when she graduated from the University of Minnesota in 1922, realized professional success from the beginning despite her gender-breaking role. She was recognized for important discoveries as an undergraduate in her native Canada before 1920, was sought after by several universities, and eventually had a high-impact career as head of the federal wheat-rust laboratories in Winnipeg. She was credited with a major role in eradicating wheat rust as a serious crop hazard in western Canada. Before this achievement, the disease had been destroying at least 30 million bushels a year. When she retired at 58 with respiratory problems aggravated by her work, crop losses from wheat rust were by then "negligible".[316] Dr. Newton was another researcher who remained single for life.

At Elsie MacGill's undergraduate institution, the University of Toronto, other women were also marking significant firsts. Helen Battle, who was born in 1903, two years before Elsie's birth, received a Ph.D. in marine zoology, a Canadian first, in 1928. Dr. Battle would later recall no feeling of discrimination at either Toronto or the University of Western Ontario where, it was said, "her career path was relatively smooth, perhaps because she never married".[317]

If constraining bias did not show until a talented female scientist became a married female scientist in such fields, it could be because zoology and the various plant-related sciences were otherwise accepted as appropriate disciplines for women. These disciplines were not, apparently, as vulnerable to discrimination as was the case in fields firmly seen as male.

The entry of women into male-dominated medical research seemed, for example, to demand a special level of heroism from women like Maude Abbott, who encountered clear discrimination simply because she was female. Abbott struggled for admittance to medical school in the late 19th century, was never granted a full professorship despite international acclaim, and was clearly underpaid in comparison to male colleagues during her years at McGill University. She is remembered and celebrated because she transcended the apparently menial tasks of her position as curator of the medical museum to produce works of importance in the study of heart disease. The level of ingenuity, dedication, and scholarship she demonstrated, however, may well have been compromised had she married.

One male-dominated discipline characterized by fieldwork and technical skill, with the potential for comparison to Elsie's discipline of engineering, is geology. In 1918, almost a decade before Elsie graduated as Canada's first woman electrical engineer, Grace Anna Stewart became the country's first woman geology graduate after studying at the young University of Alberta.[318] Stewart later earned a master's degree and pursued an impressive professional career in the United States. In 1926, Madeleine A. Fritz earned a geology Ph.D. at the University of Toronto where she launched what was later described as the only successful academic career of a woman geologist in Canada in the first half of the 20th century. Other women geologists worthy of note included academic Helen Belyea and the federal scientist Alice Wilson, a woman whose career and life were later celebrated by books and a National Film Board documentary.[319]

Stewart, Fritz, Belyea, and Wilson all never married.

Illness and Alice

As to whether the career benefits of being single could somehow be amplified by a serious illness, Alice Wilson's experience is possibly the most instructive. Like Elsie MacGill, she was a Canadian woman who not only broke barriers in male-dominated technical fields, but did so with a significant physical disability. Wilson's career was interrupted in a major way on two occasions by a combination of chronic anaemia and other illnesses. The first time was in 1904, during her third year of undergraduate studies at the University of Toronto, when bad health cut short her pursuit of a degree in modern languages. Wilson was studying languages during the day while also trying to feed her true passion for physical sciences on the side, and the combination may have induced stress and fatigue.[320]

In any case, reflection during a yearlong respite led her to quit school in favour of a job in the Mineralogy Department of the university, the first step in her career in geology. Almost two decades later, in 1921, her anaemia and other health problems forced her to spend a year in and out of hospital in New York State.[321] When she returned to work, by then at the Geological Survey of Canada, it was with a new determination to pursue a Ph.D. She would need this determined mindset, as it took until 1926, when she was 45 years old, before the bureaucratic approvals could be secured for her further studies despite her success in gaining outside scholarship support.

In both instances when her career was interrupted by illness, Alice Wilson used the period of recuperation to collect her thoughts and to muster the will to undertake something new and ambitious upon recovery and resumption of her professional life.

This process was echoed in Elsie MacGill's own life. Yet Elsie may not have been fully aware of the prior experience of other female scientists, the implications of marriage for professional women, and the context to her own 1943 decisions on career and marriage. Even if she was, she may not have considered it relevant to her own experience and prospects as a soon-to-be married engineer. She continued to hold the view that women in her field faced no impairing discrimination, that their male colleagues were generally supportive, and that their fate was largely in their own hands.

Elsie herself had an uncommon degree of sanguinity, initiative, focus, and confidence. Even though women were still being denied entry to some engineering schools and barred from specific courses in others, she continued to tell herself that "no particular barriers face women entering professional engineering in Canada".[322] In her view, if a particular institution or firm would not open the door, one had only to knock harder or go around the corner to another one. Such comments indicate that Elsie was partially blind to the reality of her situation, particularly since her relationship with widower and colleague Bill Soulsby in 1943 had been intertwined with the termination of her high-profile employment at Canadian Car and Foundry.

During these years, Elsie laughed at characterizations of her career as "a terrific uphill struggle to succeed in the face of great odds and male opposition".[323] Whether her perspective resulted from a conscious decision to disregard setbacks and rejections or an effortless approach to life, Elsie clearly kept her focus on the positive and was confident as she began a new phase in life, convinced that she would soon be employed again and that financially things would work out for the family.

As the new bride emboldened herself for the challenges ahead and considered her career options in the summer of 1943, she told herself and others that her life and career had enjoyed great support from the business community, the engineering profession, and her male colleagues — one in particular.

Bill

There was no question that the Helldiver production had been a mess, and while the debate over who was truly to blame would never be fully resolved, it was difficult in early 1943 to see any fragments of success in the experience for the former plant manager of Can-Car, Bill Soulsby. By the time he and Elsie were let go, not a single Helldiver had made it out of production at the Fort William plant. The Can-Car prototype did not fly until nearly two months later, on July 22, 1943, and the problems and tie-ups in engineering and manufacturing were to continue for months.

The impasse was only broken when Soulsby's successor, Joe Russell, declared that he had enough and ordered his workers and managers, including the new top engineer, Elsie's friend and replacement Jim Carmichael, to ignore any other changes and complete first one aircraft and then another and another based upon the design specifications to date.

By this time, Elsie and her new husband had moved to Toronto, where Bill's former colleagues from his early days at Can-Car and his years at Fairchild were sprinkled throughout the still-booming wartime aviation industry. Notwithstanding the tarnish of his dismissal and the Helldiver debacle, Bill enjoyed a good personal reputation as a solid executive knowledgeable about the aviation business and not wedded to one product or a specific area of expertise.

In fact, Eric James (Bill) Soulsby was not a technical expert and, unlike Elsie, had fallen into the aircraft industry indifferently. He was not particularly interested or adept in the mechanical and technical aspects of any particular product or sector. Rather, he wanted to make his mark as a businessman and manager. Born in Birmingham, England, on May 28, 1899, Soulsby came to Canada on his own in the wake of World War I, believing that this land of opportunity would welcome someone with drive and a bit of university education. He had studied chemical engineering at Leeds but dropped out before finishing his degree.

In his first years in Canada, he could only find work as a farm hand and labourer on the prairies, and the experience eroded his grand hopes for life in this new country. But when he drifted east through the bush and along the rail line to Fort William in the early 1920s, he got a break, finding regular work and opportunities for advancement at a pulp and paper mill. After a few months, the steady income at the mill gave him the confidence to invite his university sweetheart, still in Britain, to join him across the pond. He and his first wife, Elsie's future friend the young Helen Heaps,[324] were married in Fort William in 1925, their first child, John, appearing four years later.[325]

The couple had a foundation for family life in the New World and growing prospects. By the time the Soulsby's second child, Ann, was born less than three years later, they had moved to the Montréal suburb of St. Lambert where Bill had secured a position in the new Fairchild plant. Soulsby's move to Fairchild in those first years of the 1930s was not, therefore, the result of a special desire to enter the aviation industry even though aviation was an increasingly high profile, exciting, and dynamic feature of life in northern Ontario. Rather, the new plant represented merely a solid opportunity for an ambitious businessman to move up the ladder. In fact, Bill was regarded as "an accountant and bookkeeper" during his early days in the aviation industry. His definition of himself as an aircraft executive came later.

Soulsby's time at Fairchild overlapped Elsie's, and the two thus shared in the ups and downs of the company's exploits with new designs and dubious commercial ventures. The 1930s were a time of testing and opportunity in the Canadian aircraft industry. Failure was a frequent partner with innovation and risk, but the parallel growth in air transportation and looming war drew new companies into the industry, companies always on the lookout for skilled personnel like Elsie and Bill.

Soulsby's decision to jump to Can-Car after a few years at Fairchild would mean a return to the familiarity of Fort William. The job was offered to him mainly because he was known within the vibrant and highly networked aviation industry in Montréal, the location of Can-Car's head office as well as the Fairchild plant. Soulsby and Elsie were not alone among the key industry figures who had cut their teeth at Fairchild and gone on to influence other firms.

Fairchild was an incubator for new aircraft companies and talent. For example, in 1937, the National Steel Car Company, a firm that was to impact Bill and Elsie's lives both professionally and personally, had hired away Elsie's Fairchild boss, Frank Hyde-Beadle, and two other senior Fairchild managers, the Burlison brothers, George and William, in a single move. National Steel Car, a firm that would embrace the MacGill-Soulsby family by war's end, needed outside expertise in the late 1930s as it entered the aircraft industry with a plant in Malton, Ontario, next to a new airport that decades later would evolve into Toronto's Pearson International Airport. National Steel Car, like Canadian Car and Foundry and other manufacturers, was moving beyond its roots to ready itself for government contracts and military aircraft business by using foreign designs and components to learn the craft of airplane manufacturing. In the National Steel Car case, the foreign-designed product was the high-wing monoplane British Westland Lysander, and the customer was the RCAF.[326]

David Boyd, the Boss

When he first began work at Can-Car, Soulsby reported to David Boyd, the affable and talented production manager who would soon move back to the firm's headquarters in Montréal and would leave the firm altogether on the eve of Soulsby and Elsie's entanglement with the Helldiver project. Boyd was a great colleague, and Soulsby would have liked the arrangement to last longer. But by 1939, things were progressing so fast that the company needed someone to oversee the growth of an entire aircraft division, and Boyd was the obvious candidate. Within a year, Boyd's Can-Car division would include airplane and aviation parts plants in other parts of Ontario, Quebec, and the Maritimes as well as Fort William.

It was when David Boyd was promoted that Soulsby took over as general manager at the Fort William plant.[327] He had little time to adjust to the more senior job when war broke out, and he was faced with the double challenge of gearing up for increased production while securing supplies, staff, and equipment in a much more intense, complicated, and competitive atmosphere. Although many recognized Soulsby as dedicated, respected, and driven, others remember him as tough and intense. The staff referred to him simply as E.J. or from a distance as "E. Jesus Soulsby".[328]

Despite the sniping, Soulsby was seen, as was Elsie, as a central force in the Hurricane's success, and the glow of this success shone warmly on Boyd's reputation and career back in Montréal as well. Boyd, who liked and admired Soulsby and his chief engineer, was indebted to them.

David Boyd was well known within his industry and also enjoyed a strong reputation in Ottawa, where C.D. Howe, a powerful cabinet minister who represented Fort William in parliament, continued to dominate decisions related to war production and supply. Howe personally called upon Boyd to leave Can-Car and help out when one of the government's suppliers, none other than National Steel Car's aviation division in Toronto, started to run into problems.

The company had lost Hyde-Beadle and the Burlison brothers to de Havilland in 1940, contracts had been cancelled, delays were piling up, and the inexperience of the residual management became evident just as the company was to embark on the important task of constructing a specially modified version of the Lancaster Bomber for the new government-run transatlantic air service. The Lancaster X, as this version would be labelled, would be the first four-engine aircraft to be built in Canada. An exceptionally large aircraft, it presented new challenges for Canadian industry.

At C.D. Howe's request, Soulsby's friend Boyd accepted the post as general manager at National Steel Car's Malton plant in the spring of 1942. Soon after, the situation and the challenges worsened when Robert Magor, the umbrella company's visionary president, died. Boyd, with the support of many of the Malton plant's employees and management, petitioned Howe and the federal government to save the plant and its wartime manufacturing program from sinking into disarray by making it a government Crown corporation. Such was Boyd's influence and credibility that Howe agreed, and the plant was incorporated as the government-owned Victory Aircraft Company in December 1942, less than six months before Elsie and Bill would become available for work in Toronto.

During those six months, David Boyd had, in fact, talked informally with Soulsby about the possibility of joining the Victory plant in Toronto. Bill therefore knew immediately where he would go for work when he and Elsie were taken to the gate of the Fort William Can-Car plant in late May 1943. So strong was Soulsby's relationship with Boyd, it is likely that he and Elsie might not have been fired from Can-Car had Boyd still been with the firm in a position of influence. Elsie's new husband was thus anxious to take on a new challenge and to work with Boyd again.

Soulsby's marriage proposal to Elsie in those first days after their dismissal in Fort William was undoubtedly entangled with the practicalities of moving to Toronto and taking a job at Victory Aircraft. The marriage proposition may not have been as detached and clinical as a description of the economic benefits in shared accommodation and Toronto career opportunities. Still, these were elements of the circumstances and the times, and their wedding plans were generated within them.

Bill Soulsby had been a widower for less than a year. Yet for many months he had recognized how much he enjoyed Elsie's company and how he was moved by her personal qualities, which he would later deem "a blessing" in his life. Although the Lakehead rumour mill would be kept busy for years, those closest to the couple denied that there was any inapt "hanky-panky" before marriage and asserted that while both Bill and Elsie were lenient when it came to this kind of behaviour by others, they were strict with themselves.

Soulsby thus joined his friend David Boyd at Victory, did well, and stayed in the business and management end of the aircraft industry for the rest of his career. It was a dynamic time of exciting growth and heart-breaking setbacks, and the lives of Soulsby, Elsie, and the Soulsby children were changed by it all. The Malton aircraft plant, which employed only a few hundred people in 1938 and a few thousand in 1942, grew into an operation of nearly 10 000 workers and over a 100 000 square metres in 1944, the year after the "MacGill-Soulsby" family arrived in Toronto.[329]

Avro Before the Arrow

When the war ended abruptly the next year, the demand for Victory products plummeted. By December 1945, when the government unloaded the plant in a sale to Hawker Siddeley Aircraft Co. Ltd., the workforce had returned to its pre-war levels of a few hundred people. Bill Soulsby was among a handful of executives retained to help get Hawker's new Canadian operation off the ground. Ironically, David Boyd, the man who had been credited with most of Victory Aircraft's successes, was not. Nor was the name of the firm. Hawker renamed its enterprise "A.V. Roe Canada Ltd.", later becoming Avro. The name Avro is well known in Canada today as that of the firm associated with the controversial and mythical story of the CF-105 Arrow, a supersonic fighter jet developed in the 1950s for patrols in Canada's North. The Arrow, considered by some to be the most advanced design of its time, was cancelled as a project at the prototype stage in 1959 when Canadian government contracts were withdrawn in the face of rising costs, technical concerns, and U.S. pressure.

Bill Soulsby was no longer with the firm at this point, but he experienced the same roller coaster excitement and energy with A.V. Roe as characterized both the Arrow story and the industry as a whole during his early years with Elsie.

He was fortunate, for example, to be associated with A.V. Roe's CF-100, the Avro Jetliner, and the pioneering days of jet-engine technology. A year after Bill joined the firm, A.V. Roe took over another federal government Crown corporation, Turbo Research Ltd. In comparison with Victory Aircraft's manufacturing operations, Turbo was tiny, but its potential was immense. It had been created as a spin-off from the National Research Council of Canada (NRC) aeronautical research programs to develop new jet-engine technologies for Canadian purposes and bring them to a stage where they might be attractive to industry.

Orenda

Early in the war, Elsie's old friend John J. Green and other NRC colleagues in Ottawa travelled to Britain to tour research facilities. There they were introduced to the pioneering gas turbine engine research of Wing Commander Frank Whittle. Upon their return, they prepared a top-secret report urging the Canadian government and military to invest in this new aircraft engine technology and specifically to conduct research on the implications of the very Canadian problems associated with operating jet engines in cold weather. NRC subsequently established a cold-weather jet engine research lab in Winnipeg and put together a small team to build test facilities and conduct complementary experiments in Ontario. One day in 1944, the team members were told that the government had decided to move them out of the NRC and into a Crown corporation to be located near Toronto and to start work on prototype engines of their own design to meet Canadian needs. This company would be Turbo Research.

The team included young engineers like Winnett Boyd and Paul Dilworth who would be absorbed by Bill Soulsby's new employer A.V. Roe when it took over Turbo a few years later. In 1946, A.V. Roe was given a contract to develop a new jet engine for what would be the successful Canadian fighter aircraft, the CF-100. Originally designated TR-5 (Turbo Research 5), the test engine was run for a record total of nearly 1000 hours during its initial test program from February 1949 through to the late fall.

Turbo Research 5 became "the Orenda", a legendary aircraft product that, for a few years, was the most powerful jet engine in the world. In addition to the CF 100, the engine was also used in the Canadair CF 86 Sabre jet fighters, taking the latter to world speed records. Almost 4000 Orendas were produced at Bill Soulsby's plant in Malton between 1949 and 1956, and it saw service in the air forces of Canada, the Netherlands, Belgium, and South Africa. In a reorganization in 1955, A.V. Roe Canada Ltd. became the parent of two autonomous companies: Avro Aircraft Ltd. and Orenda Engines Ltd. Orenda's team later went on to develop the famous Iroquois engine for the Arrow. Although Avro was wounded gravely by the Arrow incident, the Orenda arm continued to thrive as an element of other aerospace firms. Bill Soulsby's responsibilities and association with Orenda was a source of both pride and many stories in the MacGill-Soulsby home.

Soulsby's role in this project, the Orenda engine development, was that of a manager and executive. Others were the creative, technical geniuses in this and other A.V. Roe programs. Soulsby's association with these people had an impact in his home as well as his work. Through it, he not only contributed to an exciting era in the Canadian aircraft sector, he also helped Elsie maintain an important window on an evolving industry that was moving into a new era and new technologies beyond her own education and experience.

After working in various parts of the Hawker Siddeley empire, Bill officially retired from the aviation industry in 1967. Even at 68 years of age, he had difficulty letting go, and Elsie would watch her husband return to his old office periodically to help his former colleagues complete reports on activities from previous years. In retirement, Soulsby also sold office equipment part-time and tried his hand at a modest business venture with a man named Weatherstone who was flogging a new, innovative window design.

As his 70th birthday approached, his appreciation for afternoon naps and love of music took more and more of his time, and he started to slow down, just a bit. But in 1943, he was a ball of energy and enthusiasm that complemented and supported his new bride in the pursuit of her own ambitions.

Elizabeth M.G. MacGill, P. Eng.

The 1943 move into the Highbourne Road home in Toronto was easy for Elsie to accept. She had lived in Toronto for four exciting years as an undergraduate student and had come back to the city for visits between classes at MIT in 1933. Much about Toronto was comfortable.

At the same time, while life in Fort William had many highs, it was not always pleasant. Even independent of the Helldiver experience, her work at Can-Car had often been an emotional roller coaster with the exciting technical successes of her Maple Leaf Trainer II and work on the Gregor Fighter being punctuated by commercial failure, and with the path to ultimate success in Hurricane production being disrupted by ongoing uncertainty over contracts and supplies. At the Can-Car factory, Elsie also felt the sting of resentment and pressure. A few staff, including female workers, saw her as icy, short-tempered, and even a mean, "crabby old bugger".[330] While such perceptions contrast sharply with the cheery, play-ful, and joke-loving optimist most often on show, even some of Elsie's admirers admit that she suffered at times from a haughtiness and sense of superiority that her mother had helped to instil and that may have served Elsie well in difficult times, but not in every circumstance.

Elsie was not often on the shop floor when at Can-Car. Although more than decade had passed since she first fell ill and she personally had come to disregard her residual paralysis, in the eyes of others she had a very significant physical disability. Her leg-lift use of the clutch when driving was both impressive and "scary" for her passengers, and her visits to the plant were memorable. Her office was some distance away, and she and her canes made the walk from one building to the next only with great difficulty.

In one celebrated instance, however, she made the effort in order to admonish plant employees and to apply the full weight of her manage-ment position. A cat had become encased in the wing of one of the aircraft being assembled. Whether by accident or design, Elsie did not care. She was incensed and, in a manner guaranteed to ensure those responsible were thoroughly embarrassed, ordered the staff to take the wing apart so the animal could be freed. Those involved were further wounded when a report of the incident in a newsletter portrayed Elsie as a tough kind of heroine.[331] The story raised her standing in many minds, but resentment and ill will persisted in other quarters, and this mix of feelings coloured Elsie's time at the plant.

Nevertheless, she would eventually look back at all aspects of the Can-Car experience fondly, even the Helldiver project. After Elsie and Bill's departure and the completion of the first planes, the Helldivers rolled off the Can-Car shop floor in the many hundreds, and the refined versions of the aircraft performed effectively in major battles in the Pacific during the latter years of the war. Fort William-made planes helped take out a Japanese naval base at Rabaul in Papua New Guinea, and later proved exceptionally effective in attacks on Japanese shipping. Decades later, Elsie would cite her role in the difficult early Helldiver engineering work with pride and even emphasize the complexity and scope of the work as a badge of honour of sorts.

Although it took a while, she found ways to laugh off the criticisms and names, clinging to a newspaper clipping describing how, in the view of the world, "a business man is aggressive; a business woman is pushy. A businessman is good in details; she is picky. He loses his temper because he is so involved in the job; she is bitchy".[332]

It was probably just as well that she and Bill were forced out of Can-Car and compelled to seek other jobs when they were. At the height of the war, opportunities for talented and experienced people like them abounded. Others in the aircraft industry, particularly other women, were less lucky when WWII ended.

The Helldiver contract with Curtiss-Wright and the U.S. Navy proved to be the boost Can-Car needed to maintain its workforce throughout the remainder of the war, but it did not keep the day of reckoning at bay forever. When the victory over Japan — VJ Day — arrived suddenly in the wake of two atomic bombs in the late summer of 1945, thousands of aircraft workers were laid off at Can-Car and many other aircraft plants just as suddenly, as demand for military aircraft evaporated overnight.

As at Victory Aircraft and elsewhere, almost all the thousands of women at the Fort William plant were let go. Their services were considered less important now, especially given the flood of unemployed men returning from overseas. Can-Car and other companies slipped back into comfortable old patterns and perceptions. In fact, it would be more than 40 years after Elsie's departure before a future incarnation of the Fort William plant would employ another female engineer, and no other woman would find a position in middle or senior management there until the 1990s.[333]

The women dismissed from the plant with the war's end were expected to return to the home, start families, and put any gains they had made in the workplace behind them as an aberration and a break from what was considered normal. Most followed the path society set out for them. Elsie, of course, did not.

For some time before her departure from Can-Car, Elsie had been contemplating other career options. She wondered specifically whether she could use her combination of experience in design, stress analysis, wind tunnel research, and production systems as the basis for a career as a professional consultant. Once again, the fact that she might be the first woman to enter into private business as an aeronautical engineering consultant did not give her pause or even enter into her thinking. Her sister's example, her husband's support, and her open mind combined to give her the confidence to take the leap without hesitation.

She opened a large office on Bloor Street in Toronto,[334] hung up her sign, and bought letterhead announcing the services of "Elizabeth M.G. MacGill, B.A.Sc., M.S.E., M.E.I.C., A.S., R.Ae.S., P. Eng". Elsie now thought of herself as an old-timer in the profession, counting her experience in decades. Still, she remained one of the very few women (or perhaps only woman) working in her specific subdiscipline within aeronautics. Given that years later she was still being cited as among the few female consulting engineers of any kind anywhere and formally recognized as the first in Canada, it is likely that once again she was marking a first as the only woman aeronautical engineer to own and operate a consulting business in North America, perhaps in the world.

As her new letterhead emphasized, Elsie had kept her maiden name, "MacGill", after marriage in a move radical by some at the time and still viewed as noteworthy enough to stimulate newspaper articles three decades later. Even long after she and others had won battles over the right of women to assert themselves and their own identities, she was still being questioned about her name and her motives for keeping it after marriage.

Some colleagues suspected it was largely a business decision. Elsie had developed a profile and reputation with the "MacGill" name in the aircraft industry, and she clearly hoped this reputation would buttress her new business enterprise. Indeed, there may have been a professional and economic element to her choice. Once again, however, it is likely that Elsie was also reiterating the influence of her mother, the still formidable Judge MacGill, who had gone under the name of Helen Gregory-Flesher during her first marriage, and of her sister, who also retained her maiden name in tandem with her husband's as Helen MacGill Hughes.

When asked about the decision, Elsie emphasized personal reasons. "A name is part of an individual", she once said, in discussing the issue. "I suppose it's a statement that I consider my personality as important as his", quickly adding "and so does he"[335] to stress her husband Bill's consistent support.

In June 1943, Elsie was 38 years old, an older bride, and a woman who had a solidified view of the world and was confident in such decisions. She knew how she felt about Bill Soulsby: someone she not only loved, but had long considered admirable, amiable, and amusing even though the tension at work and Bill's status as a recent widower had made it difficult to show her feelings before their departure from Fort William.

Only after they had left Can-Car, and about a week before their wedding, did Elsie allow herself to show her affection with the birthday gift of a cello to a man she recognized as "music struck" but who lacked an outlet to express his passion. Bill's family in England had no clear musical talent and no inclination, but he fell in love with music in all its forms in boyhood as a soprano in a choir. Elsie's gift was a source of pleasure and pride for Bill throughout his life, although he struggled with the instrument in the beginning. His colleagues at Victory Aircraft compared his playing to the sound of a "fog-bound mule", but almost 40 years later, when he had to confront life as a widower for a second time, he was composing music and playing with a degree of proficiency that comforted and distracted him with happy memories of those early summer days with Elsie in 1943.

Bill was Elsie's great love and her "dear Mr. S".

Ann, John, and Granddad Heaps

Elsie also loved his children, whom she had befriended while watching them grow and suffer in the midst of their mother's declining health and eventual death. Despite this familiarity, the job of stepmother was to be a new and uncertain adventure. It could have been awkward and difficult, particularly because Elsie was assuming her new role at the same time as she was establishing a new business and struggling to maintain her engineering skills in an era of rapid technological change.

Life at the MacGill-Soulsby home somehow worked out, partly because everyone pulled together and partly because of Elsie's organizational abilities. Due to her manufacturing and production plant background, Elsie was skilled at the division of labour, schedules, and task management. Everyone had chores linked to their particular talents and abilities.

In this organizing effort, she was acting on her own unique impulses and drawing upon unique experiences. However, she was not the only woman to apply such skills in the home. A few years later, Elsie would meet and come to know well and admire an American female engineer who exemplified in an almost mythical way the link between the management of a multi-faceted household and the management of industrial production. Although Lillian Gilbreth was initially a student of English literature and had a doctorate degree in psychology, she earned recognition as an expert in mechanical engineering, including honorary admission to Elsie's Engineering Institute of Canada on the basis of her pioneering work in time-and-motion studies, workplace efficiency, and manufacturing. Gilbreth, a widowed mother of 12 whose life was the inspiration for popular books and films under the banner "Cheaper by the Dozen",[336] would not only come to know Elsie in the 1950s, but would help promote Elsie's achievements and join her in actively supporting the Canadian women's movement.

Although Elsie's home may not have had children measured in the dozens, it did demand coordination and effort. Elsie's limited mobility made her slow and ineffective at sweeping, dusting, and general cleaning duties, which thus fell on the other members of the household. Elsie did better standing by the wringer washer feeding in the laundry and standing propped up by the sink sharing the dishwashing and drying duties with John and Ann Soulsby and sometimes their grandfather. When Ann and Elsie did the chores together, it gave them time to talk, laugh, discuss the day, and share ideas.

Elsie never overtly sought to replace Ann's mother and was so clearly a different person that the exercise would have been futile. But Elsie was someone to respect, and she and Ann became good friends. Ann knew her father loved Elsie and that they were happily married and that was good enough to build a solid relationship upon. Ann would chose her own career, her own course in life, and although the choices did not always reflect the influence of her unusual stepmother, Elsie's voice and admonishments were always floating in the background.

When Ann finished high school and went away to McGill University, she stayed in residence partly to please Elsie, who thought the experience might provide opportunities to fill what Elsie considered to be a serious void in her stepdaughter's life: not having a sister. Indeed, Ann established lifelong friendships during her lively, although abbreviated university days.

Ann did not see herself as an academic person, nor was she as studious as her stepmother, recognizing few links between Elsie's career and her own even though she too pursued courses and work in a technological field. A radiotherapy technician trained at the Montréal General Hospital, initially in diagnostics, Ann later joined the cancer treatment group at Princess Margaret Hospital in Toronto. Her work at the hospital, she believed, was coloured by more human interaction and personal involvement than the technical documents and paper-laden world that consumed Elsie much of the time. While never needing Elsie's approval, Ann was comforted decades later when her stepmother, with a tinge of envy, acknowledged the merits of a different perspective and the resulting choices her stepdaughter had made.

Elsie had fewer opportunities to influence John, the eldest of the Soulsby children. Born in Fort William in February 1929, John Soulsby was a fairly independent teenager when Elsie joined his home in 1943. He seemed almost instantly to transform into a young man after the family's arrival in Toronto, moving seamlessly out of school to the work world at the age of 16 and never looking back. He later took courses in hotel administration in Toronto and made a serious attempt to qualify as an accountant. Perhaps instilled with the story of his immigrant father's foothold success in the pulp mill and with an attachment to the forested Lakehead region of his birth, John Soulsby eventually devoted himself and much of his working life to supporting and promoting the resource industry by working with the Canadian Pulp and Paper Association based in Montréal, another city familiar to Elsie and his father and the place where John and his wife Meg would raise their own family.

Also labelled "not an academic person", and not technically trained, John Soulsby did, however, acquire an infatuation that was tied to the charged atmosphere of his youth, his stepmother's profession, and the forces that brought Elsie and his father together. One of his first jobs out of school was as "a grease monkey" helping aircraft mechanics at Trans-Canada Airlines (TCA). With this experience, he developed an aptitude for working on planes and an amateur enthusiasm for vintage aircraft, helping organize, fundraise, and work for their restoration. In fact, Elsie's stepson was working on such a project and pursuing his love of old planes at the dawn of his retirement when he passed away unexpectedly in 1996 while living in Britain.

Elsie also knew that any home she and her new husband would build together would include other people, notably Bill's former father-in-law Granddaddy Heaps, a man now entering his late sixties and still adjusting

Elsie's mother, Judge Helen Gregory MacGill, upon receiving her honorary Doctorate of Laws degree from UBC in 1938. (*Library and Archives Canada PA 203365.*)

to life in a new country and to the deaths of his wife and daughter. Bill Soulsby's first wife was an only child, and when the storm clouds gathered over Europe in the mid-1930s, she had the obligation and desire to care for her parents. They were brought to Canada to live with the Soulsby family and were fully integrated into it when illness and age took the lives of Helen Soulsby and her mother at Fort William in the fall and winter of 1942, leaving Mr. Heaps a lonely, sad, and shaken man. There was never any thought that he would not form part of Bill and Elsie's family in Toronto.

Elsie also eschewed any suggestion that her "Mr. Heaps" was a burden. In fact, he was an active and extremely handy person around the house. A cabinetmaker by profession, he compensated for his son-in-law's weakness with things mechanical and used his skills not only to help out in the MacGill-Soulsby home, but to assist others less fortunate.

Soon after settling in Toronto, Grandpa Heaps made part-time work at the Society for Crippled Civilians a part of his daily routine. Now part of the Goodwill organization, the society was established in Toronto in

1935 to provide meaningful work to people injured or disabled outside of military service. For the last decade of his life, Grandpa Heaps frequented the organization's building on George Street, where he helped disabled people in a workshop, recycling and converting donated items into useable products for sale in their retail store. For this and other reasons, he worked his way into Elsie's heart, ultimately making her the person who, about a decade after the move to Toronto, cried more intensely than anyone else at his funeral.

The Old Judge

In the years that followed, many of Elsie's admirers would recount this mid-to-late 1940s period of her life as further testimony to her superhuman capacity to juggle responsibilities and carry a burden that would overwhelm others. The list of trailblazing career, physical constraints, new husband, two teenagers, her husband's elderly former father-in-law, and all her other duties sounds daunting, but in fact — perhaps as a result of her organizing prowess — she saw her Toronto home as an integrated support system that allowed her to accomplish what she did outside the home.

She depended upon her home base from the beginning and even more so after 1945, when her ill and aging mother, who by then had retired, joined them in Toronto. The suggestion that the widowed judge would spend her final years living with Elsie had been discussed openly for some time, and Judge Helen had made it clear that this was her preference. Because Elsie had lived with her mother longer and relied on her more than had her sister and half-brothers, she felt a special bond and a sense of duty.

Even as recently as a few months before Helen's January 1945 retirement, conversations about the planned move to Toronto were filled with optimism and energy as the 80-year-old social campaigner described her intent to establish a quasi-legal consulting business, which she would run out of Elsie's Bloor Street office. But even as she spoke those words, Helen was feeling the forces that eventually dissipated her dream. Elsie's mother did eventually come to her daughter's office each day, but not to work. There she cried, slipped into confusion, and slept.

The war had brought personal heartbreak to families around the world, and Judge Helen and her clan had their share. Eric Reed Flesher, her grandson (son of Elsie's half-brother Eric Herbert Flesher) who had lived in Vancouver with her in the late thirties while he was finishing university, was listed in early 1944 as missing in action. He would survive, turning up at war's end in a German prisoner of war camp, but not before his extended family had grieved his apparent loss.

However, the greatest blow came away from the battlefield in a completely unexpected way. In the early autumn of 1944, Helen's younger son Freddy (Elsie's half-brother) died suddenly of a cerebral hemorrhage at the age of 50. The shock and sadness of Freddy's death combined with the effects of age and the impending end of her judicial career caused the famously sharp and solid mind that had served Elsie's mother for eight decades of life to break down and move into what Elsie branded the "abyss of weakness".[337] By the time Helen's daughter-in-law, Freddy's widowed second wife Margaret, brought the judge to Toronto to live with the Soulsby-MacGills, Helen was fragile in mind, spirit, and body.

Those who had not known Helen MacGill well before this time would see her simply as "a senile old lady". To Elsie, her mother still seemed engaged in the issues that had concerned much of her life, and still showed flashes of her former self, the person who once approached life with "a light touch" and who was able to "joke about herself and her work and feminism".[338]

But it was still stressful. For two years, Elsie was increasingly a mother to her mother, adding new strands to an already strong bond. Child-like, confused, and dependent, Helen would even call Elsie "Mother" at times. This inverted relationship magnified the feelings of responsibility and emotions as the end approached. Fortunately for Elsie, her sister Helen was there once again to help carry the burden, caring for her mother in Illinois for part of the time, and when Helen Gregory MacGill finally passed away, she was in Chicago with Young Helen and her family. The death came in relative peace during the night of February 27, 1947.[339]

At a memorial service in Vancouver months later, Elsie listened to what others had to say and recognized that an important and dramatic period of history had passed for her country, her family, and herself. But Elsie was herself poised on the threshold of a new era, and would soon weave her mother's example into her own life in unexpected ways, imparting texture, colour, and value upon it.

Chapter IX

The Business of Women

"Elsie Gregory MacGill was already a feminist...
the remaining four women on the commission
became feminists".[340]

With her mother's passing, Elsie recognized that visits to the city of her birth would never be the same. In the weeks that followed, Elsie's perception of the parks, buildings, and streets of Vancouver would be altered further by memorial events, public commentary, and many private conversations reflecting upon her mother's life and work in this city.

Always interested in and respectful of her mother's contributions, Elsie started to have a better understanding of the struggle and the social forces behind them and to see them as something much more than just her mother's job. This process and its impact had been magnified by the charged experience of watching her mother Helen's body and mind decline. As she performed her part in the post-burial task of reviewing papers, old clippings, and personal effects, Elsie MacGill felt their touch reach deep into her heart. Still, Elsie did not, at first, recognize these feelings as the genesis of a new career.

In early 1947, Elsie MacGill was still firmly committed to the field of aeronautical engineering and to the development of her consulting business in Toronto, although it had not gone as well as she had initially anticipated. Her husband Bill, pushed out of Can-Car along with Elsie, had managed to land on his feet and flourish as an aircraft executive in private industry. Elsie, however, at times had difficulty attracting industrial clients, and she was kept busy trying to find new ways to pursue her career.

Perhaps not surprisingly, Elsie would find the most help during her first years in business in government circles, not private industry. Through friends like John Green and J.H. Parkin, she was apprised of the major national issues in aviation through the 1940s and was eventually appointed as a member of the National Research Council Associate Committee on Aeronautical Research and its subcommittee on aircraft structures. Such official roles gave her not only a venue to work with government officials; they also kept her in touch with the latest scientific developments, emerging technical issues, and opportunities for work. Elsie naturally thrived on the technical engineering discussions, but she also seized upon the administrative processes and organizational challenges, down to providing advice on the maintenance of committee records. Although working in government had never really appealed to her, she recognized the worth of government contacts for business reasons and, to a certain extent, was starting to see the value of public service in general.

Of course with war raging, government was still the most influential force in the aircraft business when Elsie had opened her office in 1943. Indeed, the focus on mass production of bombers and fighters was the main topic of conversation in Ottawa. Yet even then higher circles in the capital were beginning to turn their thoughts to peace, reconstruction, and civilian aviation. With her pre-war bush plane background at Fairchild, Elsie was competent in the civil aircraft domain and well qualified to help her industry make the transition from military to civilian products.

The combination of these connections and interests drew her into her first major project as a consulting engineer.

A Canadian Version of the Avro York

When, during the last years of the war, Elsie was approached by government officials to conduct an evaluation of the new Canadian version of a popular British aircraft, the Avro York transport plane, she had reason to feel uneasy. There was no doubt she had the experience and specific skill set for the job, and she definitely needed the contract, but in addition there were other considerations. The plane was being developed for large-scale production at her husband's Victory Aircraft plant in Malton, and Elsie knew that Bill and his colleagues were hoping it would become their foothold in the post-war passenger and cargo plane business.

The York (Canadian) was to be a special variation of the British-designed and -built Avro York, a transport plane that, like several other

A.V. Roe products, had evolved from the Lancaster line of aircraft. In its various formats, Elsie learned, the Avro York had incorporated elements of the Lancaster's wings, tail, undercarriage, and engines. A prototype of the British York flew in the U.K. in July 1942 and large-scale production for British purposes began in 1943. Although the manufacture of British Yorks was ultimately measured in the hundreds, not thousands, the plane carved out a distinguished piece of wartime history as the personal transport aircraft of a long list of notables including Churchill, Montgomery, and Mountbatten. After the war, the planes would be recognized for their working role in the Berlin Airlift, the struggle to keep supplies flowing to West Berlin during the two years of a Soviet blockade of the city in the late 1940s.

The Canadian government became interested in adapting the plane for its own purposes shortly after its 1942 inaugural flight, seeing it as a military transport that might be of use in serving Canadian troops crossing the Atlantic. At the time that Elsie became involved in the project, Trans-Canada Airlines (TCA), the government-owned forerunner of Air Canada, was providing transport services to the armed forces. The York's longer-term potential as a civilian passenger and cargo plane was thus a major consideration for Canada.

At the height of the war, TCA and the Government of Canada were involved in a constant struggle to find suitable aircraft suppliers. Having failed to secure transport planes from the most obvious sources in the United States, the government found the York an attractive option, since Victory Aircraft, Bill Soulby's new employer, was already making Lancasters, and it seemed an easy task for the firm to build a quantity of its modified York for the transatlantic work. Victory accordingly made one pattern plane (serial number FM400).

To make the contract worthwhile to Victory and to keep the unit costs down, the government ordered 50 planes. Some thought this rash. Despite the York's growing reputation overseas, many at TCA had concerns about how the plane would perform in the unique test of service in the expansive, winter-ridden country of Canada. Even though the Canadian version of the York was to be based on components of the proven Lancaster design, its expanded square fuselage made the fundamental aeronautics different, and TCA staff, including some of Elsie's friends and the airline's superintendent of engineering, Jim Bain, had doubts.[341]

TCA engineers conducted their own studies, confirming their suspicions, but they needed a credible outside expert's word if they hoped to force cancellation of the project, to pull out of the order for another 49 planes. Likely with help from her Ottawa connections, Elsie landed the contract to provide the airline and the government with a second opinion — a good sign that her reputation as an engineer remained intact and a boost to her fledgling consulting business.

Since the original British York was already in wide service, Elsie's task may at first have seemed a straightforward march down the path already beaten by British engineers and designers. But the proposed Canadian version of the York would have many distinct features: "the floors had to be leveled, a ceiling escape hatch installed in each cabin and a new cargo door fitted... pilots' instrument panel was to be redesigned to follow North American airline practice and new radio equipment fitted. In addition, all the appropriate Canadian Lancaster X modifications were to be incorporated".[342]

Some argued that the Canadian York reviewed by Elsie had so many changes that it constituted an entirely new version of the aircraft, worthy of its own designation and Mark number, not merely the verbal qualifier "Canadian". In the end, the point was hardly worth arguing. On the strength of Elsie's evaluation, which confirmed TCA suspicions, the order for mass-produced Canadian Yorks was cancelled, and TCA reverted to using stripped-down Lancasters for its transport work. The decision certainly confirmed Elsie's stature within her industry. It may also have saved lives.

Although she was hired by federal government agencies, Elsie may have learned much about the York evaluation work through Bill since his company, Victory Aircraft, was the one lined up to build the plane for TCA. Her ultimate negative assessment, which helped kill the order, may have generated dynamic discussions around the dinner table at the MacGill-Soulsby home. Bill (who was then the Assistant General Manager at Victory) and his colleagues at the plant certainly had high hopes for their Canadian version of the Avro York. When it made its successful first flight in November 1944, Bill and his associates had celebrated with excitement.[343] But the one pattern plane was the only Canadian York ever built. It was lost in a crash in Europe in June 1949.

Sticking with the Consulting Business

Having his wife contribute to the plane's demise was not particularly welcomed, but all concerned recognized Elsie's objectivity and professionalism, and the project magnified her already substantial credibility with the federal contractors. Elsie remained involved with the government agencies throughout the rest of the war, and was actually in New York heading to Europe on "government work" in early May 1945 when V-E Day arrived and the war in Europe ended.

Back in Toronto, Bill was chewing his fingernails at the thought of her pending trip over North Atlantic waters still frequented by German subs. It was not the only time Bill might have wished that his new wife had taken a less harrowing career path. He and Elsie's friends often suggested that an easier, more comfortable life would await her if she abandoned the consulting business and returned to work as a design engineer and analyst in the employ of one of the many dynamic and growing Canadian aviation companies. A specific possibility came up with de Havilland, which had dedicated itself to an aggressive assault on the needs of bush pilots in the post-war years, one result being their wildly successful STOL (short take-off and landing) aircraft, beginning with the Beaver and the Otter. A senior engineer and future vice-president of the company, Dick Hiscocks, considered Elsie to be, without qualification, one of Canada's outstanding professional engineers and asserted forcefully that gender was irrelevant to her profile and status in the industry. He would have been delighted to have her on his team.

Elsie did some consulting work for de Havilland, but rejected the idea of applying for a full-time position with the firm. Some thought her infamous family pride was getting in the way, preventing her from seeking a permanent job despite the fact that her consulting business was at times slow. She certainly would have found it difficult to humbly apply for a subordinate engineer's position after her stint as chief aeronautical engineer with a large operation. This is one sphere in which her mother's influence might have had a "blighting" effect. While a certain amount of confidence and even the judge's notion that the MacGills might be "better than most people"[344] can be supportive to a young girl trying to overcome social constructs and other workplace barriers, such attitudes do not usually help a consultant or indeed anyone seeking fee-for-service work.

In fact, Elsie's sociologist sister Helen, who was exposed to the same influences, did not apply for a single job over her long career, though she held many, and never sought employment even when she felt the absence of paid work "rather keenly". Having been invited to take on specific tasks and positions was "a real tribute" to Elsie and Young Helen "to be sure, but it also fits in with [their] upbringing, [with the] family feeling that they... could rather expect to be at the top". Elsie's sister even may have feared "competing for a post, in case she did not win it".[345]

Elsie also suffered, sometimes more obviously than others, from such distorted thinking. But her reasons for avoiding the regimented atmosphere of a company office may have been a more complex and subtle result of her rewarding experiences in seeing and influencing the whole picture from design to manufacture and wanting to avoid a return to sub-elements and isolated tasks. In any case, her decision to stay with consulting and her global, high-level chief engineer's perspective proved to be a clear asset, for it brought her another special assignment, an assignment that would affect aviation around the globe and contribute to the betterment of international relations in general.

Helping Civil Aviation Around the World

In 1944, just as Trans-Canada Airlines was struggling over whether to develop and purchase a quantity of the modified Avro Yorks, the company's president was in Chicago along with federal cabinet minister C.D. Howe, representing Canada at a meeting later recognized as the birth of the international civil aviation industry.

The American government had invited representatives from the Allies and neutral nations to Chicago for the first-ever conference to discuss civil aviation issues ranging from technical standards and safety to sovereignty and air route cooperation. Fifty-four nations attended, and all but two of them signed the resulting Convention on International Civil Aviation. This agreement led to the creation of an interim body and, subsequently, to the permanent International Civil Aviation Organization (ICAO), a body affiliated today with the United Nations and operated as a means to secure and maintain international co-operation in civil aviation matters. The Chicago Convention thus laid the groundwork for the establishment of a common air navigation system throughout the world.

Given its air transportation boom before the war and its role as a significant player during the conflict, Canada, in collaboration with the government-backed TCA, carried considerable weight during the Chicago conference and even successfully advanced ideas in opposition to the host U.S. position. This profile carried on into the conference's aftermath, and subsequent technical meetings were hosted in Montréal by Canada. Thus when the permanent ICAO was created in April 1947, it seemed only natural to site the head office in Montréal, also home to TCA headquarters. Canadians, many of them associates and friends of Elsie MacGill, played important roles in much of the ICAO's early work, serving on many of its technical committees. One was the Sub-Committee on Airworthiness chaired by Canadian Air Vice-Marshal Alan Ferrier, a military figure with a long-standing interest in research and development and familiarity with the wind tunnel test facilities in Ottawa where Elsie had often worked before the war.[346]

In 1946, Elsie, whose review of the York had raised her profile within TCA and other government circles, was invited to participate in the preliminary meetings of the bodies that would later come together to form the ICAO. Her work with the ICAO would mostly concern stress analysis, her area of expertise, and how it related to the broader issues of safety and airworthiness. In particular, she helped draft the regulations that eventually established the international framework for design and production of commercial aircraft. Her contributions to this exercise evidently earned her the respect of the ICAO leadership and experts from other countries as it resulted in her selection in 1947 as chair of the ICAO Stress Analysis Committee, one of only five regular ICAO committees at the time.

Her appointment was seen as an exceptional honour not only for her as an individual and as a pioneering woman aeronautical engineer, but also "for Canada".[347] While her career would be marked by more vivid and tangible engineering projects and higher-profile contributions to social causes, Elsie may have had her greatest influence on her profession and indeed on all of humanity through the seemingly dry administrative and technical work of these committees. The regulatory framework they produced sent out ripples for many decades, defining innovation in civilian aeronautics and ensuring safe travel around the world. Elsie's contributions constituted a concrete and significant part of the groundwork underpinning the dramatic growth of the aviation industry in the last half of the 20th century.

The Outstanding "American" Woman Engineer

Despite the periodic sluggishness of her consulting business, Elsie thus had reason for professional satisfaction during this period. Her influential committee work was coupled with public speaking engagements, including speeches on aircraft design issues before international audiences.[348] Her appearances led to a greater profile and the start of what would become a towering monument of professional awards and international recognition fed by the publicity around her wartime work and her profile as a woman in a male-dominated field.

In 1953, the American Society of Women Engineers (SWE) made Elsie, a Canadian, an honorary member and almost immediately after named her its "Woman Engineer of the Year", awarding her its medal for "meritorious contribution to aeronautical engineering".[349] Elsie was only the second woman to be so recognized by the 3-year-old society and the first non-American. She was the unanimous choice of the prestigious Awards Committee.

In announcing the award, members of the new organization were, of course, celebrating Elsie's professional achievements and civic duty. But along with the chronicle of her engineering and organizational works, the SWE announcement also noted qualities that would come to represent Elsie MacGill in the minds of many of those who knew her personally: "a rare sense of humour and a scintillating sense of fun".[350]

Elsie was genuinely touched and even "astonished" to receive the award and the kind comments.[351] She was pleased to be recognized by an organization dedicated to the promotion of engineering careers for women, and, equally, to receive an honour that would help to strengthen Canada-U.S. ties, noting that she wished to share the honour with her fellow Canadian engineers of both sexes. As one who had worked and studied in the States in her youth, Elsie told those attending the award ceremony that while she might be a Canadian and an "outsider" to their organization, she did not consider herself to be a "foreigner" in the United States and was proud of her U.S.-based achievements. Indeed, for many years, she described herself and her family as being proudly "of this continent", as opposed to one country or the other.[352]

But although she clearly still identified with engineering as much as she did with her sex or nationality, Elsie was starting to connect with another profession: the field of business. As a consultant who lived on contracts and contacts, Elsie MacGill's days increasingly consisted less of using her technical skills and knowledge of aeronautical engineering and more of marketing those same skills through negotiations, meetings, and invoices — in other words, the stuff of running a business and interacting with interests and imperatives outside the engineering office and plant floor.

But Why?

This new world brought her into contact with more and more people who were intrigued by aeronautical engineering and the modern advances in aviation, but less attuned to the technical. Elsie was very much at ease responding to engineering colleagues interested in the scientific and mechanical aspects of her work, but less prepared for deceptively simple questions from others like "Why should we keep trying to build faster and faster airplanes? Doesn't it risk lives needlessly? Why are we not satisfied with what we have?"

While many engineers might have considered the questions naive and the answers self-evident, Elsie, now approaching the end of her fifth decade of life and past the most intense period of her engineering career, paused to reflect on such notions and to analyse why she did what she did for a living, why she approached life the way she did, and why it struck her as the right thing to do.

Applying the model of logic and sequence that infuses an engineer's training, Elsie found herself explaining her views to others by asserting that a scientific or technical goal, while a useful and maybe even essential motivation, is itself insufficient as an explanation of why someone should do a particular thing or pursue a specific career. In this, she noted that it is often difficult to determine whether an advancement, even if achieved, will ultimately be used for more good than evil or even if a particular use is inherently good. Instead, she argued that the "only conscious attempt that an individual can make to improving the species" is the "development of... [their own personal] human personality and... human capability to their greatest capacities".[353] While she could not say with certainty what the best path to such development might be, Elsie was prepared to state with confidence: "It does not appear that complacency leads to spiritual or intellectual growth." To her mind, this pointed to the merits of discontent with the norm, of always striving for something better, of trying to be the best one could be, and of pursuing one's own passion "as long as it does not impinge on others".[354]

She thus accepted the pursuit of ambitious goals as worthy, but largely because through the exertion and the quest, good things would come indirectly. Her belief in the value of confronting challenges with enthusiasm and always trying her best had been ingrained by her upbringing and her mother's example. Now it was forged into something stronger by her technically trained mind. Supported by thought and analysis, this belief became a conviction that was about to strengthen the thread of passion, connect the varied experiences of her life, and lead her into greater challenges.

Business and Professional Women

As an independent businesswoman in the early 1950s, Elsie must have struggled at times and may even have felt alone — as someone marching against a parade. In the decade after the war, the male soldiers who had returned from overseas often seemed to be taking over the working world while the many women who had flooded into it during the war were driven back into homes and their traditional roles. In fact, many institutions, including the federal government and the military, had demanded that women quit if they were married in order to open up jobs for returning veterans. Those women who continued on in factory and office jobs labelled "male" were working outside the norm, and those who started their own businesses in these fields were very rare.

Yet Elsie was not entirely alone, though she may have felt so at first, and she was far from unique as a Canadian woman in the general field of business. Even in the early 1930s, under the dark shadow of the Great Depression, there were enough entrepreneurial and educated women in Canada to justify creation of the Federation of Canadian Business and Professional Women's Clubs, building on the work of the few already existing local and provincial groups. Although its membership was modest, the Toronto branch was active and involved, and Elsie heard about it soon after arriving in the city.

Her association with the local club and the national federation would eventually embrace her soul and come to frame much of the last decades of her life. Initially, however, she did not entertain the idea of joining because she considered herself too busy with the demands of consulting, her engineering work, and a full house to engage in what seemed like peripheral social activities. Eventually, her interest in political and social issues would grow and, along with it, her appreciation of the Toronto club's mission and absorption. Even during those years of watching the group from a distance, she often contacted its leadership on the phone "asking questions about [what they] were doing, and making suggestions".[355]

Her daily literary diet would come to include "Hansard and the Votes and Proceedings of the Ontario Legislature", said one of those women leaders years later. "She always knew what was going on that affected women in business and in the professions, and what was likely to affect them either for good or for ill".[356] Clearly, the club would have loved to welcome such an energetic and knowledgeable colleague into their ranks. Although it seemed inevitable that she would join, Elsie resisted for a few years, citing engineering demands.

During this time, Elsie was visited by an equally predictable event: a broken leg. Despite her spunk, her own peculiar technique with canes, and her determination, Elsie's always frail and unsteady limbs made falling a persistent threat although she never acknowledged concern over the possibility. Perhaps inevitably, it happened in the simple circumstance of her Toronto home, where in late 1953 she tripped over an area rug. Although frustrated, Elsie, the engineer, did not blame her weakened legs. Rather she cursed the poorly designed rug. It was soon sold.

Walking had been hard without a broken leg; with one it was virtually impossible. Now, in her late forties, Elsie was tossed back a quarter century, almost precisely 25 years, to the big setback of her youth and into the prospect of sitting and staring at the walls again. During the examination and treatment of her fracture, Elsie was advised by her medical specialist that her walking might benefit from surgery on the muscles in her legs, and while this treatment would prolong her recuperation period, it would, she was told, "bring her back better than before". She agreed to do it.

Elsie might have had special reason to put her faith in innovative new medical treatments that year, particularly those aligned with her own affliction. Earlier in 1953, word had reached Canada and many other countries that Dr. Jonas Salk had developed a promising poliomyelitis vaccine. By 1955, the School of Public Health at Elsie's aeronautics alma mater, the University of Michigan, would announce successful results in the first large-scale field tests of the vaccine, which in turn launched its widespread use. Elsie was acutely aware of the discovery, for the break-throughs were particularly big news in Canada, which two years before had been hit by 9000 cases of polio, the worst such epidemic in the world at the time. Canada seized upon the Salk discovery, and was the first to bring the vaccine into production for national distribution.

As predicted, the experience of leg surgery and recuperation did change Elsie MacGill dramatically, but not in the physical way the surgeon may have envisioned.

While the thought of languishing in bed and being stuck in a wheelchair again was more than mildly unpleasant, this time around Elsie had greater confidence that the situation was temporary, and this time she was encour-aged by the first-hand example of someone who had soldiered on when struck by many such mishaps: her mother. The confluence of unexpected free time, inspiration, and a smouldering sense of unfinished business prompted Elsie to seize the opportunity and begin work on a personal project that would touch her life and her character in profound and per-haps unimagined ways: a biography of Helen Gregory MacGill.

Elsie had started gathering information and had made a few false attempts at what she called her little "bookie" in the years after her mother's death.[357] But now, with a good excuse to push the pursuit of engineering contracts and other demands to the side, Elsie threw herself obsessively into the project, devoting much of the following two years to it. The end product was a complete accounting of her extraordinary mother's life and its context. While some close to Elsie suggest that she lionized her mother to a fault and others wished for more clarity or spe-cific detail, the book proved important for many reasons.

First, the process of writing it was transformative in a professional and very personal way. It compelled a scientifically trained engineer whose early technical papers could be repetitive, awkward, and dull, to search for words conveying images, passions, and nuances. The book, *My Mother the Judge*, also marked Elsie's evolution from a researcher who measured and tested the physical world to one who sought to understand human forces in society, politics, and law. It clearly changed her.

The project took her mind and soul back over two centuries of family history, not only to her mother's Upper Canada birth and upbringing in the privileged extended family of the iconic Judge Miles O'Reilly, but beyond to early crusaders for emancipation, Loyalists, and adventurers. The branches of all sides of Elsie's family tree provided a colourful and inspiring yet logical framework for her mother's life, and helped Elsie understand the context of her own times and its social challenges.

A book can sometimes tell a reader more about the author than its subject. At the very least, the writer betrays what he or she thinks is important through emphasis, decisions about detail, and omissions. Elsie certainly regarded anything that tarnished her mother's image as awkward at best and unwanted in the narrative she was constructing. Those who knew the family history well accused Elsie of having done "a fair bit of whitewashing" in the book. Others felt she was merely unprofessional in leaving out dates and details, including any mention of her kindly German sister-in-law Rosel, Freddy's first wife, who was perversely seen as the touchstone for a family embarrassment after her husband's extramarital affair and remarriage. The degree to which Elsie felt obliged to preserve her family's image and mother's memory in a positive light was illustrated most dramatically by the fact that she purportedly destroyed letters and other documents to this end,[358] something that struck those around Elsie as "extraordinary" for a scientist who was "normally professional and exact" in her own home and her professional life. Her stepdaughter, who was among those most intrigued by these actions, was quoted as often saying that, with respect to Judge Helen, "Elsie went to her grave knowing a whole lot more than she wanted anyone else to".[359]

Perhaps because of such concerns, Elsie found the process of writing the book exhausting and swore she would never write another book. It was a highly personal and emotional exercise. Though she sprinkled only a few specific references to herself through the book, she did provide a clear window on her beliefs, feelings, and outlook on the world during the early 1950s. It was evident that, among other things, she was developing into a feminist thinker motivated and inspired by the public battles waged by her mother and her mother's contemporaries on behalf of women and children, battles exemplified by the campaign for the right to vote and, equally, by the drive to ensure women's rights and the reform of social laws.

Elsie with Prime Minister John Diefenbaker and Canada's first woman Cabinet Minister,
Ellen Fairclough, in one of the many lobbying sessions for women's rights.
(*Library and Archives Canada, Dominion-Wide Limited.*)

Elsie said that throughout her early life, prior to writing her mother's biography, she had always seen her mother as "a judge" and herself as "an engineer", each pursuing her own career and having personal priorities that "differ[ed] greatly".[360] Now, however, Elsie's research and reflection ignited an interest in issues such as penal reform, legal debates, and other elements of a life of public service that had not held her attention before.

"I am finding now, however, that many of her interests are becoming mine", she told a women's gathering in 1955, "and [now] in a small way, I work for the objectives she sought".[361]

Elsie had been approaching her fiftieth birthday when the broken leg and the associated opportunity to pause and reflect came her way. The half-century mark can often be a point at which the process of maturation has produced a level of self-confidence that allows individuals to look at their achievements and failures with a little more objectivity. For some groundbreaking women in science and engineering, this examination means recognizing that "I did well in some things because the engineering was good and I blew some jobs because the engineering wasn't very good... [but at other times] I didn't get the support I needed... that being a good engineer wasn't enough... and that I should have been making friends with so-and-so... and following unspoken rules... and this thinking allows you to start identifying where the problems really are in the system".[362]

Around this time Elsie thus began recognizing problems in the grander system and calling for change. It was a genuine turning point. Later in life and beyond, she would often be described as "an engineer and a feminist", but she might also correctly be described as "an engineer *then* a feminist" as her preoccupations and her professional pursuits clearly shifted in these middle years of the 1950s.

Emulating those who viewed suffrage as merely the first step toward a goal, Elsie saw the publication of her book as the beginning of the effort to share her mother's story and to use it is as a platform to do more with her own life. For years afterward, she sought new opportunities to promote the book, sending out free copies, contacting editors, giving interviews, and drawing upon it in speeches and other work. Her personal files filled up with book reviews, letters congratulating her on the project, notes recounting memories of her mother, and epistles from old friends commenting on her punctuation.

Blueprint for Madame Prime Minister

Many of the book reviews saw echoes of Judge Helen in her younger daughter, and some encouraged Elsie to pick up the social justice baton her mother had once carried.

Well before *My Mother the Judge* was published in 1955, Elsie, her leg now healed and with walking sticks in hand again, renewed her customary high level of activity and started applying her aroused interests and developing skill as a writer and social thinker to the challenges of the post-war era women's movement. Despite what others cited as progress and what Elsie acknowledged as the "humanized" laws prompted by voting women, she was gravely concerned that, four decades later, women had fallen far short of fully exploiting the power of the vote her mother helped to win.[363]

In a clever, oft-quoted speech to her new friends in the Federation of Business and Professional Women's Clubs, delivered around the time the book was being written,[364] Elsie condemned the still appallingly low number of female public office-holders in Canada. In this July 1954 address, she told the Federation's 14th Biennial Convention in Toronto that she found it "extremely odd that of the 262 members of the Federal House of Commons, only 4 [were]...women,... that in the provincial legislatures there [were]... only 5 women..." and that in seven of those legislatures there was "none at all".

The scorn-filled but humourous speech, entitled "A Blueprint for Madame Prime Minister",[365] was clearly patterned upon the women's parliaments organized by Helen and her suffragette colleagues to mock the male legislators in British Columbia and later staged to great effect by Nellie McClung in Manitoba. The "Blueprint" speech drew inspiration not only from Elsie's engineering language and training, but also from her concurrent research on her mother's role in the early woman's movement. It contained precise phrases and ideas she would later attribute in her book to her mother.

One example was Elsie's assertion that, being barred from king-size jobs, women had no opportunity to make king-size contributions. Yes, said Elsie, women are excluded from elected office, but there is also a long list of boards, commissions, and other public offices that had never had a female member. Yet her main message was not one of woe and despair. Her views on women's rights were her views on life in general: although there was injustice in the world, women were not impotent in the face of it and could do a lot to take their fates into their own hands.

With her own concerns and the weight of her mother's memory, Elsie was finally prompted to find the time, get involved, at long last join the Toronto Business and Professional Women's Club, and actively participate in it. Well known within the group by this point, she was "greeted with open arms". She responded to the warm welcome with enthusiasm and drive, "adding a new dimension to the ambitions of the club" with new ideas and contributing "a sense of urgency" to the pursuit of the organization's established objective "to better the condition of working women".[366]

In 1956, with the older family members gone and the children off on their own, Elsie and Bill moved into a downsized house on Bennington

Heights Drive in Toronto and started a new phase in life in a place that would be their home for the rest of their days. Bill had moved on from Victory and Avro to other business operations, and Elsie was throwing herself completely into the world of political and social advocacy with all of her might in a campaign that sometimes overlapped with an ongoing effort to promote her book.

Her friends from those days remember her working with determination in many projects, none being favoured over the other, and all the time doing the bulk of the writing, research, and communication herself. The projects took the form of briefs and policy position statements drafted and presented to elected officials at both provincial and federal levels through appearances at meetings of legislative committees, consultation sessions, and conferences. The subject matter naturally touched upon issues then seen as being of specific interest to women. But, consistent with the name of the club, the work also embraced the general concerns of people of both sexes in Canadian business.

Then, just as Elsie MacGill was building her reputation for involvement and action in this context, an opportunity to merge the blended interests of the club and her own business and to advance them on a national level came in the form of an invitation to make a submission to the landmark Royal Commission on Canada's Economic Prospects. Chaired by future Liberal finance minister and vocal nationalist Walter Gordon, the commission, which was formed amidst concern over increasing foreign ownership of Canadian industry and natural resources in 1955, completed its work by December 1956, sticking to a tough schedule and producing results in a mere 18 months. The discipline made an impression on Elsie.

Regarded as an important and comprehensive project, the Gordon Commission attracted considerable public interest. It looked at the long-term future of Canadian business and the economy in general, making amazingly accurate forecasts on population growth, the size of the labour force, and the development of specific economic sectors in Canada. Elsie was interested in many of the commission's areas of study and sought to add a unique voice to the national dialogue. Her submission, entitled "Results of Anticipated Increases in the Speed of Commercial Air Transport in Canadian Transportation Systems and Industry over the Next Quarter Century" was presented in February 1956. Elsie's paper would attract interest from many quarters as a thoughtful piece that touched on the impact of developments in nuclear engineering and education as well as in aviation and other transportation systems.

Elsie's enthusiasm for such policy issues and her capacity to mould high-profile initiatives were enough to earn her an honoured place within the world of Canadian business and professional women. A visionary leader in this context, she was also earning respect for her impressive skills as an administrator, and as a manager with an eye to technical details. Skills in sorting and filing documents, record-keeping, and correspondence were to serve her well in the lofty world of speeches and government briefs. At the Business and Professional Women's Clubs, many of her administrative systems and processes were applied and institutionalized for others to follow. Although Elsie considered a cluttered desk to be a virtuous illustration of many interests, and although her personal papers were routinely messy, folded, dog-eared, and marked up, she was invariably neat, orderly, and clear when keeping records for others.

The combination of erudition, thoughtful communication, leadership, energy, enthusiasm and attention to detail amazed even the most accomplished of her associates, who would still marvel at Elsie's output decades later. Soon, Elsie assumed official positions within the Toronto branch, setting the stage for her election in 1956 to a two-year term as president of the Federation's Ontario branch, where she continued and expanded her involvement into work that often became a full-time absorption.

Her personal files still drew correspondence, consultation documents, and other material that provides evidence of her continuing interest in aeronautical engineering during these years, the later part of the 1950s and the early 1960s. Indeed, she still attracted formal recognitions for her earlier engineering and aviation work, including accolades for her status as a business executive who had earlier been celebrated as the only woman of "the 50 Canadians responsible for the country's great industrial development"[367] during the postwar period.

But her engineering biographies and curriculum vitae show the period as empty of scientific and technical achievements. By the time she assumed the position of national president of the Canadian Federation of Business and Professional Women's Clubs (CFBPWC) in 1962, her evolution from engineer and manager into feminist advocate and leader was complete. By 1964, when her term in office ended, Elsie had built a unique national profile within the women's movement and earned respect in local communities and big-city halls of power alike. In many small towns across Canada,[368] she was known as the small woman who had ridden all night on a bus to reach them, the first national president of the Federation ever to visit their local club. Among government leaders in Toronto and Ottawa, Elsie was recognized as a formidable advocate who was "tolerant and good-humoured" in arguments, but also tenacious, devoted, and unfailingly well briefed and informed.

When, in 1964, Elsie left the presidency of the Federation, she was not in any real sense letting go of her cause. She continued, first as immediate past president and then, less officially, to contribute in many ways, particularly in what had become her special strength: writing and presenting briefs and policy papers. Elsie MacGill was a distinct and valued voice in the cause of women's rights, and she continued to provide inspiration as an engineer and business woman working in fields still considered male domains. As Canada entered the latter half of the 1960s, one in four women was working outside the home, and while this seems modest today, it was celebrated in some circles as a significant change from the ratio of one in 25 a few decades earlier.

Statistics on one facet of a social issue rarely capture its complexity and emotion, but these figures, simultaneously presenting significant change and enduring inequality, describe both the mood of the times and the approach to women's issues. Some commentators, usually male, seemed astonished that women were not satisfied at the rate of progress while other observers felt passionately that a gradual approach to an obvious injustice was insulting and illogical.

One of the latter group was Laura Sabia, a local politician from St. Catherines, Ontario, who, like Elsie MacGill, had used her position as president of a national women's organization to cultivate broader interest in women's issues and to advocate for change. Sabia had her own unique views on how to get things done, but she shared Elsie's perspective on the need for change and the importance of women taking personal responsibility for inducing it. Sabia felt that in order to gain the rights and status they deserved, Canadian women needed to change their own way of thinking, specifically to overcome a culture of submissiveness and acceptance of the unacceptable.

Sometimes, women like Sabia could point to government policy statements or specific provisions of divorce, citizenship, and property laws to delineate their issues. Other times, it was more difficult to articulate the humiliation and frustration of discrimination and what it meant to feel second class. Unlike the suffragette generation, who were mobilized, motivated, and coordinated by a clear and simple objective — the quest for the right to vote — the women's movement of the post-war period in Canada lacked a cohesion and instrument to poke at a system needing change.

The inspiration and an answer came partly from outside Canada. In 1961, the Camelot atmosphere of new ideas in the United States engendered by the early days of the Kennedy Administration in Washington included the launch of a Presidential Commission on the Status of Women. Spawned in the environment of the mushrooming civil rights movement, the commission would be headed by one of the century's most formidable forces for human rights, the former first lady and delegate to the United Nations, Eleanor Roosevelt. Roosevelt's unexpected death in the midst of the commission's work raised both its profile and public interest in the issues swirling around it. Their work also cemented the label "Status of Women" to the collection of issues variously branded women's rights, the equality of women and, later, women's liberation.

When it blew into Canada, the notion stirred a number of people, including the federal Minister of National Health and Welfare, Judy Lamarsh. Lamarsh tried but initially failed to convince Prime Minister Lester Pearson to follow the American model. Pearson reportedly balked at the idea because of media derision of the whole concept.

Nevertheless, LaMarsh, later a good friend to Elsie MacGill, played an important role inside the system and the government while others mustered the necessary external pressure on Pearson. This pressure was a result of work by many people, but Laura Sabia, then national president of the Canadian Federation of University Women, was particularly effective. Sabia was key in bringing 32 organizations together in 1966 to form the Committee for the Equality of Women (CEW). The committee, which embraced many ideals and objectives promoted by Elsie, began almost immediately to advance its collective interests under a call to the federal government to create a Royal Commission on the "Status of Women". A royal commission had the potential to induce changes in laws and national policies, and many of the women involved in CEW saw their campaign as a means to this end. Sabia had her own vision, which was simultaneously modest and grand. She saw a royal commission as a way to educate Canadians about women's issues and possibly to change attitudes. The country's prevailing attitudes about women's issues, she said, were the root of the problem.

Laura Sabia's campaign was very much a product of the same forces that propelled Elsie's involvement in the Business and Professional Women's Clubs. Both women were at the vanguard of the "second wave" of the women's movement, a natural outgrowth of the decades of social evolution following suffrage. As English Canadians, these women and their colleagues were, like Elsie, more comfortable with the process of briefs and hearings before the grand policy forum of the federal government. The notion of a "Royal" exercise in this spirit had a natural appeal.

Quebec Feminists

By the mid-1960s, women in Quebec were also banding together to advance their collective interests, notably through a new creation called the Fédération des femmes du Québec (FFQ). This provincially based grouping had a more parochial and thus more practical leaning. As such, the FFQ naturally focused its appeals at the provincial government in Québec. Provincial governments, having constitutional jurisdiction in the delivery of services in health, education, and social affairs, were involved in the real-world issues of interest to the women's organizations. The FFQ and its affiliates thus became early advocates of specific changes in services and programs while Elsie MacGill's English Canadian colleagues seemed attracted to broader policy discussions and debate under the royal commission umbrella.

It was, therefore, significant when the FFQ joined the campaign of the Committee for the Equality of Women. The pressure on the Government of Canada to respond was then magnified by a special, multidimensional credibility that spurred the growth of the movement beyond even what Elsie MacGill may have understood from her travels and study of history. For Canada, the 1960s represented a period of intensifying sensitivity to French–English relations, propelled in part by the far-ranging, multi-year, and high-profile Royal Commission on Bilingualism and Biculturalism then under way. The unity of women from the two founding cultures demanded endorsement and support.

Judy LaMarsh, for one, felt that this unified position embracing Quebec women was critical; the Government of Quebec, after all, had opposed the creation of a federal commission of inquiry on a subject it viewed as a provincial responsibility.

"I cannot see how it is any more the case than that of the Bicultural and Bilingual Commission", she said. "It seems odd to think that in some men's minds women belong predominantly to the provinces".[369]

To what extent this new bicultural feature of the campaign prompted the Pearson government to finally announce in February 1967 a Royal Commission on the Status of Women in Canada (RCSWC), it is difficult to say. Many popular accounts strongly suggest that Pearson acted primarily in the face of Sabia's ostentatious public threat to have two million women march on Parliament Hill. Other possibilities include backroom deals with the New Democratic Party members of parliament, who at the time were propping up the minority Liberal government.

In any case, Pearson was clearly aware of the presence and the persistence of the women's organizations and their leadership and sought to address this political pressure directly through the new commission. He may not, however, have been fully aware of the implications of his decision to create a commission with such far-reaching terms of reference or to give it such a broad mandate: to *"inquire into the status of women in Canada... to ensure for women equal opportunities with men in all aspects of Canadian society"*.[370] Both he and his appointed chair, CBC broadcaster Florence Bird, seemed unsure of what to do, initially emphasizing only legal questions pertaining to the position of women in the "labour market" and hinting that the issue of equal pay might be an appropriate matter for the commission to consider.[371]

Bird's early comments may have struck devoted members of the women's movement as simplistic and even uninformed. As someone who was relatively unknown both within the constituency that had advocated the royal commission and within the Canadian general public (which had questions about the commission's utility), she had a difficult task. For even though Bird was a popular journalist, broadcaster, and radio host, much of her public work had been done under the pen name "Anne Francis", making the appointment of "Florence Bird" to the important post a surprise to many Canadians.

Elsie and her sister together again at a conference in Montréal in 1960s.
(*Courtesy of Elizabeth Schneewind.*)

Bird, who was born Florence Rhein in Philadelphia in 1908 and later moved to Canada to live with her journalist husband John Bird, was drawn into her profession while living in Winnipeg during the war years. She applied her communications skills to the promotion of charitable causes and through her newspaper columns drew attention to the wartime contributions of women. So she brought a number of skills and an understanding of broader issues to the table, if not certified feminist credentials.

It made sense to wary politicians and cautious bureaucrats to appoint a chair with no obvious biases and a non-threatening aura. In fact, Laura Sabia and her menacing army of agitators were largely shut out of membership in the commission. In fact, only one of the seven commissioners was identified as "a feminist" and active in women's organizations by those directly involved in the project: "Miss Elsie Gregory MacGill". The Order-in-Council P.C. 1967-312 that established the commission identified Elsie as Miss; the chair was listed as Mrs. John Bird.

Judy LaMarsh intimated that she recommended Elsie along with other commissioners,[372] two of whom were men: Jacques Henripin and John P. Humphrey (who replaced Donald Gordon Jr. after his resignation early in the process). The other female members, Lola M. Lange, Jeanne Lapointe, and Doris Ogilvie, would later be identified as converts to feminism, transformed by the experience arrayed before them in February 1967 when they began their work on the commission. If Sabia had wished for a position on the commission for herself, she would eventually take comfort from Elsie MacGill's appointment, recognizing Elsie as someone who had sound credentials and had "been talking about equal opportunity and equal pay for work of equal value since the '50s".

"She has always been ahead of her time", Sabia would recall in later describing Elsie to a reporter. "I've seen her walk onstage with canes, hardly able to move. Then she speaks, and socks it to them. Fire and Brimstone. Wow! I'm in awe of her".[373]

In citing Elsie's appointment in her memoirs, LaMarsh referenced only one point with respect to Elsie's feminist credentials — "whose mother had been one of the first of Canada's fighters for women's rights"[374] — which suggests that Elsie's profile and credibility were at least partly a function of her 1955 biography of her mother and that her mother's achievements may even have been more important to some minds than Elsie's personal contributions to the women's movement to this point.

The commission began like most major projects with a review of existing literature, studies, essays, and research to inform the commissioners and their staff on prior thinking and any available data. Elsie MacGill may have been among the more informed within the group, but her related academic knowledge was limited. Although she had been a graduate-level researcher, a published scientist, and an active member of the women's movement, her opportunities to reflect in a formal way had been constrained.

Today feminism is well established as both a field and an influence on other areas of study. Four decades ago, there was a paucity of material to use in framing the royal commission's work. Feminist thinkers of the time were guided by a mere handful of works less than a few decades old. These included the 1949 *Le Deuxième Sexe* by French writer Simone de Beauvoir, who articulated, for many, the need for common structures to give people options independent of their sex. Within this narrow context, the commission decided to authorize and fund special studies relevant to both the specific and the general circumstances of Canadian women. While the number and scope of these studies were not as great as some might have wanted, they were constructive and advanced the commission's work in important ways.

In any case, this thoughtful, behind-the-scenes work is not what the Royal Commission on the Status of Women would come to represent for most Canadians. The commission was instead admired for its practical, real-world image, as a forum where women came from many walks of life to describe their personal lives, thoughts, and experience within Canadian society. Through public hearings, media exposure, and individual presentations, the commission's work over the following three years steadily captured the interest of the Canadian public despite a bumpy start enveloped in condescension and even ridicule from some male politicians and journalists.

"We are not getting through to men", Elsie said during the commission's early days. "They seem amused by the commission or adopt the attitude that anything to do with women has nothing to do with them".[375]

The subsequent change in attitudes came in large part from the compelling and moving testimony by women appearing before the commission at its hearings across the country. The hearings were the first of their kind to be covered on television and, more importantly, nationally on CBC Radio, thereby bringing the stories of individual Canadian women appearing before the commission into almost every Canadian home.[376] The presenters included women from small towns and aboriginal women with particular concerns and experience as well as national organizations speaking on behalf of broad interests and issues. Elsie MacGill, who had seen women from across the country arriving in Fort William and adjusting to a male work environment in her aircraft plant and who had travelled the country meeting with active women's groups while president of a national organization, was in her element in these hearings, engaged and supportive.

Elsie was one of the most active and influential members of the commission. Some suggest that she was the driving force and an even more important component of its success than the chair. For her part, Florence Bird considered Elsie to be the de facto deputy chair of the commission even though one was not formally appointed. Perhaps thinking about Eleanor Roosevelt's unexpected death in the midst of her commission's work, Bird felt early in the process that she needed to identify someone among the other commissioners to be her "confidant" and "right hand", ready to step in and continue should she herself fall seriously ill or otherwise be unable to carry on. Elsie did this and more. Bird later said that, throughout the nearly four years of the project, "Elsie was my guide, philosopher, and friend" and made her feelings clear: "the report would not have been as fine as it was if Elsie had not been there".[377]

The two women worked well as a team. Two very different personalities, they did not always agree on the implications of testimony before the commission or even on logistical plans for its hearings. But Bird enjoyed talking to Elsie and used her as a sounding board, seeking her out regularly, by phone when necessary, to hash out ideas and issues, to share their indignation, and just to laugh. The two shared qualities of patience and wisdom that allowed them to resolve their differences into a greater whole. In fact, the entire commission seemed to work in this way. Unknown to each other prior to their appointments, the seven members came to the table with varied backgrounds, biases, and suggestions, creating a situation ripe with exponential possibilities. Although it took some time to air and iron out their differences, Elsie felt it was possible to "argue like mad" and still be "careful to respect each other's ideas".

Elsie even suggested that the group became so respectful and aware of each other's opinions that it acted as an organic whole that was more than the sum of those present at a given meeting. On the rare occasion when a member missed a meeting, for example, the remaining members would take time to discuss what their missing partner "probably" would have said.

One quality Bird and some of the others did not always share with Elsie, was unbounded energy. Aside from using her status as a commissioner to be excused from jury duty in Toronto in 1968, Elsie continued to fulfill other obligations even as she tackled the commission's work with full force. The tiny, afflicted body of Elsie MacGill could soldier on morning, noon, and night, pushing the others without any visible sign of fatigue, whereas Bird, by her own admission, was often exhausted by the work and known to take long afternoon naps.

There were several reasons why Elsie was a source of vigour and support for the other members. One was her renowned sense of humour. One colleague with whom Elsie had a special bond with was Doris Ogilvie of New Brunswick, a commissioner who like Elsie's mother was her province's pioneering female judge in the juvenile courts. Judge Ogilvie and Elsie, who by then — having written her mother's story — was informed on a jurist's reality, found conversation easy and invigorating even during the most tense and trying days.

"Elsie made us laugh so much", Ogilvie would say years later. She and others saw Elsie's sense of humour as a special gift that helped solve problems and fuel the courage they all needed to advance their cause. They may not, however, have recognized the invisible hand of her engineer's training in their work. Scholarly reviews of commission records have compared Elsie's input in the structuring and development of ideas to the application of scientific principles in manufacturing.[378] Like an engineer, she constantly sought ways to optimize the use of scarce resources, to forecast the impact of creative ideas, and to build a functioning machine from a collection of parts.

It is therefore not surprising that historians and students of the commission's work see evidence that, as the commission marched through the years of hearings, briefs, and debates, Elsie was "the moving force".[379] In all, the commission was presented with a total of 469 briefs during its formal work. The briefs dealt with a wide range of well-known issues (equal pay for work of equal value, for instance), but also raised the profile of specific problems (such as the antiquated and discriminatory elements of the *Indian Act)*, and new agendas such as child care that were beginning to attract wider support in the context of changing employment patterns and demographics.

When Prime Minister Trudeau tabled the commission's final report in the House of Commons in late 1970, its 167 recommendations comprised a comprehensive collection of interests and ideas that together amounted to a call for a complete rethinking of attitudes and policies towards women in Canada. It covered all the important issues, national and local, raised in the hearings, and set priorities for all regions. It even confronted the then highly controversial and soul-wrenching issue of abortion, elevating the debate to new heights in Canada. This happened in large part because Elsie MacGill emphasized the point with a unique, separate statement on the abortion question.[380] Some referred to it as a "minority report", but Elsie was careful not to label her one-page commentary as such because she did not want to be seen as undermining the main recommendations on abortion in the full report.

Yet she felt that she could not withhold her views. The abortion issue, more than any other, caused her to reflect and to struggle. During the hearings, proponents of freer abortion laws and opponents of abortion alike presented their arguments with immense passion. Elsie recognized the "tremendous sincerity" behind all of the presentations and, like her colleagues, wrestled with the options. In the end, however, she chose to stand alone in advocating that abortion be completely removed from the Criminal Code of Canada and be made "a private medical matter between a patient and her doctor".[381] Elsie's words would echo through the abortion debate in Canada for the rest of her life and beyond. For many, it made her an icon of the feminist cause. But the full picture of her position on feminist issues is likely best captured by a reminder that her "separate statement" included a second, less-publicized issue: the idea that rights should be linked with responsibilities. In this regard, she outlined her opposition to suggested income tax rules that would confer benefits to the "marriage unit", arguing that such structures encouraged a culture of financial dependency among women, particularly young women.

Wishing to be seen as responding quickly to the report, the progressive Trudeau government announced a new cabinet position with specific responsibility for the status of women (the first incumbent was a man) as a prelude to the creation of the Canadian Advisory Council on the Status of Women.[382] Such measures were meant to be more than symbolic acknowledgements of the commission's work, the government stressed, as a basis for further action. In the meantime, however, it was thought that Elsie and her colleagues should be encouraged and appreciative of the government's gestures to date, and regard them merely as a first step.

Yet Elsie was "not really pleased".[383] When it came to implementing the commission's recommendations, "she wanted it done — yesterday!"[384]

Chapter X

Following Through to the End

"... there is Elsie, leading us all".385

With the tabling of the Royal Commission's report in December 1970, Elsie and her fellow commissioners, as per standard practice, were formally thanked for their services and told that their government appointments, salaries, and official standing had come to an end. All had personal lives and professional interests that had been subordinated for years to their work with the commission, and most felt an ache to resume where they had left off before the all-consuming project came along.

But not Elsie MacGill. A personality and mindset built upon experiential knowledge of the value of persistence, Elsie recognized that the work had really only just begun and felt obliged to continue on even though she also knew her consulting business had suffered significantly from her involvement in the commission.

Royal commissions in Canada are often notorious as majestic, expensive exercises launched to deflect public pressure from a government resistant to change. The cliché of a royal commission report is a thick, dust-covered volume (or volumes) sitting on a high shelf out of sight. If this particular commission's 167 wide-ranging recommendations were to be implemented, it would involve a concerted, if not Herculean, effort on the part of all levels of government, the private sector, and voluntary organizations all across Canada. Beyond the simple effecting of a string of individual actions, the realization of the vision set out in the report would also require a grander dialogue to communicate its contents and to change a country's way of thinking.

She was not alone, but Elsie MacGill stood out among those who felt responsible for following through on the release of the report, and she launched a drive to see it adopted in practices and policies. Indeed, her efforts to follow up the work may well have been more influential than her very substantial contributions to the commission itself.[386]

Perhaps because she saw her own hand so clearly in the commission's output, she felt an acute personal obligation to it. She thus undertook a personal campaign to share the report and to lobby for its full implementation. Without any official status, working as a volunteer, she set out in 1971 to promote the report across Canada, her speaking events often organized by groups such as her pre-commission platform, the many Business and Professional Women's Clubs.[387]

As she travelled and spoke about the report, she encountered a mixed response, most of it thoughtful and well informed, some a frivolous throwback to the early days of the commission's work, when it was the butt of such jokes and diversions as a routine call for a counter-commission for men. Abortion was of course a regular focus for questions and debates at her speaking engagements, but Elsie refrained from advancing her own views, adhering mostly to the report's official, more restrained position on the subject. Other recommendations that drew fire included the call for a $500 per year cash allowance for each child under the age of 16, a proposal some people felt ran counter to international campaigns to control population growth. Without dismissing such comments out of hand, Elsie was quick to observe that few women decide to have a baby on the basis of an extra $40 or so per month.[388]

While acknowledging that the subject of child care and nurseries seemed to attract interest in most parts of the country, she refused in her presentations to rank the recommendations in order of importance, feeling that each one represented an essential measure and an important concern even if the issue only touched a small subset of the female population. The lot of women in prisons was one issue she considered important even though it directly affected few individuals.

Predictably, Elsie was also pestered during her speaking tours to talk of her personal life, specifically her mother's influence and her own decision to keep her maiden name after marriage. Some women were still, in the early 1970s, surprised to learn that they had the legal right to keep their maiden names in Canada. By this time, Elsie, whose mother Judge Gregory MacGill had tacked her maiden name onto her husband's surname when she married seven decades earlier, found the suggestion that a

Elsie after receiving an honorary degree at the University of Toronto in 1973 (*Library and Archives Canada; photo by Robert Lansdale.*).

woman might be barred from retaining her name bewildering, particularly since it was by then a common practice for women in other countries to keep their maiden names after marriage.

In all these discussions, she proved to be an eloquent, informed and effective advocate for women's rights and the burgeoning feminist cause. Her speeches, interviews, and meetings contributed to a growing chorus stressing that the work captured in the report of the Royal Commission was not over. Spurred by new thinking and articulated in books like Betty Friedan's *The Feminine Mystique* and later Germaine Greer's *The Female Eunuch*, the women's movement was empowered even more by academic papers, scholarly debate, and new voices enunciating the early elements of feminist theory. It was at this point that Elsie's sociologist sister Helen began to reflect upon her own field and experiences as a woman and to come to the same conclusions as her younger sister had reached by a different route.

Amidst the debate over the RCSWC's report, some voices were louder, angrier, and more pointed than those who had advocated the commission a decade earlier and even stronger than the voices heard at its public hearings. While the commission was doing its work in Canada, the women's movement was evolving internationally and assuming new dimensions, including more aggressive calls for action in what would come to be branded as Women's Liberation — " women's lib". Fostered in an environment of civil-rights and anti-war protests in the United States in the late 1960s, the American Women's Liberation Movement burst forth in demonstrations aimed at drawing public attention and media interest.

Although Canadians witnessed some protest demonstrations of this type, the recommendations of the royal commission provided an alternative means of advancing such interests. They offered not only a tool for dialogue, but also a focus for collective action that involved the government and the Canadian public as well as a broad spectrum from among the advocates for women's rights.

In 1971, in an attempt to ensure the commission's enduring impact, Laura Sabia, who had been excluded from formal membership, resurrected the coalition that had originally called for the commission's creation. To this end, Sabia and others organized discussions and meetings culminating in the launch of the National Action Committee on the Status of Women (NAC), a new body demanding "action" from the federal government. It began with 30 organizations under its umbrella, all dedicated to the implementation of the royal commission report and acting in the same spirit and fashion as the campaigns that had led to the report and, a half century earlier, brought about women's suffrage. When what would later be seen as a NAC founding meeting was held in April 1972 in Toronto, the participants were not initially sure how they would proceed, but, sensing history, they had the event filmed. The footage shows a small, delicate woman in the middle of the group acting as if she was the chief organizer: "there is Elsie, leading us all," a future NAC president would say of the film years later. [389]

NAC grew into an organization with an enormous reach, embracing hundreds of smaller groups and indirectly touching millions of women in the years ahead. Elsie was active within its affiliates and participated in complementary bodies such as the Ontario Status of Women Committee.[390]

Along with its Quebec-based partner the FFQ and other bodies, NAC provided the tool to hold the government's feet to the fire. Many individuals including Sabia have claim to the role of pivotal personalities and founders of NAC, and there are so many perspectives on how the organization was born and evolved that even NAC does not venture a definitive, official description. But Elsie was certainly among the early leaders and a unique force within them. She attended every NAC public meeting throughout its early years and was extremely active behind the scenes, applying her then highly polished skill as a writer and presenter of briefs, daring strategist, and focused, methodical, engineering-style administrator enthusiastically to the cause.[391]

Because of these skills, her disarming sense of humour, and her overall effectiveness in advancing issues, Elsie was sometimes labelled the "most important"[392] person within the Canadian women's movement during the 1970s even though she did not hold important official positions within the high-profile elements of the movement.

Her seminal contributions to NAC and her involvement in the grander lobbying campaign were an enriching and rewarding experience for Elsie that would come to rival her time on the commission itself. As the months and years passed, Elsie saw the commission's recommendations pass, one by one, from words to reality in a process both painfully slow and yet very impressive: slow in the context of the obviously long-overdue change;

impressive in a world of multiple influences, government processes, and the normally glacial evolution of societal attitudes.

Within months of the report's completion, Elsie could point to a string of actions and to what she saw, even then, as its "considerable impact". She would cite steps to amend the *Unemployment Insurance Act* to allow for benefits during maternity leave; changes in the works to give women equal access to mortgages under the *National Housing Act*; and an intent to update the federal *Citizenship and Immigration Act* to ensure the equality of women. Stressing that the commission's report was directed at all levels of government and at other sectors as well,[393] Elsie also drew satisfaction from action taken on the ground by voluntary organizations such as Planned Parenthood. Unexpectedly popular as a book, the report had to be reprinted within months of its release, with other reprints to follow. The commission was soon touted as a landmark in Canadian history and its report as a central document in the formation of modern Canadian society.

To keep the pressure on the federal government, scorecards were kept on the government's progress in implementing the commission's recommendations. Within a decade, by Florence Bird's estimation, nearly 100 of the 167 would be either fully or substantially implemented.[394] Bird would later assert without qualification that by this measure the royal commission was the most successful such exercise in Canadian history.

Numbers like these are imperfect measures, and the full impact of the Royal Commission of the Status of Women is perhaps better understood by noting that women and women's issues started to affect other areas of society, areas important to the cause, such as public policy and politics. While Elsie's 1955 vision of a female Canadian prime minister would not be realized until the 1990s, women, particularly those influenced by the commission and its aftermath, began to seek and secure public office as advocated in Chapter 7 of the report ("Participation of Women in Public Life"). Many of her friends thought Elsie would make a great member of parliament, and Doris Anderson, the influential editor of *Chatelaine*, was among those who encouraged her to consider running for public office. Elsie declined the invitation, still pronouncing herself a businesswoman and engineer, not a politician.[395]

Although she had bemoaned the lack of women in positions of power for several decades, Elsie was strangely hostile to the idea of participating herself in party politics, and chided friends like Lorna Marsden when they promoted this approach as the best way to build coalitions and turn ideas into legislative and regulatory action. Elsie contended that one needed to have the freedom to criticize all political parties when necessary and to work with those who deserved support when they were on the right path.

Whereas the voice of women in the House of Commons had been limited in the 1960s to a few pioneers like Elsie's friend, Liberal cabinet minister Judy LaMarsh, the 1970s and decades beyond would witness a number of gains, although far short of equality, in the political arena. Florence Bird was appointed to the Canadian Senate, where she championed recognition of gender equality in the 1982 Canadian Charter of Rights and Freedoms. Laura Sabia ran for a seat in parliament, and although she failed, others succeeded.

One who did succeed was a young sociologist and academic from Quebec, Monique Bégin, elected as a Pierre Trudeau Liberal in 1972 and destined to join his cabinet, holding several senior positions until her retirement from politics in 1984. Bégin had been active in social issues for many years and in support of many causes, but her profile and appeal in politics came from her role as Executive Secretary of the Royal Commission on the Status of Women, essentially the administrative director of the project. She was influenced by many aspects of the work and the experience, but decades later Minister Bégin would still recall the courage and wisdom of one commissioner in particular: Elsie MacGill.

Bégin admired Elsie's "great energy and stamina… [and] the amount of work she could do"[396] and was inspired by Elsie's open mind and ability to accept as natural ideas that seemed revolutionary to others. With her political career was behind her, Bégin would write that, although as a servant of the commission she had neither the authority nor the right to break ranks, to join Elsie in what Bégin called the "minority report" on the issue of abortion, signing Elsie's report would have been her "real choice".[397] While a member of parliament, Bégin demonstrated the truth of that statement by rising in the House of Commons to call for the decriminalization of abortion in Canada, reciting Elsie's precise words — that it should be considered "a private medical matter between patient and doctor".[398]

As Elsie's influence reverberated from parliament to church-basement meeting halls across Canada, the experience and contemplation of the previous few years suffused Elsie and her perceptions of the world, specifically her treasured early identity as a professional engineer. She also started to see her field in a new light.

Whereas, 25 years earlier, Elsie was able to begin that October 1946 magazine article by saying, without qualification, that "No particular barriers face women entering professional engineering in Canada", she now spoke with frustration about the employers who would refuse to interview women for engineering positions still considered male, noting that female university graduates were finding that first job very difficult to get.

Two and a half decades of reflection and feminist experience had altered her position. She had once put the onus on women themselves; if thwarted, they should try elsewhere or just knock harder on the doors of engineering schools or firms barred to them. Now, she criticized personnel managers and recruiters as "prejudiced", rejecting the widely held notion that to succeed in engineering, women had to be better than men.

When she was young and busy, trying to master the technical side of her profession and confronting the daily pressures of the engineering shop, Elsie's focus on the job at hand had prevented her from recognizing the informal networking and gender-specific dialogue underlying professional decisions and influencing careers. Now, in the 1970s, she would jokingly jab at the aircraft business, suggesting that "having a unisex washroom" might help break down the male power clique and even level the playing field.

Elsie's more detached, clear-eyed view of the engineering profession came as she entered normal retirement years and at a time when she might have been expected to disengage from the scientific and technical aspects of her life. But as it turned out, it was also a time when she encountered more opportunities to share her views and to contribute to her former profession in a new way.

As is common in many eventful lives, Elsie's later years were marked by many accolades and formal recognitions of her achievements. Although sprinkled throughout her life, awards and honours started to flow her way with seeming regularity during the 1970s, beginning with appointment as an Officer of the Order of Canada *"for services... as a member of the Royal Commission on the Status of Women"* and also, gratifyingly, for services *"as an aeronautical engineering consultant"*. Distinct from her many professional awards, the Officer level of the Order of Canada is rewarded for outstanding public service at the national level, or for work that touches a broad spectrum of Canadian society. The investiture took place at the Governor General's residence on October 29, 1971.[399] This singular honour for national service complemented her 1967 Centennial Medal, and in 1977 was added to by the Queen's Jubilee Medal.

During these years, she received honorary doctorate degrees from a number of universities: Toronto in 1973, Windsor in 1976, and in 1978, both Queen's and York. In 1975, she had occasion to return to her childhood home to receive the Award of Distinction and honorary membership in the Alumni Association of the University of British Columbia, the institution that now noted her one term in engineering and limited early 1920s undergraduate studies in "the Shacks" with pride.

Having studied at UBC, Toronto, Michigan, and MIT, Elsie appreciated being recognized by her old schools, and enjoyed the opportunity to share her thoughts with students, colleagues, and admirers at the ceremonies where she received her honorary degrees and other awards. Sometimes, in the days leading up to a specific award or honour, she would be interviewed by the media about her achievements, and increasingly she was sought out as a unique voice at the confluence of broad social concerns notable for her experience as a woman in a traditionally male profession. She used these platforms to advance the issues she had absorbed during her time on the royal commission and to campaign against persistent injustices, particularly on behalf of less fortunate women.

During the hearings, Elsie had come face to face with many women who were clearly her equal in their capacity to adapt, endure, and confront difficult circumstance, and also with many women who were far worse off than she. The experience helped erase any residue of what Bill Soulsby saw as her mother's "silly" snobbish influence, which had manifested over the years in such mannerisms such as Elsie's derision of costume jewelry and, on occasion, in ill-considered comments such as "she is just the maid".[400] Now, more than ever, Elsie deprecated her own experience and joked about any suggestion that she had been mistreated or any inference that she had succeeded only because she was an "exceptional [woman]... who has made it in a man's world".[401]

"Engineers [in general]... are a favoured group, a relatively fortunate, educated, small middle-class group", she told a national conference marking the International Women's Year of 1975. "Women engineers rarely

Elsie receiving the Order of Canada from the Right Honourable Roland Michener, Canada's Governor General (1971). (*Library and Archives Canada PA 194420; Dominion-Wide Limited.*)

meet the conditions of deprivation and real hardship that the great mass of employed women meet: low level pay, low level work, low level working conditions".[402]

By considering the lot of others with more sensitivity, she began as well to develop more compassion and concern about her own profession of engineering and an awareness of the persistent biases impeding the careers of young women entering the field.

"They do meet handicaps in their professional development that male engineers do not", she acknowledged upon reaching the age of 70, recognizing that these handicaps not only hurt individual careers, but also prevent women engineers from making their full contribution to their country and the world.

"[Gender bias in engineering damages] the whole profession by diluting its quality, its worth, and its value to Canada",[403] she once said.

Now, despite her aversion to expounding upon the details of any difficulties in her own personal professional journey, Elsie never failed, in speeches, to let her audience know that she was a trained aeronautical engineer with close to 50 years experience, a still-active "busy practice", and an enduring interest in new developments in her field and in what she saw as a lack of vision. Because much of her most active engineering work occurred prior to the jet age, she was never quite able to move into this new era of technology as a practitioner. Yet she was able to see jet-age issues from a higher perspective — in a holistic way sometimes seen as a feminine strength. This allowed her to offer relevant and insightful observations on the modern world of engineering and technological development well into her seventies. Her speeches and correspondence during this time rang with blunt comments that revealed a fiercely quick mind still attuned to the technical as well as current social issues.

"Today we realize that to insure our survival on planet Earth it may be necessary to turn for our sources of energy, materials, food, and lebensraum to the last frontier, interplanetary space",[404] she told students at York University in June 1978. When she discussed space exploration, Elsie often blended the intricacies of international affairs, peace, nuclear arms, law, and the environment with scientific and technical issues.

She did this to impress upon young people that even though her life had witnessed many advances in engineering and science, many exciting challenges still awaited those who sought to serve humanity through this field. On some occasions around this time, she also used her platform to prod her professional engineering colleagues to strive to do better and to do more for the world, citing specific persistent and important issues such as the enduring and dangerous problem of cracks in aircraft bodies.[405]

She had many opportunities to speak about the issues facing her profession during these years. In addition to her academic honours, she continued to receive recognition as a working engineer. The award presentations would in part recall her years in the Hawker Hurricane team and the pioneering era of the 1930s aviation industry, but now those standing at the podium introducing Elsie and celebrating her achievements would also speak of her broader public-service contributions to her profession through her work with the International Civil Aviation Organization (ICAO) and her role in defining international regulations that set the context for aeronautical innovation around the world. The Engineering Institute of Canada — which had given her special credibility by accepting her as its first woman corporate or full member in 1938, and professional recognition with its Gzowski Medal in 1941 — once again formally recognized her achievements in 1973. The Julian C. Smith Award, however, spoke to her broader national contributions, her "Achievement in the Development of Canada".

Yet despite these high-level public service honours, she was especially proud of the gold medal she was awarded by the Professional Engineers of Ontario in 1979 — a first for a woman — seeing it as recognition of her professional skill as much as its stated, daunting criteria of "*making a difference in the lives of Canadians*". Even on this occasion, she managed to mock her career and profile calling it "ironic" that her gold medal was worth over ten times as much as the one given to engineer and politician C.D. Howe (because the price of gold was no longer pegged at "$35.00 CDN per ounce") even though her contributions were, in her mind, "much less".

"Perhaps, Bill and I should ask for a police escort going home tonight",[406] she added.

Of all the honours that came her way in the 1970s, the most touching and poignant recalled Elsie's youthful dreams and the year they were altered by illness. When in January 1975 she was informed that "the Ninety-Nines",[407] the International Association of Women Pilots, was awarding her the Amelia Earhart Medal, Elsie was 70 years old and had long before put aside dreams of ever flying a plane let alone being honoured as a pilot. Yet this pioneering women's organization, founded just months after Elsie's graduation in 1929, saw Elsie not only as someone who embodied the spirit and courage of the organization's first president, but also as someone who deserved a pilot's distinction, having steered the demonstration and trials of her aircraft and spent many hours as an observer on test flights. Alongside her at the medal presentation was another inspiring recipient, 84-year-old Louise Jenkins, whose exploits highlighted the bold adventure imbedded in the award. Jenkins was the first woman on Prince Edward Island to gain a pilot's license, and the pilot who set a record flying from Montréal to Charlottetown in February 1933.[408]

It was a wonderful recognition of the reality of Elsie's bravery, fundamental understanding of aircraft, and passion for flying. The medal was small enough to be worn as one would a military decoration, as she did whenever the occasion permitted, welcoming questions about both it and the Ninety-Nines. When asked to give up the medal for a museum-style exhibit in 1977, she was relieved and grateful to learn that a replica could be made so she might continue to wear it as a conversation piece, one that continues to amuse and inspire succeeding generations of her family.[409]

Other women's organization wished to celebrate Elsie's courage. In 1978, the Zonta Club of Toronto presented her with "The Outstanding Adventurer Award" for her "exemplary pioneering and adventurous spirit" and citing her work with the royal commission, where she performed, as Florence Bird later put it, with "more guts than anyone [they] had] ever known".[410]

As she passed through the eighth decade of her life, Elsie needed to call upon her courage and spirit more and more as time took its toll on friends, family, and her own body, which now felt the combined impact of age and persistent disability. Her half-brother Eric passed away in 1972 while still living in his much-loved, long-time home in Phillips Arm, British Columbia. His wife, Elsie's sister-in-law Annie,[411] followed him the year after.

It was difficult. Despite the distance, Eric had worked hard over the years to keep in touch with his sisters, whom he still called "HelNelsie" well into old age. For many decades, the siblings kept in touch through weekly letters, carbon-copied and passed around through the mail. Elsie might have felt the thread to her family and childhood had grown a little thinner with his death, but another generation along her lines was budding across Canada and the United States. Her brother's son, another Eric, the one who had been a prisoner of war, had married and was now a father, and Young Helen's daughters were also married. Elsie's namesake niece, Elizabeth "Elsie" Schneewind, had three daughters including another Elizabeth, and Elsie's stepson John Soulsby had made Elsie a step-grand-mother three times over.

She soldiered on, never acknowledging any significant pain or discomfort. When, 50 years after her illness and 25 after her broken leg, she started using a wheelchair once again, she said it was to make life easier for her friends and family, whom she feared would have to wait for her slow-moving legs when out doing errands. Elsie made this claim even though her husband Bill often joked that she seemed to speed up markedly "whenever she's shopping for clothes".

During these years, nevertheless, Elsie became active in a variety of other ways. She contributed to a range of community and cultural organizations, being named, for example, as a life member of the Art Gallery of Ontario for her support of the gallery's programs. She continued to work in public service roles both federal and provincial. For instance, she became the first woman member and then, after January 1980, the first woman chair of the Ontario Building Code Branch's Building Materials Evaluation Committee.[412] There she took her aeronautical design and stress analysis expertise to a new field aligned with public safety and, periodically, to issues pertaining to the needs of people with disabilities.

Even though she did everything she could to avoid being seen as disabled, she now lent her support to the disabled, accepting, for example, a position on the Canadian Organizing Committee (COC) preparing for the International Year of the Disabled in 1981, and making substantial contributions to the COC's planning work and its special report on the disabled in Canada.

With age, she struggled more obviously with her canes and needed the wheelchair more and more. It was an adjustment. For most of the half century of her disability, Elsie had dismissed her condition as "troublesome, but irrelevant"[413] to her work and her personal life. Still, she understood the stigma attached to disability and had great empathy for others facing the psychological and physical hurdles.

"I know it takes an effort to harden your heart to use it — at least it did me... I put it off as long as I could", she told a friend faced with using a wheelchair for the first time and needing encouragement.

Elsie was never anxious to see a doctor or surrender even a sliver of her independence. When weakened muscles and disability compelled her to use a catheter to drain urine from her bladder, she would regularly insert the tube herself. This self-treatment may have been a factor in the development of a urinary tract infection in early 1980. Antibiotics were prescribed, and she took them and felt better for a while, but did not follow up with the doctor as quickly as Bill and her stepchildren advocated, even when her breathing became laboured.

"He's a urologist", she said. "Lungs are not his department".[414]

The link between certain medications and the scarring of lung tissue is still a question for debate in the medical community, but years later Elsie's family would see the antibiotics she was prescribed as the trigger for the hacking cough and shortness of breath that followed.

Even with this discomfort and obvious fatigue, Elsie decided that she and Bill should take a short trip in late September 1980 to visit her sister Helen. Helen was living in Cambridge, Massachusetts, with her now-venerated sociologist husband Everett, who had, nearly two decades earlier at the age of 64, settled at Brandeis University to start the final phase of his career. There, he built the university's first graduate department of sociology, passing the last years of his scholarly life in the lofty academic atmosphere of Cambridge.[415]

Despite her weaknesses and chronic problems, Elsie could intimate that she would be helping her sister, who had her own challenges by this time. Everett, the esteemed researcher, author, and professor who had headed the American Sociological Association, had been elected as a member of the American Academy of Arts and Sciences, had been sought after for his wisdom around the world, and had been "much loved"[416] by Elsie, was showing the first terrible signs of what would be labelled a Parkinson's-like disease.

Shortly after her arrival in Cambridge, Elsie's condition worsened. Helen took her to the MacGill Hughes' family doctor. From there she was rushed to the Harvard-affiliated Mount Auburn Hospital in Cambridge where the staff informed her that the scarring of her lungs had progressed

Elsie near the end of her life when she resumed using a wheelchair. (*Courtesy of Helen Hughes Brock.*)

to the point that the air sacs were being replaced by thick fibroid tissue.[417]

Pulmonary fibrosis was added to Elsie's medical biography.

Over the next month, her ability to transfer oxygen into her bloodstream steadily declined, and she started to fade away. The situation was clearly serious, and Bill felt he could not miss a day from her side. His daughter Ann came from Toronto to see Elsie for Thanksgiving and returned a few weeks later when her brother John, living in Montréal, joined her to visit with their ailing stepmother for what would be the last time.

As her family and friends considered the prospect of not having Elsie in their lives much longer, they reflected upon what they would miss most and what they would recall about her. There were many things: her intellect, her commitment, and her caring. Bill Soulsby thought simply once again that she was "a blessing". Elsie's sister was flooded with touching and evocative memories. She would soon be writing out those recollections for a memorial service speech that emotion would prevent her from delivering herself.

The list of Elsie's admirable qualities was long in most people's minds, but it rarely included her disability. Instead, the most commonly cited quality and element of Elsie's life would, perhaps surprisingly, be her wonderful capacity for playfulness, her childlike sense of humour, and "merry heart".[418] The jokester who cheered the work of the royal commission and who spiced up speeches to engineering groups also brought thousands of chuckles and smiles to her home and her friendships. Elsie was both witty in a clever way and a whimsical comic who kept humorous clippings and wrote parodies of songs.

She could sound gruff, act dismissively when someone talked about her "tough time" or call her a "hero", and even presented herself as a "curmudgeon", as she did in her last high-profile media interview weeks before her trip to Cambridge.[419] Yet she always did these things and made her wise cracks with smiles, "chuckles", and a twinkle in her eye. Friends would tease her about the magazine interview, suggesting she was such a light-hearted joker that she couldn't make a convincing curmudgeon even when she tried.

In her final hours, when she seemed weighed down, unable to speak, and weak in her hospital bed, she smiled, winked, and lifted her arm to scribble a Groucho-style moustache on a smiley face picture drawn by her grand-niece.[420]

In the days and hours before closing her eyes forever on November 4, 1980, Elsie MacGill often looked on the face of her sister, a reflection of her mother's example and the golden thread of her childhood that had weaved through the ups and downs of her whole life, and she felt the love of Bill Soulsby,[421] the man Elsie had met at the height of her engineering career.

These were the great, intertwined influences and passions of that dramatic and important life.[422]

Epilogue

"Those of us who would like the world to be populated with more courageous and creative people than it currently holds might be well advised to conduct more systematic studies of family environments and other conditions that produce women engineers"[423]

They were bright, energetic, young women poised at the threshold of interesting careers and lives. Some were talking with friends in the hallways; others were eating and laughing in the cafeterias; but most were settled into their seats in the sanctuary of a university classroom. Snow covered the ground and the tops of the cars outside. Christmas and holidays were just a few weeks away, and a few decorations hung from the walls of the building.

Several of the young women felt a little stiff, sore, and tired having spent the day working in laboratories, drafting rooms, and shops. Because they wanted careers as professional engineers, they knew they would need the practical experience of a machinery setting and the factory floor as well as their academic studies at the École Polytechnique, which is affiliated with the Université de Montréal.[424] For this reason, they took courses in the evening.

There was little warning. A slight, boyish figure appeared suddenly in their midst. At first, the professor and the 60 young men and women in the evening engineering class barely noticed his entrance, and thought he was making a strange joke when he waved the small-calibre rifle at them. He ordered the men to one side of the room, the women to the other. No one moved until he fired into the ceiling. Herding the men outside, as he barked "J'haïs les féministes", Marc Lépine then walked about slowly and calmly, firing rounds at the terrified young women, some pleading for their lives and crying. His gun jammed at one point, but he unlocked it and resumed his hunt for women. He strolled through other floors of the building, ultimately killing 13 female students, one female clerk, and one male: himself. He wounded 13 others that night, including some young men who tried to protect their female friends. But women were the gunman's target.

It was the evening of December 6, 1989.

Less than a decade had passed since Elsie MacGill's death, and while her now 86-year-old sister and other friends felt that Elsie's life had been cut short, even they were relieved to know she had been spared the numbing pain of this night.

Sixty years earlier, Elsie had herself been cut down while still in university by a scourge that was never given a proper diagnosis. The trauma that befell Canadian society that night in 1989 was equally difficult to comprehend. Newspaper and television reporters were quick to brand Lépine "a madman" on a "rampage" within a scene of "pandemonium". But to many observers, terms like rampage and madman seemed both inadequate and incongruous, given the first-hand descriptions of a calm, focused, methodical hunter.

In the days, weeks, and years to come, details of the gunman's life and intent were revealed. He and his mother had evidently been abused; he had failed to gain entrance into engineering studies at the École Polytechnique; and he blamed women for his troubles. He specifically saw the rise of women's rights, the assertion of women in what were labelled "non-traditional" roles in society, and feminist thinkers as his enemies. His assault on the students, soon known as "the Montreal Massacre", was premeditated and deliberate. In fact, police investigators found evidence that he intended to target particular high-profile Canadian women, not all known as feminists, but successful and recognized for their work.

Public reaction to the tragedy was described variously as outrage, sadness, shock, horror, and anger. The massacre was discussed and analysed from many perspectives and against many agendas, and seen by some as a manifestation of the broader plague of domestic violence. Others felt that Lépine was not merely a lone force, an insane individual, but rather an extreme expression of a pervasive resentment of the advancement of women in society and in professions previously considered the exclusive domain of males.

For the victims and their families, all talk of politics and social issues was of little consolation. There is no question, however, that December 6, 1989, constitutes a milestone in the development and growth of Canadian society. In the months that followed, female students reported a decline in sexist jokes around Canadian university campuses, while at least some, if not all, male engineering students demonstrated a sensitivity and degree of compassion for their female colleagues not always evident in the past. Over the longer term, the impact of that day can be seen in revised gun-control laws, in the awareness of issues around aggression, and in the scholarly literature of several fields.

The thoughtful study spawned in part by these events evolved into entirely new, and in some ways uniquely inspired research: an interdisciplinary blend of the technological interest in science and engineering professions with historical studies informed by feminist perspective and thought. In the broader context of feminist history, this interest has even stirred a new look at Elsie MacGill's life and work as a meeting of engineering and feminism that not only injected a new point of view to the field of engineering, but also brought an engineer's technical approach to the issue of feminism as exemplified by her disciplined, managed, and methodical contribution as the "Moving Force on the Royal Commission on the Status of Women".[425]

The December 6, 1989 murders also coincided with a marked change in the number of women pursuing careers in engineering in Canada. It was the inverse of the gunman's wishes.

When discussing trends and policies related to the enrolment of women in engineering studies in Canada over the following decade, scholars began to speak in terms of the pre- and post-1989 eras.[426] The post-1989 decade saw remarkable increases in the total and relative numbers of female engineering students at universities across Canada.[427] At some institutions, it meant a doubling of the ratio, and even though women remained a distinct minority within Canadian engineering schools, the change was significant.

Fuelling the trend, the 1990s — a decade of exponential growth in technically driven industrial development in Canada, the United States, and around the world — gave a huge boost to both the profile of engineers and their opportunities to find work, a boost likely to have attracted more people of both sexes to the field. The boom in high technology, the growth of the Internet, and other related phenomena, also alerted women to the notion of a career in engineering.

But some students of the trends and international comparisons looked for distinctly Canadian forces at work, traceable to that sad day in December 1989. The event certainly accelerated and magnified the level of public discourse on the issue of gender and engineering education, stimulating a degree of interest and curiosity about the field among some of the young girls who in the 1990s would attend university.[428]

Beyond this blunt effect, the event also stimulated constructive reflection and action. When trauma rips a hole in the fabric of a life or society, new light sometimes shines through. In much the same way as Elsie's paralysis 60 years earlier compelled her to regroup, reflect, and then recover and resume her career with new energy, Canadian society and its institutions rebounded to launch a suite of programs and special initiatives to promote engineering careers to women and to increase their numbers within the profession. These initiatives would range from targeted recruitment activities at private-sector firms to special scholarship and mentoring programs at individual universities such as Elsie's alma mater, the University of Toronto.[429]

The response also included national promotion campaigns and new programs highlighted by the creation of the Canadian Committee on Women in Engineering, a multiparty initiative led by the Department of Industry, Science and Technology and the Canadian Council of Professional Engineers. The committee's report and recommendations set out an action plan for increasing the involvement of women in engineering that was implemented over the next decade by university deans, private employers, and professional associations across Canada.

One individual organization moved to act was the National Research Council of Canada (NRC), the host of much of Elsie MacGill's early wind tunnel research work for Fairchild Aircraft and a body she served later in life as a special advisor on aeronautical issues. Victims of the December 1989 shootings included NRC employees. Two NRC guest workers, Hélène Colgan and Nathalie Croteau, were slain, and their NRC colleague France Chrétien suffered multiple bullet wounds. Months before the shooting, the three young women had joined what was later to be known as the Polymer Composites Group at the NRC Industrial Materials

Institute (NRC-IMI), a large research facility not far from the former site of Elsie's Fairchild plant in Longueuil, Québec. Their colleagues at NRC included some who were present in that classroom at l'École Polytechnique when shots were fired and bodies fell to the floor. Another of the survivors, Nathalie Provost, a young woman who was shot three times after trying to reason with the gunman, came to work at another NRC institute after recovering from her wounds.

In an attempt to respond to the tragedy, NRC established a program to encourage female students to pursue scientific and engineering studies and careers. NRC's Women in Engineering and Science (WES) program was officially launched in 1991. It was a program open to female undergraduates in the first year of postsecondary education, offering them two and sometimes three 16-week job placements in NRC engineering and science laboratories during summer breaks throughout their university years. The positions paid well and gave the students hands-on experience in laboratory research. The first class of 25 WES students graduated from the program in 1994. Later, up to 75 would be accommodated within the program at any one time. They came from cities and towns all across Canada to work in fields from biochemistry and photonics to robotics and aeronautical engineering.

Over the 1990s, hundreds of exceptional young women with diversified interests and passion — the brightest of the bright — came to Canada's national laboratories to work and learn. Many at NRC were energized by their presence and inspired by their example. The WES students were supported in turn by NRC scientists who were assigned as mentors, role models, and research supervisors. To what degree this influence was a deciding factor or merely an encouragement to inherent excellence, it remains an astounding fact that the last formal evaluation of the program revealed that 92 percent of the young women who participated in it went on to complete graduate school, with the majority earning doctorates.

However, even with some 300 participants, the program directly supported only a small fraction of the many women in science and engineering in Canada and is but one limited example of many programs and initiatives started or bolstered during the 1990s. Yet its impact was amplified because part of the WES job description required the women in the program to act as role models, to visit their own and other high schools and to speak about their experiences, interests, and opportunities, possibly generating ripples that will touch lives for many years to come.

Despite the initial impact of these initiatives, the first years of the new century have seen a levelling off and decline in the relative share of female enrolment in Canadian engineering schools,[430] viewed by some as just another phase of what experts tag "cycles of advancement and retrenchment".[431] The vision of women participating in equal numbers in engineering remains elusive. The number of women undergraduate engineering students in Canada has slipped once again below 20 percent, with women being well represented only in the same sub-disciplines, such as chemical engineering, that were the first to feel the presence of women nearly a century ago.[432]

Despite the increases in post-1989 engineering-school enrolments, senior levels of the profession in Canada still reflect the extremely low female enrolment rates of earlier decades. Women accounted for less than 10 percent of the country's total population of active registered professional engineers in the early years of the 21st century, and expert observers see a need for new thinking aimed at "transforming the organizational structures"[433] and a renewed focus on the challenge of attracting women to the field and supporting them within it.

Building upon the CCWE initiative, the engineering profession has sought to address the issue in many ways, one example being the creation by the Canadian Council of Professional Engineers of the Award for the Support of Women in the Engineering Profession. Candidates for the award are judged from many perspectives, including professional achievements, contributions to the profession, and contributions to their communities. But the CCPE, which comprises the bodies empowered with accrediting all 160 000 professional engineers in Canada, identifies one quality far above all others in judging one's effectiveness in the support of women in engineering: "recognition as a role model", a criterion accounting for a full 70 percent of the factors considered in determining who receives this award.

The importance of role models to the profession suggests that engineers can make a special contribution as parents who encourage their daughters, as well as their sons, to follow in their footsteps. Professor Elizabeth Cannon, the first female Dean of Engineering at the University of Calgary, the wife of another engineer, and a mother who expects one day to speak proudly of "her daughter, the engineer", says that the key lies in being "passionate and positive" about one's life and profession.

"She saw that I enjoyed what I did, and that I was making a difference", Professor Cannon said in discussing her daughter's 2006 decision to enroll in engineering and the difficulty of engaging more young women in the field.

As Canada, the United States, and many other countries continue to struggle with this persistent issue, they are empowered by an exceptional role model, a role model who remained consistently "passionate and positive" in the face of what many would see as daunting obstacles: Elsie Gregory MacGill, a woman who herself had been bolstered throughout the ups and downs of life by her mother the judge's positive, passionate example.

Branded well before her passing as "the Number One Canadian woman engineer to look up to",[434] Elsie MacGill, a woman who is remembered in part for avoiding celebration as a role model and considering such talk of her career "tiresome", remains, despite the recognitions that came her way, among the magnificent, largely untapped sources of inspiration for all human beings.

Extracts from Separate Statement by Elsie Gregory MacGill

Report of the Royal Commission on the Status of Women (1970)

Abortion

"I think that abortion should no longer be regarded as a criminal offence but as a private medical matter between patient and doctor.

"I foresee with fear that unless the prohibitions and penal ties provided in the Criminal Code are repealed promptly, they will linger on for a decade or two more to harass and punish women".

Income Taxation

" Income Tax Legislation can encourage or discourage the financial dependency of one group of individuals on another... In Canada a great many wives are financially dependent on their husbands and this appears to be a factor in the lower wage rates paid to women as compared with those paid to men.

Our findings indicate that anticipation of this dependency often saps the initiative of young girls to take advantage of educational opportunities, and focuses their attention on acquiring a husband-provider.

... For these reasons, I am against the introduction of the "marriage unit" basis [of taxation]..."

Elsie Muriel Gregory MacGill
(1905–1980)

Chronology and Family Tree

O'Reilly – Gregory

Miles O'Reilly

Elsie's maternal great-grandfather, Upper Canada judge

Born: May 18, 1806, near Niagara Falls
Died: Aug. 11, 1890, in Hamilton, ON.
Married: Jane Racey (born Apr. 7, 1813, in NY State, died Dec. 10, 1893) in 1831
Four children: James, Helen Elizabeth, Miles, and **Emma**, Elsie's grandmother

Emma (O'Reilly) Gregory

Elsie's maternal grandmother, early suffragette

Born: Apr. 5, 1835, in Hamilton
Died: June 12, 1907, in Vancouver
Married (1): Charles H. Jarvis (born 1831; died Sep. 18, 1857, in Hamilton)
One son: Miles ("Milo"), born Sep. 18, 1857, in Hamilton, died 1911 in Winnipeg
Married (2): **Silas Ebenezer Gregory** (born June 3, 1823, near Montréal, died Apr. 4, 1911, in Vancouver) in 1863 in Hamilton
Two daughters: **Helen Emma** (Elsie's mother) and Herbert Everett (born 1870, died 1943 in San Francisco)

Helen Emma Gregory MacGill

Elsie's mother, the judge

Born: Jan. 7, 1864, in Hamilton
Died: Feb. 27, 1947, in Chicago
Married (1): farmer and surgeon **Charles Frederick Lee Flesher** (born Aug. 26, 1869, in Ontario, died Aug. 10, 1901, in Minnesota)
Two sons: **Eric** and **Freddy Flesher**
Married (2): **James Henry MacGill**, in St. Paul, Minnesota, Sep. 16, 1902 (q.v.)

Eric Herbert Flesher

Elsie's half-brother

Born: June 2, 1891, in Lawrence, California
Died: Aug. 7, 1972, in Phillips Arm, B.C.
Married: Ann Olga Reed (born Dec. 4, 1891, in Barbados, died Oct. 5, 1973, in Phillips Arm, B.C.)
One child: **Eric Reed Flesher**, Elsie's nephew (born Nov. 23, 1917, in Vancouver, taken prisoner in Germany 1944, released 1945). In 1954, Eric married Grace Elizabeth Thomson. Their daughter, Grace Anne Flesher, Elsie's grandniece, was born June 3, 1956.

Frederick Phillip (Freddy) Flesher

Elsie's half-brother

Born: May 10, 1894, in San Francisco
Died: Sep. 17, 1944, in Portland, Oregon
Married (1): Rosel Staltsonberg (born in Germany; after divorce Rosel Shone of Vancouver) in 1922
Married (2): Margaret Andrews (born Aug. 7, 1908, died 1947) in 1934

MacGill

James Henry MacGill

Elsie's Father

Born: 1869 in Springfield, ON
Died: Jan. 10, 1939, in Vancouver
Married: **Helen Emma Flesher (née Gregory)**, Elsie's mother, in St. Paul, Minnesota, Sep. 16, 1902
Two daughters: **Helen** and **Elizabeth (Elsie)**

Helen Elizabeth Gregory MacGill Hughes

Elsie's sister, "Young Helen"

Born: Aug. 24, 1903, in Vancouver
Died: Apr. 29, 1992, in Baltimore, MD
Married: **Everett Cherrington Hughes** (born Nov. 30, 1897 in Beaver, OH, died Jan. 5, 1983, in Cambridge, MA) on Aug. 18, 1927, in Vancouver
Two daughters: **Helen** and **Elizabeth**

Helen Hughes Brock

Elsie's Niece

Born: July 21, 1938, in Montréal
Married: **Sebastian Paul Brock** (born 1938 in London, U.K.)

Elizabeth Hughes Schneewind

Elsie's Niece

Born: May 11, 1940, in Chicago
Married: **Jerome Schneewind** (born 1930)
Three children (Elsie's grandnieces): Sarah Katherine, Rachel Miriam, and Hannah Elizabeth. Among her children Hannah has a daughter (Elsie's great-grandniece) named Elizabeth.

Elizabeth ("Elsie") Muriel Gregory MacGill

Born: Mar. 27, 1905, in Vancouver

Died: Nov. 4, 1980, in Cambridge, MA
Married: **Eric James (Bill) Soulsby** on June 4, 1943, in Kankakee, IL

Soulsby

Eric James (Bill) Soulsby

Elsie's husband

Born: May 28, 1899, in Birmingham, U.K.
Died: Apr. 26, 1983, in Toronto
Married (1): **Helen Heaps** (born Apr. 11, 1899 in Keighley, U.K., died Sep. 26, 1942, in Fort William) on Aug. 30, 1925, in Fort William
Two children: **John** and **Ann**

John Frank Soulsby

Elsie's stepson

Born: Feb. 16, 1929, in Fort William
Died Jan. 6, 1996, in U.K.
Married: Margaret Anne Chadwick on July 6, 1958
Three children, Elsie's step-grandchildren: Rohan, Alison, and Joanna
The next generation, Elsie's step-great grandchildren, are Aidan, Nicole, and Megan Thorstensen-Woll Soulsby

Ann Soulsby

Elsie's stepdaughter

Born: Jan. 28, 1932, in St. Lambert, Quebec
Died: Aug. 24, 2007, in Toronto

Elsie Gregory MacGill

Sampling of Awards and Honours

1927   University of Michigan: Graduate School Fellowship

1940   Engineering Institute of Canada: Gzowski Medal

1953   Gaveart Gallery Tribute to 50 Business Leaders: only female

1953   American Society of Women Engineers: Achievement Award

1967   Centennial Medal of Canada

1971   Officer of the Order of Canada

1973   Engineering Institute of Canada: Julian C. Smith Award

1973   University of Toronto: Honorary Doctor of Letters

1975   Ninety-Nines International Assn. of Women Pilots: Amelia Earhart Medal

1975   University of British Columbia Alumni Association Award of Distinction

1976   University of Windsor: Honorary Doctor of Science

1977   Queen's Jubilee Medal

1978   York University: Honorary Doctor of Science

1978   Queen's University: Honorary Doctor of Science

1979   Ontario Association of Professional Engineers Gold Medal

1980   University of Toronto Engineering Alumni Association: Hall of Distinction

Memberships, Recognitions, and Achievements

Member/P.Eng - Association of Professional Engineers of Ontario (APEO)

- First female corporate member
- Member of APEO program committees
- Chair of APEO Committee on Examination Syllabus (Aeronautical Engineering)

Fellow of Engineering Institute of Canada (F.E.I.C.)

- First female corporate member of E.I.C.
- Chairman Lakehead Branch of E.I.C.
- National Councillor of E.I.C. (1965–1968)

First female member of Association of Consulting Engineers of Canada. M.A.C.E.C.

- Member of the Board of Directors, Ontario Chapter, 1966–1969
- 1974 honorary life member

Chartered Engineer (U.K.), C.Eng.

Fellow of the Royal Aeronautical Society, London England (F.R.A.S.)

First female Fellow of the Canadian Aeronautical & Space Institute (F.C.A.S.I.)

Member of the American Institute of Aeronautics & Astronautics (M.A.I.A.A.)

Award member of the Society of Women Engineers, U.S.A. Aw. S.W.E.

Member of the Canadian Society of Mechanical Engineers. M.C.S.M.E.

Member Iota Alpha (Beta Chapter) — honorary engineering fraternity

Life member of Canadian Federation of Business & Professional Women's Clubs

- National President 1962–1964 and many other positions

Life member of Toronto Business & Professional Women's Club

- Club established Elsie Gregory MacGill Scholarship Annual Award for female student in science and engineering in 1955

Member of Soroptimist Club of Toronto

Life member of the Art Gallery of Ontario

Fellow of the Royal Society of Arts (England)

Public Service

Member of National Research Council Associate Committee on Aeronautical Research

- Member of sub-committees on aircraft structures

Technical Advisor at United Nations International Civil Aviation Organization (ICAO)

- Advisor to meetings to draft International Airworthiness Regulations
- Chairman Stress Analysis Committee

Commissioner on Canadian Royal Commission on the Status of Women (1967–1970)

Member of the Ontario Status of Women Committee

Commissioner/Chair Ontario Building Materials Evaluation Commission (1976)

Appointed to Canadian Organizing Committee for International Year of Disabled 1980

Elsie Gregory MacGill

Chronology of Aircraft and Companies

Fairchild

1920	Sherman M. Fairchild forms Fairchild Aerial Camera Corp. in U.S.
1922	Fairchild Aerial Surveys Ltd. (Canadian subsidiary) formed
May 1929	Fairchild Aircraft Ltd, a Canadian manufacturer, incorporated
Spring 1930	Fairchild's Longueuil plant opens; builds U.S.-designed planes
March 1930	Fairchild Sales Manager WWI hero Billy Barker dies in crash
Feb 1931	Francis Percival Hyde-Beadle joins Fairchild as Chief Engineer
Late 1934	Elsie MacGill joins firm as Hyde-Beadle's assistant
May 1938	Elsie MacGill leaves firm

Fairchild Super 71

1933	Fairchild begins work on this first all-metal, Cdn-designed plane
Oct. 1934	Prototype first flown on floats at Longueuil, Quebec
1935–36	Two modified Super 71Ps are completed with Elsie's help
1937	One Super 71P crashes on a lake in Manitoba.
January 1938	RCAF reports negative experiences with planes
April 1940	Second Super 71P taken out of service in Camp Borden
October 1940	Original Super 71 strikes a log and is written off

Fairchild 82

1934	Fairchild begins developing Model 82
July 1935	82 model first flown; others made with Elsie's help
1939	82 manufacture suspended for war, never resumed

Fairchild 45-80 Sekani

1936	New Fairchild GM Vanderlipp starts design work
Summer 1937	Prototype first flown on floats; Hyde-Beadle leaves firm
Fall 1937	Elsie plays a lead role in modifying/improving design
Spring 1938	Fairchild abandons Sekani development after two planes

Canadian Car & Foundry Co. Ltd.

1909	Company founded from merger of rail-car makers
1937	Fort William plant, closed in 1922, reopens for aircraft business
August 1938	Elsie MacGill joins firm
May 1943	Elsie MacGill leaves firm
1955	Firm and plant bought by Avro (part of Hawker Siddeley)
1994	Bombardier takes over Fort William plant

Grumman G-23 Goblins

December 1931	U.S. prototype first flown.
November 1936	CC&F obtains U.S.-made demonstrator plane.
February 1938	First CC&F planes test flown, one sold to Nicaragua and one to Japan.
March 1938	Shipments of 34 planes to Turkey, in reality Spain, begins
May 1938	Illegal shipment of six "Turkish" planes stopped at Saint John
Mid-1938	One sent to Mexico. Elsie advises on construction of five more
Fall 1940	Last 15 delivered to RCAF for East Coast patrols

Maple Leaf I Trainer

June 1937	CC&F secures manufacturing rights for "Wallace Trainer"
April, 1938	Plane of Wallace design tested at Fort William for Nicaragua
March 1938	CC&F tests design with "unsatisfactory performance"

Maple Leaf Trainer II

Fall 1938   Mexico expresses interest in high-altitude version of Trainer

October 1939   Prototype plane on Elsie's new design tested at Fort William

October 1940   Prototype aircraft and parts for others sent to United States

April 1941   Mexico ends Maple Leaf II contract with CC&F

August 1941   Modified Maple Leaf II flies in Mexico

1942-1944   Mexican Air Force builds additional planes based on CC&F design

Canadian Car & Foundry

Gregor Fighter FBD-1

Fall 1937   Michael Gregor hired by CC&F

December 1938   Elsie does stress analysis; prototype rolled out at Fort William

January 1940   FBD-1 breaks down during New York to Miami race

May 1940   Transfer to Mexico blocked by Canadian Defence Department

1945   Plane burned in hangar fire at St. Hubert, QC

Hawker Hurricane

November 1935   Prototype first flown in U.K.

November 1938   CC&F given first contract for 40 Hurricanes in Fort William

January 1940   Elsie leads engineering shop; first Canadian Hurricane flown

July 1940   10 Canadian Hurricanes lost in transit across Atlantic

August 1940   Canadian-built Hurricanes participate in Battle of Britain

Summer 1941   Production increases despite lack of supplies

Feb/March 1943   Elsie's two winterized Hurricanes tested

Curtiss-Wright Helldiver

May 1942	Contract for 1000 planes given to Canadian Car & Foundry
May 1943	Elsie's struggle with design changes ends with her dismissal.
July 1943	CC&F prototype first flown; mass production follows

Burnelli CBY-3

1936	CC&F acquires manufacturing rights to Burnelli lifting fuselage
1938	Elsie advises on design; plan to build planes postponed
December 1943	Construction of CBY-3 begins at CC&F Montréal plant
July 1945	Prototype, the only version of the plane made, first flown

Victory/Avro Canada/Orenda

1941	National Steel Car (NSC) Malton, ON, to build Lancaster X
Spring 1942	Elsie's friend David Boyd joins National Steel Car
Nov. 1942	Government forms Victory Aircraft, takes over Malton NSC plant
June 1943	Elsie's husband E.J. Soulsby joins Victory Aircraft
December 1945	Avro Canada formed, takes over Victory Aircraft; Boyd leaves
May 1946	Avro Canada takes over Turbo Research Ltd.
January 1954	Hawker Siddeley splits firm into Avro and Orenda Engines
February 1959	Canadian Government terminates CF-lO5 Arrow contract
1967	Soulsby retires after career with Hawker Siddeley/Orenda

Avro 685 York (Canadian)

1942	Canada establishes a transatlantic air service
1943	Victory Aircraft gets order for 50 York (Canadian) aircraft
1943	York (Canadian) program cancelled after Elsie MacGill's review
November 1944	One York (Canadian) completed for first flight at Malton, ON
	Avro York (Canadian) lost in Berlin Airlift

Various sources, notably, M. Molson and H.A. Taylor, *Canadian Aircraft Since 1909.* Stittsville, ON: Canada's Wings, Inc., 1982.

Notes and References

Abbreviations for sources of information used in Notes and References

BCA	British Columbia Archives, Victoria
DBD	Dick Bourgeois-Doyle, the author
EGM	Elsie Gregory MacGill
EHS	Elizabeth Hughes Schneewind, Elsie's niece
HGM	Helen Gregory MacGill, Elsie's mother
HHB	Helen Hughes Brock, Elsie's niece
HMH	Helen MacGill Hughes, Elsie's sister
JHP	John Hamilton Parkin
LAC	Library and Archives Canada, Ottawa: Elsie Gregory MacGill Papers, MG 31 K7.
NRC	National Research Council of Canada

Note: Materials gathered by the author for this book can be accessed at NRC Archives, NRC Canada Institute for Scientific and Technical Information, National Research Council of Canada, 100 Sussex Drive, Ottawa, ON, K1A 0R6, under the heading "Dick Bourgeois-Doyle — NRC Author Fond: Elsie Gregory MacGill Biography".

Preface
1. Remarks by HMH, read by EHS at Elsie's memorial service on Nov. 26, 1980, at Knox College Chapel, University of Toronto.
2. John L. Garvey, M.D., University of Michigan Department of Neurology, University Hospital, Ann Arbor, June 15, 1929. Medical referral letter for Elsie; LAC.
3. Some of the symptoms and signs characteristic of infectious poliomyelitis and consistent with Dr. Garvey's report and family descriptions of Elsie's experience are recounted here as per the Medline Plus Service of the U.S. National Library of Medicine, http://www.nlm.nih.gov/medlineplus/ency/article/001402.htm,, and the U.S. National Institutes of Health description on transverse myelitis through http://www.ninds.nih.gov/index.htm, both accessed Jan. 20, 2006. However, another possible diagnosis has been suggested. Dr. Chris Richardson, a virologist at Dalhousie University, Halifax, NS, says (pers. comm., Feb. 2008) that Elsie's symptoms could be indicative of Guillain Barré, an inflammatory autoimmune disease that typically strikes after an acute infection (Elsie had "flu"). A serious and quite variable disease, it usually starts in the legs, is often preceded by tingling, and can result in paralysis, though symptoms in most cases abate with time

(only 5–10 percent of patients are left with severe disability). Like polio, it attacks the peripheral nerves, though other systems may also be affected. Some medical historians believe that Franklin Roosevelt suffered from Guillain Barré rather than polio.

4. See endnote no. 2.
5. See endnote no. 1.
6. EGM, *My Mother the Judge: A Biography of Judge Helen Gregory MacGill.* Toronto: Ryerson Press, 1955, 205, and repeated by Elsie in other venues. Hereafter this book is referred to as *My Mother the Judge.*
7. HHB, quoted by her sister EHS at Elsie's memorial service.

Chapter I — The Golden Thread

8. *My Mother the Judge*, xv. Much of this chapter and part of the next draws on Elsie's biography of her mother; on a 1977 biographical essay by HMH; and on family-tree information provided by EHS and HHB, Elsie's nieces.
9. *My Mother the Judge*, xiv.
10. *My Mother the Judge*, xv.
11. EGM. Speaking notes for Mar. 28, 1953, meeting of the Society of Women Engineers, where she received their achievement award; Society of Women Engineers Archives, Walter P. Reuther Library of Labor and Urban Affairs, Wayne State University, Detroit, MI.
12. Obituary of Elsie in Ontario Region Bulletin of the Engineering Institute of Canada, Jan. 1981.
13. Dr. Lorna Marsden, President of York University, former Canadian senator and early president of the National Action Committee on the Status of Women, speaking in "Rosies of the North", Kelly Saxberg (dir.). Montréal: National Film Board of Canada, 1999.
14. *My Mother the Judge*, xi, quoting her mother.
15. A. Kloppenborg, A. Niwinski, E. Johnson, and R. Grueter, eds., *First Century: A City Album/1980–1985.* Vancouver/Toronto: Douglas & McIntyre, 1985.
16. Robert A.J. McDonald, Making Vancouver: Class, Status, and Social Boundaries 1863–1913. Vancouver: UBC Press, 1996, xii.
17. Ibid. 202. Even in 1911, British-born residents accounted for as much as 30 percent of the total population of Vancouver.
18. *My Mother the Judge*, 91.
19. *My Mother the Judge*, 95.
20. HHB to DBD, Oct. 28, 2007.
21. *My Mother the Judge*, 48.
22. HMH, "Wasp/Woman/Sociologist", Society 14 (1977): 69–80.
23. *My Mother the Judge*, 56.
24. *My Mother the Judge*, 79.

25. *My Mother the Judge*, 98.
26. *My Mother the Judge*, 106.
27. *My Mother the Judge*, 80.
28. *My Mother the Judge*, 87.
29. *My Mother the Judge*, 99.
30. HMH, "Wasp/Woman/Sociologist", Society 14 (1977): 69–80.
31. *My Mother the Judge*, 15.
32. Elsie's birth certificate; LAC.
33. *My Mother the Judge*, 105.

Chapter II — My Mother, the Suffragette

34. N.L. McClung, In Times like These, (Toronto and Buffalo: University of Toronto Press, 1972), p. 35
35. P.E. Roy, Vancouver: An Illustrated History. Toronto: James Lorimer and National Museum of Man, National Museums of Canada, 1980, 87, describes this era.
36. *My Mother the Judge*, 108.
37. The different spelling of their name and their denials did not prevent many people from suggesting that Elsie and her sister were related to the founder of McGill University.
38. Vancouver School Board, District 39: Roberts School Overview, Sep. 2006, http://www.vsb.bc.ca/schools/Elementaryschools/03939031/Profile/schooloverview.htm
39. HMH, "Wasp/Woman/Sociologist", Society 14 (1977): 69–80, describes the relative privilege of West End children at the time.
40. EGM. Two-page handwritten note later marked by Elsie as 1911 or 1912; LAC.
41. P. Blanchard, *The Life of Emily Carr.* Toronto: Douglas and MacIntyre, 1987, 124–125, describes Carr's studio at 1465 West Broadway, Vancouver.
42. I. Dilworth, Foreword to Emily Carr, *Klee Wyck*. Toronto, Vancouver: Clarke, Irwin, 1941, i.
43. J. Barton, "An Expansive Sense of Place, Emily Carr's Victoria", *Vernissage, The Magazine of the National Gallery of Canada,* Spring 2006, 12. Carr's parents died two years apart, leaving Emily an orphan at 16. In 1890, at 19, she convinced her guardian to allow her to attend a San Francisco art school, where she stayed into the years when Helen lived in the area.
44. *My Mother the Judge*, 133.
45. *Ibid.*
46. *My Mother the Judge*, 106.
47. *My Mother the Judge*, 100.
48. *My Mother the Judge*, 187. Among organizations cited at Helen's memorial

were the Women's Institute, the I.O.D.E., the King's Daughters, the Women's Canadian Club, the Canadian Daughter's League, the National Council of Women, honorary membership of the American Women's Club, life member of the Women's Benefit Association, founder of the Vancouver Business and Professional Women's Club, and Phi Delta Delta, the international women's legal fraternity.

49. V. Strong-Boag, Introduction to N.L. McClung, *In Times like These*. Toronto and Buffalo: University of Toronto Press, 1972, vii.

50. *Ibid.*

51. N.L. McClung, *In Times like These*, 35.

52. *My Mother the Judge*, 154.

53. *My Mother the Judge*, 133.

54. http://www.thecanadianencyclopedia.com/index.cfm?PgNm=TCE&Params=A1ARTA0006236, accessed Dec. 8, 2005.

55. HGM, *Daughters, Wives, and Mothers in British Columbia: Some Laws Affecting Them.* Vancouver: Moore Printing, 1912, cited in *My Mother the Judge*, 137.

56. I. Howard, *The Struggle for Social Justice in British Columbia: Helena Gutteridge, the Unknown Reformer.* Vancouver: UBC Press, 1992, 93. Racism infiltrated the movement when some of its protagonists argued for the rights of white, British-born women over those of recently immigrated men. In the lead-up to the 1916 referendum on suffrage in British Columbia, the Mount Pleasant Suffrage League in Vancouver declared the "occupation of these shores by hordes of dark-skinned immigrants from the Far East" to be a "menace" that women, once enfranchised, could help eradicate.

57. *Ibid.*, 33. Emmeline Pankhurst, a British suffragette whose "direct action" militancy landed her in jail on occasion and whose Women's Social and Political Union recruited Helena Gutteridge in her early twenties, later came to Canada and Vancouver for extended periods.

58. *Ibid.* 65. Earlier, Helen and other Conservative suffragettes had formed the Equal Franchise Association over differences with groups led by Helena Gutteridge.

59. *Ibid.*, 126.

60. *My Mother the Judge*, 154, where Helen Gregory MacGill is described as the first woman in Canada to be appointed to the bench with the formal title of "Judge", in this case as a judge of the Juvenile Court of Vancouver. However, as Elsie elaborates, Helen's friend "Emily Murphy and, later, Alice Jamieson [had been appointed over the previous year by Alberta as] magistrates and commissioners to act as judges of the Juvenile Court in Edmonton and Calgary respectively, and [Alberta] had commissioned Annie Burwash Langford of Calgary as J.P."

61. HMH, "Wasp/Woman/Sociologist", *Society* 14 (1977): 69–80.

62. A. Kloppenborg, A. Niwinski, E. Johnson, and R. Grueter, *First Century: A City Album/1980–1985.* Vancouver/Toronto: Douglas & McIntyre, 1985.
63. HHB to DBD, Oct. 28, 2007.
64. *My Mother the Judge*, 184.
65. HHB to DBD, Oct. 28, 2007.
66. "Soroptimist of the Month: High Flying Designer", *The American Soroptimist*, Nov. 1953, 3. Elsie and her sister attended the West End's King George Secondary School, then at Nelson St. and Burrard in a building previously occupied by the Dawson Elementary School.

Chapter III — Toronto and Ann Arbor

67. "Jumbo jets, women's pleas engross Elsie MacGill", *Montreal Gazette*, Sep. 13, 1968.
68. D. Jones, "Doing it her way was Elsie's way of flying", *Toronto Star*, Mar. 16, 1985.
69. *My Mother the Judge*, 183.
70. D. Jones, "Doing it her way…"
71. In 1922, the year before Elsie and her sister left UBC for Toronto, public and student complaints about the crowded UBC facilities culminated in a large protest march, known as "the Great Trek", that induced the provincial government to finally begin construction at UBC's present-day Point Grey site. http://www.library.ubc.ca/archives/hist_ubc.html.
72. University of Michigan press release, May 12, 1975. Refers to events related to the experience of Pauline Sherman, the first woman faculty member (1960) in the U. of M. Department of Aerospace Engineering; LAC.
73. EHS to DBD, email, Feb. 2, 2007.
74. HMH, "Wasp/Woman/Sociologist", *Society* 14 (1977): 69–80.
75. "Short History of Toronto" fact sheet by the City of Toronto, http://www.toronto.ca/culture/history/history-shortversion.htm, accessed Jan. 20, 2006.
76. W. Stewart Wallace, *A History of the University of Toronto 1827–1927.* Toronto: University of Toronto Press, 1927, 142.
77. R. White, *The Skule Story: The University of Toronto Faculty of Applied Science and Engineering, 1873–2000.* Toronto: Faculty of Applied Science and Engineering and the University of Toronto Press, 2000, 122.
78. M. Gosztonyi Ainley, "Last in the Field?", in *Despite the Odds: Essays on Canadian Women and Science*, ed. M.G. Ainley. Montréal: Véhicule, 1990, 25–62.
79. N.R. Ball, *Mind, Heart, and Vision: Professional Engineering in Canada 1887 to 1987.* Ottawa: National Museum of Science and Technology/ National Museums of Canada, 1987, 153.
80. R. White, *The Skule Story*, 73.

81. J. Hamilton Parkin, *Aeronautical Research in Canada, 1917–1957*, Vol. I. Ottawa: National Research Council of Canada, 1983, 140. Hereafter this two-volume memoir is cited as "Parkin memoirs."

82. John Fox, Nov. 1980. Handwritten note by a fellow student in the U. of T. class of 1927, written for Nov. 1980 memorial service; Soulsby family papers.

83. R. White, *The Skule Story*, 120.

84. Parkin memoirs, Vol. I, 141.

85. HHB to DBD, Oct. 28, 2007.

86. *Ibid.*

87. HMH, "Wasp/Woman/Sociologist", *Society* 14 (1977): 69–80, 74.

88. HGH to Dr. Seager, Dec. 3, 1923. Helen's address is given as 1165 Nelson Street, Vancouver; LAC.

89. "1873–1973 Career Profiles of U. of T. Women Engineering Graduates." Pamphlet marking the centenary of the Faculty of Applied Sciences, University of Toronto; LAC.

90. JHP to G.R. Spradbrow, Mar. 22, 1927; JHP papers, Vol. 28, NRC Archives, Ottawa.

91. Parkin memoirs, Vol. I, 141.

92. W. Stewart Wallace, *A History of the University of Toronto 1827–1927*. Toronto: University of Toronto Press, 1927, 106.

93. M.L. Friedland, *The University of Toronto: A History.* Toronto: University of Toronto Press, 2002, 285.

94. *Ibid.* 302.

95. Reported as the phrase used by Professor T.R. Roseburgh when he presented Elsie to the Chancellor of the U. of T. at the convocation where she received her honorary degree. "Canadian … Women in Aviation", *Canadian Aviation*, Feb. 1940, 19.

96. See Chap. II herein. The Persons' Case advanced by the "Famous Five" turned on the definition of "qualified persons" in legislation governing appointments to the Canadian Senate. The case was instigated in a letter from the five to the Governor General of Canada and concluded on Oct. 18, 1929, when the Privy Council in London, U.K., overturned a negative Supreme Court of Canada decision pursuant to the British North America Act of 1867.

97. D. Fraser, "Elsie Gregory MacGill: Aeronautical Engineer", *The Archivist*, Jan.–Feb. 1987, 8–9, is among the sources that name the Austin Motor Company as the firm that drew Elsie to the U.S. and provided her with a base from which to apply for aeronautics studies at the University of Michigan.

98. While the most likely scenario is the one described in the main text of this book (that Elsie went to Pontiac to work for the U.S. engineering firm named Austin, which she described to her family as "an engineering firm", not an

automaker), there is a remote possibility that Elsie may have been recruited by the British Austin Motor Co., as others suggest. By 1927, the year Elsie graduated from the U. of T., Austin had started exporting cars (Austin Sevens) to North America, and that spring the company sent the works director of its Longbridge plant in the U.K., Charles Engelbach, to develop the firm's presence in N. America and to investigate the possibility of establishing manufacturing facilities there. (Minutes of Austin Motor Company Board Meeting of May 25, 1927 [doc. ref.: MSS.226/AU/1/1/1], Modern Records Centre, University of Warwick, Coventry, U.K., courtesy of Liz Wood, Assistant Archivist, email to DBD Aug. 22, 2007.) Engelbach reported back to Austin's board of directors with great enthusiasm, encouraging them to expand their interests in the U.S. If Elsie MacGill was recruited at this time, it could have been in an atmosphere of optimism and the ambiance of Austin's ambitions for growth in America. But it could not have been to work in an automobile manufacturing plant. Only a few years later did Austin finally establish U.S. manufacturing facilities, which operated only briefly as part of the Austin empire until difficult times in the Depression saw them dissolve into a pool of mergers and restructuring. (Auto editors of *Consumer Guide, 50 Years of American Automobiles 1939–1989*. New York: Beekman House, 1989, 9.) Austin never had an auto plant in Michigan, and Pontiac historical records have no mention of even an office. So, if Elsie was hired by the Austin Motor Company, as some secondary records suggest, the atmosphere may have been optimistic at first, but would quickly have turned to disappointment and frustration for the young, energetic and ambitious engineering grad.

99. More than one company operated under the Austin name in the U.S. around this time. Austin Engineering, cited here as Elsie's most likely employer, had strong aviation industry ties and was building an auto plant, "the world's largest building for the Oakland Motor Car Company" (later Pontiac and GM) in Pontiac, as described at http://www.theaustin.com/html/history.html, accessed Dec. 10, 2006.

100. Email from Marvin M. Epstein, official Austin archivist and author of "*The Austin Story*", on behalf of Austin retirees and other experts in the company's history, Oct. 14, 2007.

101. JHP to G.R. Spradbrow, Mar. 22, 1927, describes the options for aeronautical engineering students at the time; JHP papers, Vol. 28, NRC Archives, Ottawa.

102. The first record of Elsie at the University of Michigan is a graduate student directory card dated Nov. 17, 1927. Later cards are dated Nov.26, 1928, and May 19, 1929. There is no mention in her file of research related to a firm named Austin. Information courtesy of Megan Cooney, Graduate Reference Assistant, U. of M. Archives, Bentley Historical Library, U. of M., via email and interview.

103. Remarks by U. of M. President Mary Sue Coleman at the "Celebration of University History", Oct. 4, 2006. History and Traditions Committee, http://www.umich.edu/pres/speeches/061004history.html, accessed Oct. 24, 2006.

104. R. Bordin, *Women at Michigan: The "Dangerous Experiment," 1870s to the Present*. Ann Arbor: University of Michigan Press, 1999, 19.

105. University of Michigan News Service, "Michigan Today", Summer 2004, at http://www.umich.edu/news/MT/04/Sum04/story.htmlengine, accessed Sep. 20, 2006.

106. "The History of Diversity at the University of Michigan", Bentley Historical Library, University of Michigan. http://umich.edu/bhl.refhom/diversity.htm, accessed Sep. 29, 2006.

107. University of Michigan Aerospace Engineering Department information sheet on Felix Pawlowski; http://www.engin.umich.edu/dept/aero/about/pawlowski.html, accessed Jan. 7, 2006.

108. M.E. Cooley with the assistance of V.B. Keatley, *Scientific Blacksmith*, Ann Arbor: University of Michigan Press, 1947, 115.

109. University of Michigan Aerospace Engineering Department, http://www.engin.umich.edu/dept/aero/about/pawlowski.html, accessed January 7, 2006.

110. The first M.S.E. (Aeronautical Engineering) at Michigan was awarded to W.F. Gerhardt in 1918.

111. R. Bordin, *Women at Michigan: The "Dangerous Experiment," 1870s to the Present*. Ann Arbor: University of Michigan Press, 1999, 32–33.

112. Mortimer E. Cooley. *Scientific Blacksmith*.

113. *The University of Michigan, An Encyclopedic Survey: The Department of Aeronautical Engineering*. Ann Arbor: University of Michigan Press, 1181–1189, via http://www.hti.umich.edu/u/umsurvey/, accessed Sep. 30, 2006.

114. E.A. Stalker, *Principles of Flight*. New York: Ronald, c1931.

115. "Canadian ... Women in Aviation", *Canadian Aviation*, Feb. 1940, 19, in which Professor Pawlowski cites one or two women working in the aviation industry in England and continental Europe in the 1920s.

116. JHP to Jas. L. Henning, Winnipeg, Mar. 3, 1931; JHP papers, Vol. 28, NRC Archives, Ottawa.

117. "Canadian ...Women in Aviation", 19.

118. Convocation program, University of Michigan, Thursday, May 9, 1929 (the same day as her admission to University Hospital) lists Elizabeth Muriel Gregory MacGill as a fellowship student in the M.S.E. program; LAC.

119. HMH, read by EHS at Elsie's memorial service.

120. Drawn from descriptions of related nervous-system diseases. Encyclopædia Britannica Premium Service, http://www.britannica.com/eb/article-75738, accessed Jan. 18, 2006.

121. Her home address, on personal correspondence, was 322 North State St., Ann Arbor, close to the campus and to University Hospital; LAC.
122. John L. Garvey, M.D., University of Michigan Department of Neurology, University Hospital, Anne Arbor, June 15, 1929. Medical referral letter written for Elsie; LAC.
123. Remarks by HMH, read by EHS at Elsie's memorial service.
124. *Ibid.*
125. *My Mother the Judge*, 205
126. EHS to DBD, Feb. 2, 2007.
127. EGM to Dr. Margaret Lourie, Director, Women's Studies Program, University of Michigan, Ann Arbor, May 13, 1974; LAC.

Chapter IV — Roots and Wings

128. EGM, "Women on the Wing", *Chatelaine*, August 1931, 15; LAC. Also cited in J.F. Vance, *High Flight: Aviation and the Canadian Imagination*. Toronto: Penguin Canada, 2002, 128, 301.
129. Elsie was there to help her mother through the 1926 recovery, having come home to Vancouver from Toronto that summer. Telegram dated June 9, 1926 "Elizabeth Muriel Gregory MacGill, Correspondence outward, 1926–1951", BCA.
130. Reference to Elsie designing a flying boat during this time of recuperation: comes from a doc. (#53027) entitled "Women can be Engineers", "Elsie MacGill Soulsby", 46. Society of Women Engineers Archives, Walter P. Reuther Library of Labor and Urban Affairs, Wayne State University, Detroit, MI.
131. "Canadian … Women in Aviation", *Canadian Aviation*, Feb. 1940, 20.
132. EGM, "Women on the Wing", *Chatelaine*, Aug. 1931, 42; LAC.
133. F.H. Ellis, *Canada's Flying Heritage*. Toronto: University of Toronto Press, 1954, 294.
134. *Ibid.*
135. J.F. Vance, *High Flight: Aviation and the Canadian Imagination*. Toronto: Penguin Canada, 2002, 129.
136. History of Vancouver Airport Authority, http://www.yvr.ca/authority/history/history.asp?id=1930, accessed Nov. 4, 2007.
137. J.R.K. Main, *Voyageurs of the Air: A History of Civil Aviation in Canada 1858–1967*. Ottawa: Queen's Printer, 1967, 86.
138. On Mar. 28, 1931, Elsie wrote to the University of Michigan asking that her academic "credentials" be sent to New York University, saying she hopes to undertake a research program in aeronautics there. Phone interview with Megan Cooney, Graduate Reference Assistant, Bentley Historical Library, University of Michigan, Nov. 2, 2007.

139. G. Burkowski, *Can-Car: A History 1912–1992*. Thunder Bay, ON: Bombardier Inc., 1995, 45.

140. Elsie's aunt, her father's sister, lived in Toronto and provided Elsie with a eastern base for the early years of her resumed career. In Aug. 1933, Elsie's home address was Sussex Court, Sussex and Huron Streets, Toronto; LAC.

141. C.E. Planck, *Women with Wings*. New York and London: Harper & Brothers, 1942, 219–220. Other women engineering students at MIT during the 1930s included Elsa Gardner, who had worked in a variety of technical roles in the aviation industry since WWI; Margaret Whitcomb, who earned her undergraduate degree in the Aeronautical Department and went on to earn a master's degree in metrology; and Rose Lunn, who took a master's in aeronautical engineering and continued postgraduate research while working with Curtiss-Wright.

142. Elsie is listed as a member of the MIT Class of 1934 in Marilynn A. Bever, "The Women of MIT, 1871 to 1941: Who They Were, What They Achieved". Thesis for the Department of Humanities, MIT, Cambridge, MA, 1976, 154.

143. JHP to Jas. L. Henning, Winnipeg, Mar. 3, 1931; JHP papers, Vol. 28, NRC Archives, Ottawa.

144. Timothy J. Cronen, Scope and Content Note, Jerome Clarke Hunsaker Papers, National Air and Space Archives, National Air and Space Museum, Smithsonian Institution, Washington, DC, 1994.

145. Parkin memoirs, Vol. I, 172.

146. "Hunsaker, Jerome C." Encyclopædia Britannica Premium Service at http://www.britannica.com/eb/article-9041552, accessed July 21, 2006.

147. W.F. Trimble, *Jerome C. Hunsaker and the Rise of American Aeronautics*. Washington/London: Smithsonian Institution Press, 2002, 145.

148. *Ibid.*, 146, citing S. Ober, *The Story of Aeronautics at MIT, 1895 to 1960*. Cambridge, MA: Department of Aeronautics and Astronautics, MIT, 1965.

149. EGM, "Danger! Women Thinking". Address to the opening banquet of the Quota Club International convention in Banff, AB, June 27, 1955. Reprinted as "Elizabeth Muriel Gregory MacGill", *The Quotarian*, Oct. 1955, 4–6; BCA.

150. W.F. Trimble, *Jerome C. Hunsaker and the Rise of American Aeronautics*. Washington/London: Smithsonian Institution Press, 2002, 146.

151. F.H. Ellis, *Canada's Flying Heritage*. Toronto: University of Toronto Press, 1954, 297, cites the 1935 start date at Fairchild, as does Elsie's later curriculum vitae. However, other facts suggest that she initiated a relationship with the firm, perhaps acceptance of the job offer, in late 1934.

152. S. Ober, *The Story of Aeronautics at MIT, 1895 to 1960*. Cambridge, MA: Department of Aeronautics and Astronautics, MIT, 1965.

153. According to Fairchild's numbering system, the first digit, "7", denoted the

number of people (passengers plus pilot) the plane could carry, the second digit the model number.

154. Larry Milberry, *Air Transport in Canada*, Vol. I. Toronto: CANAV Books, 1997, 105, and supported by essays for the U.S. Centennial of Flight Commission, http://www.centennialofflight.gov/essay/aerospace/Fairchild/aero25.htm, accessed Jan. 24, 2006.

155. W.E. Knowles Middleton, *Mechanical Engineering at the National Research Council of Canada, 1929–1951*. Waterloo: Wilfred Laurier Press, 1984, 31–32.

156. P. Pigott, *On Canadian Wings: A Century of Flight*. Toronto: Hounslow, 2005, 59. The prototype CF-AXA was flown around the time of Elsie's arrival at Fairchild. But she did work on the further development and refinement of the aircraft, among the most successful of the firm's projects in Canada during the period, with two dozen sold.

157. Parkin memoirs, Vol. II, 441.

158. "Wind Tunnel Tests on a 1/10 scale model Fairchild Super 71 Aircraft." Report No. PAA-17, Apr. 10, 1934, NRC Laboratories, Ottawa; and Report No. PAA-23, Aug. 8, 1935.

159. J.J. Green, obituary of Elsie, *Canadian Aeronautics and Space Journal*, 26 (1980): 349–351.

160. Parkin memoirs, Vol. II, 442.

161. Kenneth M. Molson, *Canada's National Aviation Museum: Its History and Collections*. Ottawa: National Aviation Museum/National Museum of Science and Technology, 1988, 31.

162. P. Pigott, *On Canadian Wings: A Century of Flight*. Toronto: Hounslow, 2005, 58. The Super 71P(CF-AUT) crashed on Morrison Lake, MB, Aug. 6, 1937; the original Super 71, based at Sioux Lookout, ON, hit a log on take-off in Oct. 1940.

163. "Wind Tunnel Tests on a 1/10 scale model Fairchild Super 71 Photographic Seaplane." Report No. PAA-48, Oct. 1, 1938, Division of Mechanical Engineering, NRC, Ottawa.

164. "Wind Tunnel Tests on Fairchild 'Sekani' landplane and skiplane with fixed wheel undercarriage." Report No. PAA-39, Feb. 8, 1938, Division of Mechanical Engineering, NRC, Ottawa. Elsie's friend J.J. Green conducted the tests under her guidance as the Fairchild engineer on site. Her former U. of T. professor, now an NRC director, J.H. Parkin, approved the work. Report No. PAA-48, Oct. 1, 1938, Division of Mechanical Engineering, NRC.

165. L. Milberry, *Aviation in Canada*. Toronto: McGraw-Hill Ryerson, 1979, 113.

166. J.J. Green, obituary of Elsie, *Canadian Aeronautics and Space Journal*, 26 (1980): 349–351.

167. DBD interview with Ann Soulsby, Toronto, Mar. 3, 2005.
168. J.J. Green obituary of Elsie, 349, and personal files of Ms. Anne Soulsby, Toronto, 2005.
169. Can-Car was founded as part of a merger of Canadian firms in 1912. It and its Fort William/Thunder Bay plant passed through many hands over the years, including Hawker Siddeley and, in the 1990s, Bombardier.
170. "Civil Service of Canada, Junior Engineer — Department of National Defence, Ottawa, $1800 per annum." LAC.
171. HMH, "Wasp/Woman/Sociologist", *Society* 14 (1977): 69–80, p.76.
172. A farewell dinner for Young Helen and her husband was held at McGill on May 10, 1938, around the time of Elsie's departure for Fort William. At the dinner Prof. W.D. Woodhead presented a humorous poem written in their honour; BCA.
173. Departure date cited in letter from EGM to her family, May 1938; LAC.

Chapter V — The Maple Leaf of Mexico

174. "Introducing The Maple Leaf Trainer", *Canadian Aviation*, August 1940, 20. A U.S. Navy test pilot was later quoted as calling her plane "one of the sweetest jobs I ever handled"; Gordon Burkowski, *Can-Car: A History 1912–1992*. Thunder Bay, ON: Bombardier Inc., 1995, 46.
175. F.H. Ellis, *Canada's Flying Heritage*. Toronto: University of Toronto Press, 1954, 298.
176. Formally Bishopsfield, but also identified in some sources as Bishop's Field. Then the only airport in Fort William, it was owned by Canadian Car and Foundry, which operated it with a private license acquired on the eve of Elsie's arrival at the Lakehead.
177. DBD interview with Jim Carmichael (Elsie's former Can-Car colleague), Ottawa, Jan. 26, 2008.
178. Parkin memoirs, Vol. II, 468–469.
179. One of these reports was a specially commissioned study ordered by Can-Car around the time Elsie was hired in early 1938. "Wind Tunnel Tests on a 1/24 scale model of the Burnelli three-engined Aircraft." Report No. PAA-42, May 12, 1938, Division of Mechanical Engineering, NRC, Ottawa.
180. K.M. Molson and H.A. Taylor, *Canadian Aircraft Since 1909*. Stittsville, ON: Canada's Wings, Inc., 1982, 170.
181. The plane was recovered from a Nicaraguan scrapyard and eventually restored with parts from another single plane now on display at the National Museum of Naval Aviation in Pensacola, Florida.
182. G. Burkowski, *Can-Car: A History 1912–1992*. Thunder Bay, ON: Bombardier Inc., 1995, 32–38, provides a fuller description of the company's adventure with the Goblins and the intrigue of the Spanish sale.

183. L. Milberry, *Sixty Years: The RCAF and CF Air Command 1924–1984.* Toronto: CANAV Books, 1984, 189.

184. P. Pigott, *Wings Across Canada: An Illustrated History of Canadian Aviation.* Toronto: Dundurn, 2002, 53.

185. EGM to W.J. Wheeler, Toronto, Jan. 27, 1966. "Test flights were carried out in September 1939 with J.V. Hatton flying as test pilot and me as observer"; LAC.

186. Obituary of J.J. Green, *Canadian Aeronautics and Space Journal*, 26 (1980): 349–351, 349. Green conducted tests on the Gregor Fighter design in Ottawa in the summer of 1938, described in "Wind Tunnel Tests on a 1/10 scale model single seater fighter biplane." Report No. PAA-45, June 30, 1938, Division of Mechanical Engineering, NRC, Ottawa.

187. "Canada's first fighter: shot down by bad timing", *Ottawa Citizen*, Dec. 17, 1988. Russian-born Michael Gregor had designed Russia-B, the first successful Russian-designed aircraft, before fleeing his native country for the United States in the wake of the Bolshevik Revolution.

188. L. Milberry, *Aviation in Canada.* Toronto: McGraw-Hill Ryerson, 1979, 111.

189. EGM to William J. Harvey, Montréal, 1964. Her address is given as 3 Bennington Heights Drive, Toronto; LAC.

190. Larry Milberry, *Sixty Years: The RCAF and CF Air Command 1924–1984.* Toronto: CANAV Books, 1984, 189. (Many other sources also identify December 17, 1938, as the date of the FDB-1 Gregor fighter's first flight, but research by aviation historian and author Jonathan Kirton, Rigaud, Quebec, shows that the plane was merely rolled out in Fort William for photos on this date and that the inaugural flight, in fact, took place months later in St. Hubert, Quebec (February 1939) when the planes flight logbook and registration certificate were acquired by Can-Car in Montréal.)

191. While the EIC membership was a significant first, such breakthroughs would eventually seem routine to Elsie. As well as being the first female to graduate in two engineering disciplines, she established many firsts over the years, e.g., first female Registered Professional Engineer in Canada and first woman to join other professional organizations, including the Association of Professional Engineers of Ontario.

192. Parkin memoirs, Vol. I, 141.

193. EGM to her family, May 27, 1938, sent from Longueuil, QC; LAC.

194. Lester Gardner, Institute of the Aeronautical Sciences., New York, to EGM, June 10, 1936; LAC.

195. A.M. Springer, "The Development of An Aerospace Society: The AIAA at 70". Paper presented to the 39th Aerospace Sciences Meeting and Exhibit, Jan. 5–12, 2001, Reno, NV; http://www.aiaa.org, accessed Sep. 10, 2006.

196. P. Wakewich, "'The Queen of the Hurricanes': Elsie Gregory MacGill: Aeronautical Engineer and Women's Advocate", in *Framing Our Past:*

Constructing Canadian Women's History in the Twentieth Century, eds. S. Cook, L. McLean, and K. O'Rourke. Montréal and Kingston: McGill-Queen's University Press, 2001, 396–401, 400.

197. Institute of Aeronautical Sciences, New York to EGM at Fairchild, Longueuil, QC, May 23, 1936 describes context. This quote is from Elsie's reply on June 6, 1936, to L.D. Gardner, Secretary of the Institute. Gardner indicated that she could not be admitted to the organization because its dinners were held at men-only venues. LAC.

198. Can-Car's first attempt, the Maple Leaf I Trainer, also known as the Wallace Trainer, had been designed by an American, Leland Stamford Wallace, a long-time colleague of Michael Gregor, and was evidently built with the intent of sales to Nicaragua, as the prototype tested in Fort William Apr. 18, 1938, bore identification (GN-3) from that country. K.M. Molson and H.A. Taylor, *Canadian Aircraft Since 1909*. Stittsville, ON: Canada's Wings, Inc., 1982, 165.

199. BCATP entry, *Canadian Encyclopaedia* online, accessed June 2006.

200. "Introducing the Maple Leaf Trainer", *Canadian Aviation*, Aug. 1940.

201. EGM to Mr. William J. Wheeler, Toronto, Jan. 27, 1966; LAC.

202. K.M. Molson and H.A. Taylor, *Canadian Aircraft Since 1909*. Stittsville, ON: Canada's Wings, Inc., 1982, 167.

203. G. Burkowski, *Can-Car: A History 1912–1992*. Thunder Bay, ON: Bombardier Inc., 1995, 46, referencing Molson and Taylor and Can-Car sources.

204. The Society of Women Engineers, 2003 Achievement Award brochure, The Society of Women Engineers, Chicago, IL.

205. http://www.aa.washington.edu/people/alumni/award/1994.html, accessed Aug. 10, 2006.

206. C.E. Planck, *Women with Wings*. New York and London: Harper & Brothers, 1942, 220.

207. J. Lee, D.S. Eberhardt, R.E. Breidenthal, and A.P. Bruckner, "A History of the University of Washington Department of Aeronautics and Astronautics 1917–2003". Seattle, WA: Department of Aeronautics & Astronautics, University of Washington, 2003; http://www.aa.washington.edu/about/history/AA_History.pdf, 15.

208. A. Canel, R. Oldenziel, and K. Zachmann, eds., Introduction to *Crossing Boundaries, Building Bridges: Comparing the History of Women Engineers, 1870s–1990s*. Amsterdam: Harwood Academic, 2004, 7.

209. A. Vogt, "Women in Army Research: Ambivalent Careers in Nazi Germany", in *ibid.*, 189–210, 201.

210. C.E. Planck, *Women with Wings*. New York and London: Harper & Brothers, 1942, 218–219.

211. *Ibid.*, 6.

212. EGM to her family, Dec. 1, 1939. Address given is 1306 Ridgeway Street, Fort William; LAC.

213. F.H. Ellis, *Canada's Flying Heritage.* Toronto: University of Toronto Press, 1954, 298.

214. L. Milberry and H.A. Halliday, *The Royal Canadian Air Force at War 1939–1945.* Toronto: CANAV Books, 1990, 142.

215. "Introducing The Maple Leaf Trainer", *Canadian Aviation*, Aug. 1940, 20.

216. *Ibid.*

217. DBD interview with Ann Soulsby, Toronto, Mar. 3, 2005.

218. J. Martin, "The Great Canadian Air Battle", *Canadian Military Journal*, Spring 2002: 65–69. Over 3000 Canadian and Allied pilots and crew were killed in Canada during WWII training and operations with an average of five fatal crashes and 12 deaths per week during 1942, 1943, and 1944.

219. EGM, "Practical Forms for Flight Test Reporting". Paper presented to the General Professional Meeting of the Engineering Institute of Canada, Toronto, Feb. 9, 1940; LAC.

220. S. Flores Ruiz, "Mexican Naval Aviation (1917–1979)", *Journal of the American Aviation Historical Society*, 25 (1980): 181–186.

221. EGM to K.M. Molson, Nov. 22, 1965; Canada Aviation Museum and Archives, Ottawa.

222. EGM to the president of Republic Aviation Corporation, Long Island, NY, Aug. 20, 1958; LAC.

223. K.M. Molson and H.A. Taylor, *Canadian Aircraft Since 1909.* Stittsville, ON: Canada's Wings, Inc., 1982, 167. "The Maple Leaf II was exported to the Columbia Aircraft Corp.… on Long Island in October 1940." ." Also, a 16 August 1940 letter from the Civil Aeronautics Authority in Washington to the Controller of Civil Aviation in Ottawa says that a J.W. Kenney of Columbia Aircraft, Port Washington, New York State, had purchased "a Maple Leaf Trainer II and pertinent technical data from the Canadian Car and Foundry Company" as quoted by J. Kirton in email to DBD, 31 March 2008. Interestingly, Can-Car Vice-President L.A. Peto had stated only four months earlier (letter dated 18 April 1940 to CCA) that Can-Car planned to fly the Maple Leaf II directly to Mexico.

224. J.R. Ellis, compiler, *Canadian Civil Aircraft Register 1929–1945.* Ottawa: CAHS Publications, nd.

225. DBD interview with Gabriel Parrish, Vice-President, Valley Stream New York Historical Society, and Columbia employee (1941–1946), Oct. 30, 2006. Parrish states that Columbia did not own, operate, or manufacture such a trainer at either its Port Washington or Valley Stream plants after the summer of 1941.

226. Republic Aviation was bought by Elsie's former employer Fairchild in 1965, with the merged enterprise becoming Fairchild Republic by 1971. B.

Gunston, *World Encyclopedia of Aircraft Manufacturers: From Pioneers to the Present Day*. Annapolis, MD: Naval Institute Press, 1993, 251.

227. José Villela Gomez, *Breve historia de la aviacion en México*, D.F. Mexico (s.n.) 1971, 228–230.

228. The intelligence report quotes the Mexican newspaper *Excelsior* for Aug. 8, 1941, and the newspaper *El Nacional* for Aug. 8, 1941. Newspaper photos show the aircraft on land and in the air. Dan Hagedorn, Archives Research Team Leader and Adjunct Curator, Latin American Aviation, Archives Division, Smithsonian Institution, National Air and Space Museum, Washington, DC, in the U.S. National Archives at College Park, MD. Hagedorn says "It was clear to me that this 'pattern' aircraft was in fact the elusive Maple Leaf", suggesting that the plane may have been the Fort William prototype plane, modified for Mexican requirements, and that "the Ares aircraft... which bears a nearly identical appearance to the Maple Leaf was in fact built in a quantity reported as being between 10 and 12". Information per Nov. 16, 2006, email from Hagedorn, and Nov. 17, 2006, interview at the National Air and Space Museum, Washington, DC.

229. Article in Mexican newspaper *El Nacional* of Aug. 8, 1941, cited by D. Hagedorn in email to DBD, Nov. 16, 2006.

230. K.M. Molson and H.A. Taylor, *Canadian Aircraft Since 1909*. Stittsville, ON: Canada's Wings, Inc., 1982, 167, says the series is identified as Ares Num. 2, a name that echoes the Maple Leaf Trainer II. But other sources state that each of the ten Ares trainers was identified by a number (Ares 01, 02,03,04,05,06,07,08,09,10).

231. "Introducing The Maple Leaf Trainer", *Canadian Aviation*, Aug. 1940, 225–250.

232. U.S. military intelligence report, Mar. 26, 1943 (declassified 1/3/'96), copied in U.S. National Archives, Washington, courtesy D. Hagedorn, Smithsonian National Air and Space Museum.

233. Coronel José Franciso Teran Valle, Military and Air Attaché, Embassy of Mexico, Ottawa to DBD, Dec. 11, 2006, confirms this and other facts cited here with respect to the Ares, and for Mexico's negotiations with Can-Car on the Maple Leaf II Trainer.

234. S. Flores Ruiz, "Mexico Fashions an Aerial Poncho/History of the Mexican Air Force", *Air International*, 21 (1981): 248.

235. M.C. Meyer and W.H. Beezley, eds., *The Oxford History of Mexico*. Oxford/ New York: Oxford University Press, 2000, 536, 540.

236. Also referred to as Luis Noriega and Noriega Medrano. Schwab, Stephen I., "The role of the Mexican expeditionary air force in World War II: Late, limited, but symbolically significant", *Journal of Military History*, 66 (2002): 1119.

237. *Ibid.*, 1115.

238. Sig Unander Jr., "World War II: Mexican air force helped liberate the Philippines: The only Mexican air force unit to serve overseas during World War II fought to liberate the Philippines", *Aviation History*, reproduced (nd) at http://www.historynet.com/magazines/aviation_history/3028341.html?page=1&c=y, accessed Aug. 15, 2007.

239. J.R.K. Main, *Voyageurs of the Air: A History of Civil Aviation in Canada 1858–1967*. Ottawa: Queen's Printer, 1967, 264.

240. In the decade after the war, Can-Car's Fort William plant manufactured Harvards and a Beech trainer as a last effort in the aircraft industry before moving on to other products, including buses and other transit system equipment.

Chapter VI — The Ice Queen of the Hurricanes

241. F.K. Mason, *The Hawker Hurricane*. Manchester, U.K.: Crécy, 1987, 50.

242. *My Mother the Judge*, 227.

243. EGM to her family, May 7, 1938; (LAC).

244. EGM to her family, Dec. 1, 1939, from Fort William; LAC.

245. DBD interview with Jim Carmichael, Elsie's Can-Car colleague, Jan. 26, 2008. He and Elsie regarded Mitchell as a "romantic" figure.

246. "Messerschmitt, Willy." Encyclopædia Britannica Premium Service, http://www.britannica.com/eb/article-9052244, accessed Feb. 18, 2006.

247. "Hawker Siddeley", U.S. Centennial of Flight Commission Essays, http://www.centennialofflight.gov/essay/Aerospace/Hawker/Aero51a.htm, accessed Feb. 5, 2006.

248. A hurricane or "a tropical cyclone generates winds that exceed 119 km (74 miles) per hour". "Tropical cyclone", Encyclopaedia Britannica Premium Service, http://www.britannica.com/eb/article-9106251, accessed Feb. 18, 2006.

249. P. Pigott, *On Canadian Wings: A Century of Flight*. Toronto: Hounslow, 2005, 81.

250. Victor M. Drury, Can-Car president, was also President of the Conservative Party of Canada. G. Burkowski, *Can-Car: A History 1912–1992*. Thunder Bay, ON: Bombardier Inc., 1995, 49.

251. F.K. Mason, *The Hawker Hurricane*. Manchester, U.K.: Crécy, 1987, 50.

252. K.M. Molson and H.A. Taylor, *Canadian Aircraft Since 1909*. Stittsville, ON: Canada's Wings, Inc., 1982, 378.

253. These citations and much of the detail of this work is as described in a special issue of *The Standard Photonews*, Montréal, July 20, 1940. Caption of photo entitled "Hurricanes Made in Canada".

254. Pamela Wakewich, "'The Queen of the Hurricanes': Elsie Gregory MacGill: Aeronautical Engineer and Women's Advocate", in *Framing Our Past:*

Constructing Canadian Women's History in the Twentieth Century, eds. S. Cook, L. McLean and K. O'Rourke. Montréal and Kingston: McGill–Queen's University Press, 2001, 396–401. "Women's participation in aircraft production at Can-Car began in January 1938 with the hiring of a small group of women to sew fabric [for] wings and tails for aircraft."

255. *The Standard Photonews*, Montréal, July 20, 1940. Caption of photo entitled "Aircraft Boss".

256. G. Burkowski, *Can-Car: A History 1912–1992*. Thunder Bay, ON: Bombardier Inc., 1995, 84–85: "From being an almost exclusively male workforce, the Can-Car staff included around 350 women or 10 percent of its employees by the start of 1941, and 2,707 or 40 percent of its 6,760 in March 1944."

257. Citation in Canada Aviation Museum Hawker Hurricane exhibit panel, Aug. 2006: Hurricanes were credited with downing over 80 percent of all enemy aircraft destroyed in the Battle of Britain.

258. DBD interview with Jim Carmichael, Ottawa, Jan. 26, 2008.

259. Samuel Kostenuk and John Griffin, *National Museum of Man/National Museums of Canada RCAF Squadron Histories and Aircraft 1924–1968*. Toronto/Sarasota: Hakkert, 1977, 21: "the first squadron of the RCAF to engage the enemy, to score victories, to suffer combat casualties, and to win gallantry awards".

260. http://www.airforce.forces.gc.ca/hist/hist_battle_e.asp, accessed Feb. 18, 2006.

261. Among sources noting the influence of Canada in planning the air war is: J. Terraine, *The Right of the Line: The Royal Air Force in the European War 1939–1945*. London/Sydney/Auckland/Toronto: Hodder and Stoughton, 1985, 464.

262. K. Saxberg (dir.), "Rosies of the North". Montréal: National Film Board of Canada, 1999.

263. G. Burkowski, *Can-Car: A History 1912–1992*. Thunder Bay, ON: Bombardier Inc., 1995, 63.

264. Parkin memoirs, Vol. II, 468.

265. K.M. Molson and H.A. Taylor, *Canadian Aircraft Since 1909*. Stittsville, ON: Canada's Wings, Inc., 1982, 379.

266. J. Montagnes, "Girl designs new trainers", *The New York Times*, Oct. 13, 1940; LAC.

267. "The Queen of the Hurricanes" (True Comics), cited in J.F. Vance, High Flight: Aviation and the Canadian Imagination. Toronto: Penguin Canada, 2002, 264 (undated in LAC, but cited as Jan. 1942 by Michigan State University Libraries, Special Collections Div; at http://www.CBC.ca ("Queen of the Hurricanes"); and in other sources). Predictably, the comic offered a faint and flawed representation of the events of her life, causing some confusion and jealousy.

268. Although C.E. Planck, in *Women with Wings*. New York and London: Harper & Brothers, 1942, did not attribute this statement directly to Elsie, she was the only female aviation figure cited in his book who met the description of an aeronautical engineer in a large manufacturing firm in 1942.

269. *Ibid.*, 6.

270. Type-written speaking notes with Elsie's handwritten edits and notes; LAC.

271. J. Montagnes, "Girl designs new trainers", *The New York Times*, Oct. 13, 1940; LAC.

272. EGM, "Simplified Performance Calculations for Aeroplanes". Paper presented to the Ottawa branch of the Engineering Institute of Canada on Mar. 22, 1938, when Elsie was at Fairchild and not yet a member, and published in *Engineering Journal* in Aug. 1938, after she had arrived at Can-Car.

273. EMG, "Performance Design Hampers Mass Production of Aircraft", *Canadian Aviation*, Sep. 1940, 22–23, 26. An earlier article on the same theme ("Mass production of aircraft") appeared in *Canadian Aviation* in Aug. 1940, 26–28.

274. K.M. Molson and H.A. Taylor, *Canadian Aircraft Since 1909*. Stittsville, ON: Canada's Wings, Inc., 1982, 378.

275. For a full description of early aircraft-ski research in Canada see Chap. 3, "The Science of Skis in the Sky," in DBD, *George J. Klein: the Great Inventor*. Ottawa: NRC Research Press, 2004.

276. Parkin memoirs, Vol. II, 435.

277. J.J. Green and G.S. Levy, "The Wind Tunnel Development of a Streamlined Ski for the Hawker Hurricane Aircraft". NRC Report MA-72, Nov. 1939, cited in W.E. Knowles Middleton, *Mechanical Engineering at the National Research Council of Canada, 1929–1951*. Waterloo, ON: Wilfred Laurier University Press, 1984, 73.

278. Parkin memoirs, Vol. II, 436.

279. K.M. Molson and H.A. Taylor, *Canadian Aircraft since 1909*. Stittsville, ON: Canada's Wings, Inc., 1982, 380. Tests were conducted at Rockcliffe airbase in Ottawa in Feb. and Mar. 1943. Earlier attempts to conduct tests in Fort William were thwarted by weather conditions.

280. *Proceedings of the Sixth Meeting of the Subcommittee on Aircraft Skis of the Associate Committee on Aeronautical Research*, Feb. 16, 1943. Ottawa: NRC, Ottawa, 2; JHP papers, Vol. 40, NRC Archives.

281. *Proceedings of the Eighth Meeting of the Subcommittee on Aircraft Skis of the Associate Committee on Aeronautical Research*, Sep. 11, 1944. Ottawa: NRC, 1; JHP Papers, Vol. 40, NRC Archives, Ottawa.

282. J.L. Orr, D. Fraser, J.A. Lynch, and C.K. Rush, NRC Commonwealth Advisory Aeronautical Research Council. Report No. MD-34, CC 91. Ottawa: NRC Canada Institute for Scientific and Technical Information, 1.

283. W.E. Knowles Middleton, *Mechanical Engineering at the National Research Council of Canada, 1929–1951.* Waterloo: Wilfred Laurier Press, 1984, 132: The "June 12, 1945, Canadian Patent 428135 was awarded to T.R. Griffiths and J.L. Orr [of the National Research Council in Ottawa]" for their electrical heater system for aircraft propellers. "Most of the equipment for de-icing propellers made after the War was made, under licence and otherwise, on the principles in this patent."

284. K. Munson, *Aircraft of World War II.* London: Ian Allan, 1974, 91: Hawker built 10 030 itself. The grand total was 14 533, counting those produced by Can-Car and others.

285. K.M. Molson, *Canada's National Aviation Museum: Its History and Collections.* Ottawa: National Aviation Museum/National Museum of Science and Technology, 1988, 158.

Chapter VII — A Dive into Hell

286. U.S. air crews and pilots quoted in reference to the SB2C Helldiver in Peter Pigott, *On Canadian Wings: A Century of Flight.* Toronto: Hounslow, 2005, 111.

287. U.S. Centennial of Flight Commission, http://www.centennialofflight.gov/essay/Aerospace/Curtiss/Aero2.htm.

288. A few months later the Canadian operations of Fairchild were also subcontracted to produce 300 Helldivers, which they did. The eventual Can-Car total was recorded as 894. Kenneth Munson, *Aircraft of World War II.* London: Ian Allan, 1974, 50.

289. http://www.cenntennialofflight.gov/essay/Aerospace/Curtiss_wright/Aero9.htm, accessed Mar. 13, 2005.

290. According to Gordon Burkowski, *Can-Car: A History 1912–1992.* Thunder Bay, ON: Bombardier Inc., 1995, 73, the platforms were "40 feet by 48 feet". Burkowski is the source of much of the general information in this section.

291. *Ibid.,* 75.

292. *Ibid.,* 76.

293. "Initially, single women were selected, but when labour shortages continued, married women without children were hired." Pamela Wakewich, Helen Smith, and Jeanette Lynes, "Women's Wartime Work and Identities: A Case Study of Women Workers at Canadian Car and Foundry Co. Ltd., Fort William, ON, 1938–1945", in S. Cook, L. McLean, and K. O'Rourke, eds, *Framing Our Past: Constructing Canadian Women's History in the Twentieth Century.* Montréal and Kingston: McGill–Queen's University Press, 2001, 410.

Chapter VII — "My dear Mr. S" and a New Era

294. *My Mother the Judge*, 238
295. Ann Soulsby to DBD via email, Dec. 2 & 3, 2006. Elsie and Bill's civil wedding is recorded as taking place in Kankakee, IL, south of Chicago, although it was celebrated at her sister's home in Chicago and often recounted as having taken place there.
296. "Elsie MacGill wed in Chicago: Bride Outstanding Canadian Woman", unspecified newspaper clipping; LAC.
297. *My Mother the Judge*, 105.
298. H. MacGill Hughes, *News and the Human Interest Story*. 1940, reprint, New York: Greenwood, 1968, xxiii.
299. *Ibid.* vii.
300. HMH, "Wasp/Woman/Sociologist", *Society* 14 (1977): 69–80, 69.
301. *Ibid.*, 74.
302. *Ibid.*, 73.
303. *Ibid.*, 75.
304. *Ibid.*, 70.
305. *Ibid.*
306. *My Mother the Judge*, 205.
307. HMH, "Wasp/Woman/Sociologist", *Society* 14 (1977): 69–80, 76.
308. E. Hughes, *French Canada in Transition.* Chicago: University of Chicago Press, 1943, one of Hughes' classic works, reflects this collaboration with Elsie's sister.
309. Hoecker-Drysdale, "Women sociologists in Canada: Three careers", in *Despite the Odds: Essays on Canadian Women and Science*, ed. M. Gosztonyi Ainley. Montréal: Véhicule Press, 1990, 152–176, 167. In notes to follow, this book is abbreviated to *Despite the Odds.*
310. *Ibid.*, 165.
311. M. Gosztonyi Ainley, Introduction to *Despite the Odds*, 17–21, 21.
312. M. Gosztonyi Ainley, "Last in the field? Canadian women natural scientists, 1815–1965", in *Despite the Odds*, 25–62, 42.
313. *Ibid.*, 61.
314. R.A. Richardson and B.H. MacDonald, *Science and Technology in Canadian History: A Bibliography of Primary Sources to 1914.* Thornhill, ON: HSTC Publications, 1987, cited in *Despite the Odds*, 65.
315. M. Gilett, "Carrie Derick (1862–1941) and the Chair of Botany at McGill", in *Despite the Odds*, 74–87, 75.
316. R.H. Estey, "Margaret Newton: Distinguished Canadian Scientist", in *Despite the Odds*, 236–247, 245.
317. M. Gosztonyi Ainley, "Last in the field? Canadian women natural scientists, 1815–1965", in *Despite the Odds*, 25–62, 43.

318. M. Gosztonyi Ainley, "Last in the field? Canadian women natural scientists, 1815–1965", in *Despite the Odds*, 25–62.

319. *Ibid.*

320. B. Meadowcroft, "Alice Wilson, 1881–1964: Explorer of the Earth Beneath Her Feet", in *Despite the Odds*, 204–219.

321. *Ibid.*

322. EMG, "Position of Women in Canada in the Engineering Profession". *Saturday Night*, Oct. 19, 1946, 28.

323. "Soroptimist of the Month: High Flying Designer", *The American Soroptimist*, Nov. 1953, 4.

324. Helen (Heaps) Soulsby was born Apr. 11, 1899 in Keighley, Yorks., U.K. She married Bill Soulsby in Aug. 1925 in Fort William, and died in Sep. 1942.

325. John Frank Soulsby was born Feb. 16, 1929, at Fort William, ON, and died Jan. 16, 1996, in the U.K.

326. K.M. Molson, *Canada's National Aviation Museum: Its History and Collections.* Ottawa: National Aviation Museum/National Museum of Science and Technology, 1988, 41.

327. G. Burkowski, *Can-Car: A History 1912–1992.* Thunder Bay, ON: Bombardier Inc., 1995, 56.

328. *Ibid.*

329. Although the name "MacGill-Soulsby" did not exist in any official sense, on occasion Elsie would be addressed as Mrs. MacGill-Soulsby or Mrs. Soulsby by those who may have assumed her use of her maiden name was merely a professional gesture.

330. G. Burkowski, *Can-Car: A History 1912–1992.* Thunder Bay, ON: Bombardier Inc., 1995, 46.

331. Elsie's former Can-Car colleague Jim Carmichael, unpublished manuscript on Can-Car history and interview with author, Jan. 26, 2008, Ottawa.

332. From a faded, unidentified newspaper clipping; LAC.

333. G. Burkowski, *Can-Car: A History 1912–1992.* Thunder Bay, ON: Bombardier Inc., 1995, 90.

334. Correspondence from the period gave her address as 365–370, 86 Bloor Street West, Toronto.

335. J. Sharp, "A Name in Vain", *Vancouver Province*, June 13, 1972.

336. Gilbreth's application of industrial production and workplace efficiency methods to their home was described by two of their children, Frank Bunker Gilbreth, Jr. and Ernestine Gilbreth Carey, in two books — *Cheaper by the Dozen* (1949; filmed 1950) and *Belles on Their Toes* (1950; filmed 1952) — and inspired less factual accounts by others.

337. *My Mother the Judge*, 240

338. EGM, "Danger! Women Thinking". Address to the opening banquet of the

Quota Club International convention in Banff, AB, June 27, 1955. Reprinted in *The Quotarian*, Oct. 1955, 4–6, as "Elizabeth Muriel Gregory MacGill"; BCA.

339. HGM was born Jan. 7, 1864, in Hamilton, ON. She is buried in Vancouver's Mountain View Cemetery.

Chapter IX — The Business of Women

340. M. Bégin, "The Royal Commission on the Status of Women in Canada: Twenty Years Later" in *Challenging Times*, Part I, eds. C. Backhouse and D.H. Flaherty. Montréal & Kingston: McGill–Queen's University Press, 1992, 21–38, 28.

341. P. Pigott, *National Treasure: The History of Trans Canada Airlines*. Madeira Park, BC: Harbour Publishing, 2001, 181. Another senior TCA engineer at the time was J.T. Dyment, a close friend Elsie met at the U. of T. and who she would count as a close colleague until her death.

342. K.M. Molson and H.A. Taylor, *Canadian Aircraft since 1909*. Stittsville, ON: Canada's Wings, Inc., 1982, 78.

343. K.M. Molson, "World War Two Aircraft Production in Canada", *The Journal of the Canadian Aviation Historical Society*, 30 (Winter 1992): 138–148, 139.

344. HHB to DDB, Oct. 28, 2007, the source of this and other quotes on the MacGill family's sense of pride.

345. *Ibid.*

346. C.D. Howe, Minister of Reconstruction and Chairman of the Delegation; H.J. Symington, President, Trans-Canada Air Lines; J.A. Wilson, Director of Air Services, Department of Transport. http://www.icao.int/cgi/goto_m.pl?icao/en/hist/history02.htm, http://www.icao.int/icao/en/chicago_conf/index.html, http://www.icao.int/cgi/goto_m.pl?/icao/en/chicago_conf/committees.html,http://www.icao.int/cgi/goto_m.pl?/icao/en/chicago_conf/delegates.html.

347. J.J. Green, obituary of Elsie, *Canadian Aeronautics and Space Journal*, 26 (1980): 350.

348. Such as her speech "The Initiative in Airliner Design", which admonished American industry for falling behind in the gas turbine engine age, to the Convention of the Society of Women Engineers, Chicago, Sep. 5, 1952; Society of Women Engineers Archives, Walter P. Reuther Library of Labor and Urban Affairs, Wayne State University, Detroit, MI.

349. J.J. Green, obituary of Elsie; http://www.swe.org/stellent/idcplg?IdcService=SS_GET_PAGE&ssDocName=swe_000999&ssSourceNodeId=63, accessed June 13, 2006

350. *The Journal of the Society of Women Engineers*, June 1953: 5; Society

of Women Engineers Archives, Walter P. Reuther Library, Wayne State University, Detroit, MI.

351. Elsie's letter of acceptance to Miss Marie Reith, Chairman of the Awards Committee, Mar. 14, 1953; Society of Women Engineers Archives.

352. In an Oct. 30, 1951, letter to M. Brown of the Business and Professional Women in Vancouver, Elsie not only expressed pride that her family stretched back generations on this continent, but also in the fact that the American states (then territories) Wyoming and Colorado had granted women the vote before other jurisdictions abroad. "Elizabeth Muriel Gregory MacGill, Correspondence outward, 1926–1951"; BCA.

353. Elsie's remarks to the Mar. 28, 1953, meeting of the Society of Women Engineers in New York where she received her award; Society of Women Engineers Archives, Walter P. Reuther Library of Labor and Urban Affairs, Wayne State University, Detroit, MI.

354. *Ibid.*

355. Elsie's friend Margaret Hyndman, QC, at Elsie's memorial service.

356. *Ibid.*

357. For example, EGM to "Miss Wright", Feb. 26, 1948, soliciting information on her mother's, grandmother's and cousin Sarah's involvement in the Women's Auxiliary of the Anglican Church; BCA.

358. An exception in this context may be a love poem written by her half-brother Freddy that Elsie saved; BCA.

359. HHB to DBD, Oct. 28, 2007.

360. "Danger! Women Thinking", an address given by Elsie Gregory MacGill, P. Eng, to the Opening Banquet of the Quota Club International Convention in Banff, Alberta, June 27, 1955 and reprinted in *The Quotarian*, Oct. 1955, 4–6; BCA.

361. *Ibid.*

362. DBD interview on June 19, 2006, with Dr. F.M. (Mary) Williams, Director General, NRC Institute for Ocean Technology, St. John's, NL. Dr. Williams held the NSERC/Petro-Canada Chair for Women in Science and Engineering, Atlantic Region, Memorial University, 1997–2002.

363. Elsie's mother had at times been more positive about what women had accomplished in the political world. In an article published in the May 16, 1936, issue of *Liberty Magazine*, she strongly asserted that "Canadian women have NOT failed in politics", reciting social reforms they had induced. Cited in a Nov. 26, 1947 letter from Elsie to the editor the Phi Delta Delta, Detroit, MI; BCA, "Elizabeth Muriel Gregory MacGill, Correspondence outward, 1926–1951".

364. E. Gregory MacGill, "A Blueprint for Madame Prime Minister", Address at the Banquet on July 27, 1954, the Federation of Business and Professional Women's Clubs 14th Biennial Convention, Royal York Hotel, Toronto,

Canada, NRC Archives, NRC Canada Institute for Scientific and Technical Information, Ottawa.

365. EGM, "A Blueprint for Madame Prime Minister". Banquet address, 14th Biennial Convention of the Federation of Business and Professional Women's Clubs, Royal York Hotel, Toronto, July 27, 1954.

366. Margaret Hyndman, QC, Elsie's memorial service.

367. "Top feminine business brains go into session", *Vancouver Province*, May 16, 1963.

368. After attending a 1963 Conference in Vancouver, for example, she made side trips to Kitimat, Prince Rupert, Prince George, Fort St. John, Dawson Creek, and Peace River in "Top feminine business brains go into session", *Vancouver Province*, May 16, 1963.

369. J. LaMarsh, *Memoirs of a Bird in a Gilded Cage.* Toronto/Montréal: McClelland and Stewart, 1968, 301.

370. CBC TV broadcast, accessed Feb. 3, 2006, http://archives.cbc.ca/IDC-1-73-86-410/politics_economy/status_women/clip1CBC

371. CBC TV broadcast, accessed Feb. 3, 2006, http://archives.cbc.ca/IDC-1-73-86-410/politics_economy/status_women/clip1.

372. *Memoirs of a Bird in a Gilded Cage*, 302.

373. "Ahead of her time", *Today Magazine*, Sep. 13, 1980.

374. *Memoirs of a Bird in a Gilded Cage*, 302.

375. "Jumbo jets, women's pleas engross Elsie MacGill", *Montreal Gazette*, Sep. 13, 1968.

376. http://radio.cbc.ca/programs/thismorning/sites/politics/women_010308.html.

377. Florence Bird, speaking notes for Elsie's memorial service.

378. C. Sissons, University of Ottawa, "Elsie MacGill: Feminist Engineer and 'The Moving Force' of the Royal Commission on the Status of Women, 1967–1970". Paper presented at the 14th Biennial Conference of the Canadian Science and Technology, Historical Association, Sep. 29 – Oct. 2, 2005, Canada Science and Technology Museum, Ottawa.

379. *Ibid.*

380. Other commissioners including Elsie's friend Doris Ogilvie opposed the liberalized abortion proposals in the commission's report even though they were more restrained than Elsie's. International human-rights advocate and fellow commissioner John Peters Humphrey issued a lengthy separate report, distancing himself from significant portions of the report, specifically the notion of quotas to induce equality, in a move he admitted was difficult in part because he feared that his position might be viewed as "Male prejudice".

381. *Report of the Royal Commission on the Status of Women in Canada.* Ottawa: Information Canada, 1970, 429.

382. The first Minister Responsible for the Status of Women was the Hon. Robert K. Andras, appointed May 1971; the first woman to hold the post (from Sep. 1981, a whole decade later) was the Hon. Judith Erola.
383. "Status report impact already felt — commissioner", *The Montreal Star*, May 11, 1971, Lifestyles section.
384. DBD interview with Ann Soulsby, Toronto, Mar. 3, 2005.

Chapter X — Following Through to the End

385. Dr. Lorna Marsden, now President of York University at Elsie's memorial service.
386. DBD interview with Dr. Lorna Marsden, Nov. 20, 2006.
387. "Status report impact already felt — commissioner", *The Montreal Star*, May 11, 1971.
388. *Ibid.*
389. Dr. Lorna Marsden, at Elsie's memorial service.
390. P. Wakewich, "'The Queen of the Hurricanes': Elsie Gregory MacGill: Aeronautical Engineer and Women's Advocate", in S. Cook, L. McLean, and K.O'Rourke, eds, *Framing Our Past: Constructing Canadian Women's History in the Twentieth Century.* Montréal and Kingston: McGill–Queen's University Press, 2001, 400–401.
391. DBD interview with Dr. Lorna Marsden, Nov. 20, 2006.
392. Dr. Lorna Marsden, at Elsie's memorial service.
393. Just over a quarter of the commission's recommendations were directed at non-federal organizations.
394. "Ten Years Later", CBC TV broadcast, Senator Florence Bird interview with Patrick Watson, Dec. 29, 1980, http://archives.cbc.ca/IDC-1-73-86-418/politics_economy/status_women/clip8, accessed June 29, 2006. Bird cited the figures 43 fully and 53 substantially implemented.
395. Described in an exchange of letters between Anderson and Elsie, June/July, 1971; LAC.
396. Hon. Monique Bégin, Minister of National Health and Welfare, to E.J. Soulsby, Dec. 16, 1980; LAC.
397. M. Bégin, "The Royal Commission on the Status of Women in Canada: Twenty Years Later", in Constance Backhouse and David H. Flaherty, *Challenging Times*, Part I. Montréal and Kingston: McGill–Queen's University Press, 1992, 30.
398. House of Commons debates, Jan. 28, 1975, 2685, cited in *ibid.*
399. The other Order of Canada recipients in 1971 included hockey stars Jean Beliveau and Gordie Howe, harness racer Hervé Filion, and another aeronautical engineering figure Phil Garratt of de Havilland Aircraft, the

man whose Moth series trainer aircraft had edged out Elsie's Maple Leaf II for contracts with the RCAF.

400. HHB to DBD, Oct. 28, 2007, quoting Ann Soulsby.
401. EGM. Speaking notes for "Action 75 Plus", International Women's Year Conference, Ottawa, Oct. 15, 1975, Panel Number 2; LAC.
402. *Ibid.*
403. *Ibid.*
404. Kathleen Rex, "Aircraft pioneer wants controls on flying space", *The Globe and Mail*, June 12, 1978.
405. EGM. Speaking notes on the occasion of receiving the gold medal of the Professional Engineers of Ontario, Hotel Toronto, Toronto, Oct. 27, 1979; LAC.
406. *Ibid.*
407. http://www.canadian99s.org/articles/p_macgill.htm, accessed June 30, 2006.
408. (Hamilton) *Mountain News*, Feb. 5, 1975; LAC.
409. EHS's middle daughter, Rachel, Elsie's grandniece, is now the proud possessor of the replica of the Amelia Earhart medal. She named her cat Amelia, expanding opportunities to reference the medal.
410. Senator Florence Bird to E.J. Soulsby, Nov. 7, 1980.
411. Ann Olga Flesher.
412. Ontario Ministry of Consumer and Commercial Relations, "An amazing woman". *Intercom*, 4, no. 7 (1980).
413. "Soroptimist of the Month: High Flying Designer", *The American Soroptimist*, Nov. 1953, 4.
414. DBD telephone interview with Ann Soulsby, Jan. 24, 2005.
415. Obit, Everrett C. Hughes, *Boston Globe*, Jan. 8, 1983.
416. This special note ("much loved") about the then-ill Everett Cherrington Hughes was included in the program for Elsie's memorial service. Everett died just over two years later in Jan. 1983 at the same hospital in Cambridge. He did not have Alzheimer's Disease, as some reports stated, but his Parkinson-like ailments had been magnified by a stroke shortly before his death. His wife Helen lived another decade, dying in 1993 of progressive supra-nuclear palsy, another Parkinson-like disease, while living in a nursing home in Baltimore, MD, near the home of her daughter, Elizabeth Schneewind.
417. Ann Soulsby to DBD via email, July 17, 2006.
418. E.J. Soulsby at Elsie's memorial service.
419. "Ahead of her time", *Today Magazine* (a weekly supplement in the *Toronto Star* and other Canadian papers), Sep. 13, 1980.
420. EHS. Personal remarks at Elsie's memorial service.

421. Bill Soulsby died suddenly while walking through a local grocery-store parking lot in Toronto in April 1983.
422. Like her mother and other family members, Elsie is buried at Mountainview Cemetery in Vancouver.

Epilogue

423. Quotation from Ruth Schwartz Cowan, Chair of the Honors College, State University of New York at Stony Brook, in A. Canel, R. Oldenziel, and K. Zachmann, eds., Foreword to *Crossing Boundaries, Building Bridges: Comparing the History of Women Engineers, 1870s–1990s*. Amsterdam: Harwood Academic, 2004, xv.
424. "Commemorating the École Polytechnique Victims and Tracing the Roots of NRC's Women in Engineering and Science Initiative." Zone News (online internal NRC employee news site), Dec. 6, 2004.
425. C. Sissons, "Elsie MacGill: Feminist Engineer and 'The Moving Force' of the Royal Commission on the Status of Women, 1967–1970". Paper presented at the Canadian Science and Technology Historical Association Conference, Ottawa, Sep. 2005, and more fully explored in C. Sissons, "Engineer and Feminist: Elsie Gregory MacGill and the Royal Commission on the Status of Women, 1967–1970", *Scientia Canadensis*, 29 (2006): 75–97. Ms. Sissons, a graduate student at the U. of Ottawa, is working on a Ph.D. dissertation entitled "Elsie Gregory MacGill: Engineering the Future and Building Bridges for Canadian Women, 1918–1980".
426. M. Frize and R. Heap, "The Professional Education of Women Engineers in Ontario and Quebec (1920–1999): Enrolment Patterns". Website of the Memorial University Chair for Women in Science and Engineering, http://www.mun.ca/cwse/Frize,Heap.pdf, accessed Aug. 4, 2006.
427. NSERC/Nortel Networks Joint Chair for Women in Science and Engineering in Ontario, National Statistics, women in accredited engineering programs: In 1998 = 12.3% of undergraduates; in 1998 = 19.5% of undergrads; 20.7% of the graduating class; 22.7% of master's enrolments; 15.4% of doctoral enrolments. Women faculty members in engineering programs in 1998 = 7.7%; http://www.carleton.ca/wise/natstats.htm, accessed Mar. 28, 2006.
428. DBD interview June 19, 2006, with Dr. F.M. (Mary) Williams, Director General, NRC Institute for Ocean Technology, St. John's, NL. NSERC/ Petro-Canada Chair for Women in Science and Engineering, Atlantic Region, 1997–2002, Memorial University.
429. Among other initiatives, the U. of T. Faculty of Applied Science and Engineering created Women Engineers Mentoring Students (WEMS) to link female alumnae with female engineering students.

430. C. Alphonso, "Engineering a balance of genders: Two female deans try to draw more women into their field; their daughters are hooked", *The Globe and Mail*, Sep. 12, 2006: "While women make up about 60 percent of the undergraduate population, and nearly half of the student body in law and medicine, they have fallen to just 20 percent of the first-year engineering class, down from nearly 30 percent five years ago."

431. Carleton University Engineering Professor Monique Frize, quoted in Pauline Tam, "Workshop to tempt girls to study engineering, science: School enrolment falls off after decades of gains", *The Ottawa Citizen*, Oct. 9, 2006.

432. http://www.ccpe.ca/e/prog_women_1.cfm, accessed Mar. 28, 2006.

433. University of Ottawa historian Ruby Heap, colleague of Professor Frize, cited in Pauline Tam, "Workshop to tempt girls…", Oct. 9, 2006.

434. Claudette Lassonde, President of Women in Science and Engineering, to EGM, 1979, cited in D. Fraser, "Elsie Gregory MacGill Aeronautical Engineer", *The Archivist*, Jan.–Feb. 1987, 8–9, 9.

Acknowledgements

My first thought in thanking the many people who helped me with this book is to acknowledge the debt I owe to Elsie MacGill herself: for leading an inspiring and interesting life and for touching those who supported me directly, notably her stepdaughter Ann Soulsby. Ann's kindness, sense of humour, and generosity made this project particularly enjoyable. Her sad passing in late summer 2007 now makes this book's recollections of Elsie's later family life particularly poignant. I am grateful in the same spirit to Elsie's nieces, Elizabeth Schneewind in the United States and Helen Brock in Oxford, U.K., who provided me with detailed material and insights on family history.

I am grateful to Elsie MacGill as well for helping to document her life through her own writings and records. As any student of Elsie's life knows, she was a fierce collector and producer of notes, letters, and other scraps of paper, which now occupy close to five metres of shelf space in the holdings of Library and Archives Canada. As a resident of Ottawa, I am fortunate to have easy access to this material as well as many other files related to the companies and organizations Elsie served. Elsie's writings, of course, included the well-known book about her mother Helen, which chronicled many important family events in a format rarely available to a biographer and in a way that, sometimes between the lines, conveys the core messages of Elsie's own story.

Elsie's life shows up in other archival holdings as well. As I was often unable to conduct research on-site, I would like to say a distinct thanks to individuals who sorted through material and helped me refine my requests for copies and references from a distance. These people certainly include Deborah Rice of the Society of Women Engineers Archives at Wayne State University in Detroit, Rachel Mills at the British Columbia Archives in Victoria, Carol Haber at the Vancouver City Archives, and Elizabeth Andrews of Archives and Special Collections at the Massachusetts Institute of Technology in Cambridge.

Here in Ottawa, I enjoyed superb support from the Ottawa Public Library Interlibrary Loans Service and from Fiona Smith Hale, Manager of Information Resources, and her colleague Ian Leslie at the Canada Aviation Museum Library. My work also benefited from facilitated access to the NRC Canada Institute for Scientific and Technical Information's

Archives and the 78 volumes of the John Hamilton Parkin Papers on aeronautical research in Canada it holds. In this regard, I am once again indebted to Archivist Steven Leclair.

In working to answer the question of what happened to Elsie's prototype Maple Leaf Trainer II, I was encouraged and helped by a number of individuals including Coronel Francisco Teran Valle, Military and Air Attaché, Office of the Embassy of Mexico, and Mr. Gabriel Parrish, Vice-President, Valley Stream Historical Society, Long Island, New York. I am also indebted to my Spanish-speaking colleagues, notably Mr. Louis Robayo, who reviewed Mexican documentation with me. However, I most grateful to the staff of the Smithsonian Institution's Paul E. Garber Preservation, Restoration and Storage Facility in Suitland, Maryland, and to Mr. Dan Hagedorn, Archives Research Team Leader and Adjunct Curator, Latin American Aviation Archives Division, Smithsonian National Air and Space Museum. He took time not only to meet with me and facilitate my own research at their facilities, but also to undertake original research on my behalf.

Among those who knew Elsie personally and agreed to be interviewed for this book, the delightful and astute Jim Carmichael, Elsie's carpool friend and aircraft industry colleague from the 1930s and 1940s, deserves special mention. Others who must be cited for a combination of encouragement and other input are engineer and editor Fred Beale, Parks Canada's Historical Services Branch researcher Arnold Roos, University of Ottawa doctoral student Crystal Sissons and her supervisor Professor Ruby Heap, York University President Lorna Marsden, and Professor Jeremy Mouat, Athabasca University, as well as Suzanne Kettley, Robert Forrest, Gerry Neville, Professor Paul Cavers, Stephanie Haddad, and their colleagues of the Monograph Program of NRC Research Press. I am also beholden to the anonymous reviewers of my manuscript for their kind comments and more importantly for their prods toward improvement. June Hall not only checked, deleted, and corrected through her editing, but often helped better express subtle ideas and improved the quality of the writing overall.

Finally, in this and everything I do, I am blessed by special family support from my intrigued editors-in-law, my amused children, my wonderful wife Michèle, and the others who make my own life story worth experiencing.

Index

A

Abortion 240, 244, 249, 269
acute infectious myelitis ix, 71
Aerial Experimental Association 90
Anderson, Doris 248
Ann Arbor ix, 64–74, 76, 79, 89, 104, 188
Ares planes 134, 298
Austin, Austin Company, Austin Motor Company 61–62, 288–289
autogiro aircraft 81
Avro, A.V. Roe 200–202, 214–216, 229, 279, 281–282
Aztec Eagles (Escuadron 201) 135–136

B

Balbuena airfield 129, 134–135
Baldwin, Casey 174
Banting, Frederick 59
Barreda, Roberto de la 132, 134
Battle, Helen 192
Battle of Britain 151–152, 162, 170, 280
Battle of Canada 127
Beaverbrook, Lord (Max Aiken) 146–147, 151
Bégin, Monique 249, 308
Bell, Alexander Graham 90, 174
Belyea, Helen 193
Bennington Heights Drive 228
Bird, Senator Florence 234–236, 238, 239, 248
Bishopsfield Airport 105, 153
Blueprint for Madame Prime Minister 227–228
boundary layer effect 69
Boyd, David 110, 140, 159, 178, 197–200, 281
British Columbia Minimum Wage Board 38
British Commonwealth Air Training Plan (BCATP) 118, 126–127, 137
Brock, Helen Hughes 102, 185, 186, 272, 312
Broken leg(s) 12, 78, 223, 226, 256
Browning armaments 144
Buccaneer Bay Cottage 13, 16, 22, 34, 43
Burlison brothers 197–198
Burnelli flying wings 106–107
Bush, Vannevar 82
Byrd, Admiral 163

C

Camm, Sydney 143, 147
Canadair CF 86 Sabre jet fighters 201
Canadian Car and Foundry (Can-Car, CC&F) 99–101, 104, 105–114, 116–119, 126–137, 140, 146–159, 164, 165, 170, 174–181, 195, 197–199, 202–204, 206, 279–281
Canadian Council of Professional Engineers 264, 266
Canadian Federation Business and Professional Women's Clubs 222, 228, 230, 231, 275
cancer 31, 77–78, 139, 142, 208
Cannon, University of Calgary Dean Elizabeth 266
Carmichael, James, "Jim" 147, 196
Carr, Emily 29–30, 54, 285
CBY-3 Loadmaster 106, 108
CF-100 200–201
CF-105 Arrow 200
CF-114 Tutor jet trainers 117
Chatelaine Magazine 79, 248
Columbia Aircraft 130–131, 297

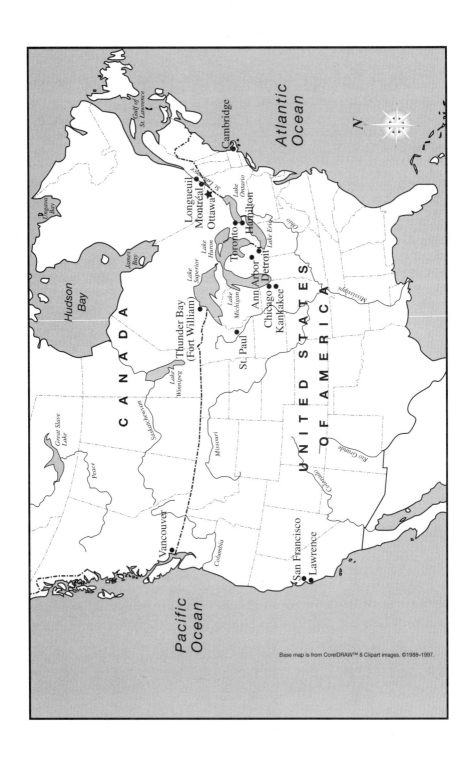

Base map is from CorelDRAW™ 8 Clipart images. ©1988–1997.

Dick Bourgeois-Doyle, Director of Corporate Governance at the
National Research Council of Canada (NRC), has headed a number of special projects since joining the NRC Executive Offices
in 1987. He previously served as Chief of Staff to the Minister of
Science and Technology and the Minister of Fisheries and Oceans
and was start-up manager of successful technology and public
relations firms. A former broadcaster and journalist, Bourgeois-
Doyle has contributed to many books, articles, TV features, and
radio programs on science history.

National Research
Council Canada
Conseil national
de recherches Canada

Also available in the NRC Biography Series
Également de la collection de biographies du CNRC

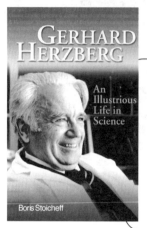

Gerhard Herzberg:
An Illustrious Life in Science

By / Par

Boris Stoicheff

Co-published with McGill-Queen's University Press
Co-édité par Mc-Gill-Queen's University Press
468 Pages 2002
Hardcover / Édition reliée

ISBN 0-660-18757-4; NRC 44462
ISSN 1701-1833; CNRC 44462

$49.95 CAN; Other countries: $49.95 US
49,95 $CAN; À l'étranger : 49,95 $US

George J. Klein:
The Great Inventor

By / Par
Richard I. Bourgeois-Doyle

289 Pages 2004
Hardcover / Édition reliée

ISBN 0-660-19322-1; NRC 46323
ISSN 1701-1833; CNRC 46323

$49.95 CAN; Other countries: $49.95 US
49,95 $CAN; À l'étranger : 49,95 $US

To order books / Pour commander

Order Office / Bureau des commandes
NRC Research Press / Presses scientifiques du CNRC, National Research Council / Conseil national de recherches
Ottawa, ON K1A 0R6, Canada. Telephone / Téléphone : 613-990-2254;   Fax / Télécopieur : 613-952-7656
E-mail / Courriel : pubs@nrc-cnrc.gc.ca;   Order online / Commandes en ligne : http://pubs.nrc-cnrc.gc.ca

01/09/2008

NRC·CNRC

Canada